THE LITERARY
LEGACY
of
C. S. LEWIS

THE LITERARY LEGACY
of
C. S. LEWIS

CHAD WALSH

SHELDON PRESS

LONDON

First published in the United States in 1979 by
Harcourt Brace Jovanovich, Inc.
757 Third Avenue, New York, N.Y. 10017

First published in Great Britain in 1979 by
Sheldon Press
Marylebone Road, London NW1 4DU

Printed in Great Britain by
Billing & Sons Limited, Guildford, London and Worcester

ISBN 0 85969 289 2

Acknowledgments are due to the following for permission to quote
from the material listed:

Bantam Books, for the Afterword to C. S. Lewis, *A Grief Observed*,
1976. Afterword © 1976 by Chad Walsh. Some passages were incorporated
or paraphrased.

The Bodley Head, for excerpts from C. S. Lewis, *The Last Bottle*,
The Magician's Nephew, *Out of the Silent Planet*, *Perelandra*, and
That Hideous Strength.

Cambridge University Press, for excerpts from C. S. Lewis, *The
Discarded Image*, *Experiment in Criticism*, *Selected Literary Essays*,
Spenser's Images of Life, and *Studies in Words* (2nd ed.).

Collins Publishers, for excerpts from C. S. Lewis, *The Pilgrim's*
(*Continued on p. 262*)

for
Walter Hooper

CONTENTS

	Preface	ix
1	The Shape of His Sensibility	3
2	Epistles to a Young Tempter	21
3	The Almost Poet	35
4	Visionary Worlds	59
5	The Womb of Space	83
6	The Parallel World of Narnia	123
7	The Road Taken Too Late	159
8	The Hopeful Critic	179
9	Apostle at Large	201
10	A Backward and Forward Look	243
	Bibliography	253
	Index	265

PREFACE

In 1949 I published *C. S. Lewis: Apostle to the Skeptics,* the first book devoted wholly to Lewis. As the years went by, I was content to leave to others any further book-length exploration of Lewis's achievement.

Gradually the lacks in my book became clearer in my mind, and I began to think of a new and larger book with a different focus. So early a book obviously said nothing about the large number of works by Lewis published after mine had been frozen into print. The Chronicles of Narnia, for example, were a picture in Lewis's mind but little or nothing on paper when *Apostle to the Skeptics* was published.

Also, I came to suspect that my early book had exercised a baleful influence on many other scholars. While I had some things to say about him simply as an important writer, I had concentrated on his religious odyssey and the way this found expression in a variety of literary genres. Lewis scholarship has sometimes seemed a branch of hermeneutics rather than literary criticism. Only in recent years has much attention been given to him not as a religious writer but as a writer—one whose work is well worth reading and studying simply as literature.[1]

---

[1] A particularly rewarding attempt to apply normal approaches of literary criticism to Lewis's fiction is now available in a multi-author book, *The Longing for a Form: Essays on the Fiction of C. S. Lewis,* edited by Peter J. Schakel (Kent, Ohio: Kent State University Press, 1977).

My old delight in Lewis never left me, and gradually I began to think, How would it be if I wrote a book in which I examined all his major works from the middle distance of a half-generation after his death?

It seemed better to start from scratch, rather than revise and expand the old book. I have no intention of neglecting the religious significance of Lewis's books; after all, one would not write about Dante and say nothing of Heaven and Hell. But this time I wish to pay Lewis the just compliment of assuming that he was an unusual and significant writer, and that his work can be studied like that of any other author.

What I have done by way of preparation is simply to reread all of Lewis's published works (and some unpublished ones) together with almost all the books about him, and many of the articles. The result is really one long essay on the achievement of C. S. Lewis. I am sure that many of my insights came from books and essays I have read, and where I can recall specific influences, I have gratefully acknowledged them in footnotes. My apologies to any scholars whose ideas I may have echoed without recalling their source —but such negligence, I trust, is the sincerest flattery.

One other reason for this book. Soon after Lewis's death, I wrote an essay in which I predicted that his reputation would suffer a sharp decline, to be followed by a partial revival. I am glad to report that I was a poor prophet. There was little or no decline in Lewis's readership, and at the moment it is steadily rising. One of his American editors happily assured me, "The sale of his books is going through the roof." His work seems to have staying power.

The danger is that Lewis may become a cult figure and the study of his life and work turn into hagiography. Already at least two evangelical campuses boast of possessing *the* wardrobe through which one enters the magic land of Narnia. This curious cult of relics, so contrary to historical Protestantism, is an indication of the hold that Lewis and his works have on one of the largest and most rapidly growing expressions of American Christianity. Meanwhile, C. S. Lewis societies have sprung up, much like the Browning societies of earlier times, to present regular programs and publish their debates. A professional actor offers Lewis impersonations for $1,000 an evening.

Lewis, however—and this is why I wrote this book—is not a writer for one season or one public. His Roman Catholic readership has been large from the beginning, and many Jewish boys and girls, or children of no religious background, have responded to all seven Narnia tales, sometimes aware of the Christian symbols and sometimes not, but in any case reading the books because they are very readable. That is the right approach. Literature first.

Many have helped me along the way; the list would be intolerably long. I wish to express particular thanks to Professor Clyde S. Kilby and the Reverend Walter Hooper. The former opened to me the magnificent Marion E. Wade Collection at Wheaton College, Wheaton, Illinois, and the latter introduced me to the rich resources of the Bodleian Library, Oxford, and has been infinitely helpful throughout.

Beloit College has always been supportive of my research and writing; I am especially grateful for a sabbatical leave when I was at the early stages of this book. While finishing it, I held the J. Omar Good visiting professorship at Juniata College, and this carried with it a reduced teaching load and adequate secretarial assistance, two priceless boons for any writer. Therefore my thanks to Juniata, and in particular to the reference librarian, Sally Barnett, and to the three secretaries who labored so faithfully to meet my deadline—Kaylene Corbin, Verna Horne, and Cheryl L. Curfman.

Chad Walsh

THE LITERARY
LEGACY
of
C. S. LEWIS

THE SHAPE OF HIS SENSIBILITY

It was Lewis's good fortune that he and his older brother, Warren ("Warnie") were left alone a good deal. After their father, a successful solicitor, moved the family in 1905 to a roomy house on the far outskirts of Belfast, and before school closed in upon them, the two boys (aged six and nine) took possession of the huge and mysterious attic. They made it their world, where they exercised their imaginations. Here Lewis wrote his first (and still unpublished) books, dealing with the adventures of talking animals. A mile or so in the distance they could see, often through a drizzling Irish rain, the mysterious Castlereagh Hills, which were to reappear in *The Pilgrim's Regress* as a symbol of the heart's unknown desire.[1]

After the move to the new house, Little Lea, young Lewis had his first experience of "Joy" or "Romance," to use his terms. As he describes it in *Surprised by Joy,* he was standing by a flowering currant bush when suddenly he re-

---

[1] For a complete biography of Lewis, see Roger Lancelyn Green and Walter Hooper, *C. S. Lewis: A Biography.* Lewis's account of his early life is contained in *Surprised by Joy.* Some biographical portions of this present book are taken, in modified form, from the Afterword I wrote for the 1976 Bantam edition of Lewis's *A Grief Observed.*

membered the toy garden in a cookie tin that his brother had once created:

> . . . there suddenly rose in me without warning, as if from a depth not of years but of centuries, the memory of that earlier morning at the Old House when my brother had brought his toy garden into the nursery. It is difficult to find words strong enough for the sensation which came over me; Milton's "enormous bliss" of Eden . . . comes somewhere near it. It was a sensation, of course, of desire; but desire for what? Not, certainly, for a biscuit tin filled with moss, nor even (though that came into it) for my own past.[2]

This baptism by "Joy" was to be repeated throughout his life at irregular intervals. Sometimes the trigger was literary, as when he read Longfellow's *Saga of King Olaf* and came to the lines, "I heard a voice that cried, / Balder the beautiful / Is dead, is dead."[3] The effect was overpowering:

> I knew nothing about Balder; but instantly I was uplifted into huge regions of northern sky, I desired with almost sickening intensity something never to be described (except that it is cold, spacious, severe, pale, and remote) and then, as in the other examples, found myself at the very same moment already falling out of that desire and wishing I were back in it.

The attic paradise came to an end. First Warnie, then Jack (as Clive insisted on being called) went forth to boarding school. In the case of the younger brother, there was a succession of them, all of which he detested with varying degrees of intensity. Meanwhile, his mother had died of lingering cancer, deepening his already dark doubts about the goodness and omnipotence of God.

It seemed that no school was right for Lewis. His father finally turned to an Ulster Scottish schoolmaster at Great

---

[2] *Surprised by Joy* (New York: Harcourt, Brace & World, 1955), p. 16.
[3] P. 17.

Bookham, Surrey. W. T. Kirkpatrick, then retired, had tutored Warnie and got him to the point where he received prize cadetships at Sandhurst. Was it not possible, Mr. Lewis wondered, that the "Great Knock," as he was called, could perform a similar miracle with the intransigent Jack?

Anyone wishing a loving character sketch of the Scottish schoolmaster—modified of course by Lewis's creative imagination—will find it in the person of MacPhee in *That Hideous Strength*. Kirkpatrick was an atheist of the stern and moral nineteenth-century type, a secular puritan. He was also a relentless logician. If young Lewis committed the most trifling offense against the canons of logic, he would be sternly rebuked and shown the errors of his reasoning. Lewis loved it, and those who find a bit too much logic-chopping in his books say he never recovered from it.

Though he did not know it yet, the outlines of the adult Lewis were beginning to emerge: the ruthless logician combined with the quester for the source of the mysterious "Joy" that he intermittently experienced.

Residence at Kirkpatrick's home was more than a continuous seminar in logic. Lewis had to learn Greek, among other things. The experiment was successful. He competed for a scholarship and won one at University College, Oxford. Meanwhile, World War I had broken out. The Irish were exempt from conscription, but Lewis seems never to have seriously considered taking advantage of this dispensation. Perhaps having a brother in the professional army discouraged any pacifist thoughts, though there is little reason to think Lewis would have inclined that way in any case. He decided to make a bargain with himself. He would offer himself for training as a reserve officer, but until he was called up, he would let the war take care of itself. He refrained from newspapers and went about his academic days as though they would never be interrupted.

The army, of course, did not forget. Lewis was soon in training; then, as a second lieutenant, he was sent to that part of the French front where the Germans made their final, all-out attack. Wounded by a British shell that fell short, he was moved from one hospital and rest home to another, and eventually demobilized. He returned to Oxford, almost as though nothing had happened. Except for a few short poems, his writing shows little trace of the war experience.

From 1919 to 1924 he was a student at University College. In effect—to use the American term—he was doing a "double major" (Latin and Greek literature and philosophy and ancient history; plus English literature). It was his hope that this combined background would aid him in securing an academic position, as it eventually did when in 1925 he was appointed fellow in English language and literature at Magdalen College.

Lewis's early years as an Oxford don coincide with the period when his religious quest was coming to its climax. The unmerited and painful death of his mother destroyed any easy confidence in a God who was both good and all-powerful. The matron at one of his schools was a religious dabbler, flirting with spiritualism and theosophy, and Lewis found her ideas liberating; he felt one could play around with them without being asked to affirm them literally. The influence of Kirkpatrick was obviously another factor, strengthening the atheistic position that Lewis had already reached. Even the study of the classics led Lewis into deeper skepticism. He noticed that the editors of texts always assumed that the classical divinities were products of human imagination; was there any reason to put Jehovah in a different category?

The story of Lewis's return to Christianity is told in great detail by Lewis himself in *Surprised by Joy*. Briefly, he took two paths finally leading to the same destination. On the first path, he pursued the clues offered by moments of "Joy" and found he could make sense of them only by assuming a fourth dimension to existence; this turned out to be another name for God. The second path was that of logic and reason. Ironically, the very intellectual tools that the atheistic Great Knock had taught him eventually turned him in the other direction. He found that belief in God made more sense, was better logic, than disbelief. During the year that he taught philosophy (before securing a permanent appointment in English) he reached the point of believing in "the God of the philosophers," which he still insisted was not "the God of popular religion." When he tried to distinguish between these two Gods in lectures and tutorial sessions, he ran into increasing difficulties, and found himself moving—almost in spite of himself—toward an explicitly Christian concept of God. He still did not know what to make of Christ, but finally, in a letter to his boyhood friend Arthur Greeves (October 18, 1931), he describes his formal capitulation:

> . . . the idea of the dying and reviving god (Balder, Adonis, Bacchus) . . . moved me provided I met it anywhere *except* in the gospels. The reason was that in Pagan stories I was prepared to feel the myth as profound and suggestive of meanings beyond my grasp even tho' I could not say in cold prose "what it meant." Now the story of Christ is simply a true myth: a myth working on us in the same way as the others, but with this tremendous difference that *it really happened.* . . .

Lewis's return to Christianity had resounding literary consequences. It not only led him to write such outright apologetics as *Mere Christianity,* but it also, and more importantly, baptized his imagination, giving him new subject matter and themes, and most important of all, a set of symbols through which he could operate. One must remember that this was a baptism both of the head and of the heart. Had only the path called "Joy" been followed, Lewis might have been merely another George MacDonald, though a better stylist. The second path, that of reason and logic, gives an intellectual firmness to books that might otherwise be more feeling than thought.

At about the same time that he capitulated to Christ, an important change in Lewis's psychology took place; perhaps the two events are not unrelated. He turned outward, not in the sense of becoming a great extrovert and jolly good fellow, but rather in losing interest in his own subjective feelings.

He began to concentrate instead on the public world about him, which for him consisted mainly of literature, religion, and a small circle of close friends.

Owen Barfield, one of Lewis's closest and oldest friends, discusses the change in an Introduction written for *Light on C. S. Lewis.* As he sees it:

> What I think is true is, that at a certain stage in his life
> he deliberately ceased to take any interest in himself except
> as a kind of spiritual alumnus taking his moral finals. I
> think this was part of the change to which I have referred;
> and I suggest that what began as deliberate choice became
> at length . . . an ingrained and effortless habit of soul.
> Self-knowledge, for him, had come to mean recognition
> of his own weaknesses and shortcomings and nothing
> more. . . . As far as I am able to judge, it was this that lay
> behind that distinctive combination of an almost supreme
> intellectual and "phantastic" maturity, laced with moral
> energy, on the one hand, with—I can find no other phrase
> for it—a certain psychic or spiritual immaturity on the
> other, which is detectable in some of his religious and
> theological writings; and occasionally elsewhere: for
> example, in the undergraduate humour of Weston and
> Devine's humiliation before Oyarsa in *Out of the Silent
> Planet* and the opera-bouffe climax of *That Hideous
> Strength* . . . is this Kathleen Raine's "a kind of boyish
> greatness"?[4]

These comments must be modified when considering certain of Lewis's later books, but in general they ring true to anyone who knew Lewis. He was at the same time remarkably open and remarkably shut. The world of his mind was freely available to friends and public. The world of feelings and intuitions was sparingly shared, or conveyed in such transformed style as to seem divorced from its source.

Little has been said here about Lewis's daily life. During his time as an undergraduate and his early years as a

---

[4] *Light on C. S. Lewis,* Jocelyn Gibb, ed. (New York: Harcourt, Brace & World, 1965), p. xvi.

don—before he began earning significant money from his writing—he lived in a state of great financial stringency. Partly this was because in 1919 he and Mrs. Janie Moore (mother of Paddy Moore, a friend of Lewis's who was killed in the war), together with her daughter Maureen, established a combined household. This arrangement puzzled many of his friends, some of whom sought Freudian explanations. The simplest explanation may be the best: Lewis was simply keeping his promise to look after Paddy's mother if her son did not return from the war. Most, though not all, of Lewis's acquaintances describe Mrs. Moore as bigoted and bossy. They tell how she used him like an extra servant and would interrupt his tutorial sessions with phone calls on trivial matters. At any rate, he took care of her until her failing mind required a nursing home, and he visited her there almost every day until her death in 1951.

Another tormenting problem gradually emerged. Warnie became an alcoholic. Periodically he would have to enter a hospital for treatment. There might be months of abstinence, then a massive relapse. Though often drunk, Warnie was always a gentleman, and in his drier periods he wrote notable books in the field of French seventeenth-century history. Still, he was a constant anxiety to Lewis, who never knew when he would have to come to the rescue. On July 6, 1947, we find him writing to the poet Ruth Pitter:

> My brother, thank God, was out of danger when I reached him on Monday morning last but one at the unearthly city of Drogheda where almost every building is a church or a tavern and what men do but pray and drink or how life is supported I can't conceive . . . you hear more wit and humor in one day of London than in a week of Drogheda. My brother was in the care of the most charming nuns.

In the midst of household confusions and anxieties about Warnie—and with a correspondence that constantly grew as his fame increased—and in the midst also of his daily chores as an Oxford tutor, Lewis somehow managed to find the time to write more than fifty books. One advantage he had: he early developed a style that was distinctively his, and he seldom had to make extensive changes after his first draft.

The 1950's saw two major turning points in Lewis's life. One was his marriage to Joy Davidman Gresham, discussed in Chapter 9. With his wife came two stepsons. The other was his appointment to a specially created chair, "Medieval and Renaissance English Literature," at Cambridge. This gave him much more time for writing.

Lewis and J. R. R. Tolkien first met in 1926, and out of their friendship evolved the Inklings. This group of personal and professional friends would meet Thursday evenings at Lewis's rooms, and often at Tuesday noon in the Eagle and the Child (commonly called the Bird and Baby), a small pub specializing in remarkable cider. The evening meetings were usually devoted to reading aloud some portion of a book in progress, followed by straightforward criticism. After the charismatic Charles Williams joined the group (the Oxford University Press, for which he worked, moved from London to Oxford during World War II) the Inklings reached their high point. At a meeting one might find Lewis reading a chapter from *Perelandra,* or Williams reading from *All Hallows' Eve,* or Tolkien from the future *Lord of the Rings.* These meetings served as a major stimulation. John Wain, a junior member of the Inklings, recalls the sessions in Lewis's college rooms:

> I can see that room so clearly now, the electric fire pumping
> heat into the dank air, the faded screen that broke some
> of the keener draughts, the enamel beer-jug on the
> table. . . . There would be no fixed etiquette, but the
> rudimentary honours would be done partly by Lewis and
> partly by his brother, W. H. Lewis, a man who stays in my
> memory as the most courteous I have ever met—not
> with mere politeness, but with a genial, self-forgetful
> considerateness that was as instinctive to him as breathing.
> Sometimes, when the less vital members of the circle were

in a big majority, the evening would fall flat; but the
best of them were as good as anything I shall live to see.[5]

A more structured and public organization was the Socratic Club, where formal papers on religious questions were
presented and debated. Lewis was the principal champion of
the Christian view, and with his formidable dialectic ability
proved a scourge to most, if not quite all, the unbelievers
who ventured into what was really a Christian lion's den.

It was a quiet life, Lewis's years at Cambridge and
Oxford, and he would not have had it otherwise. His increasing fame as a writer (and briefly as a radio personality)
eroded his privacy a little, but he maintained it as best he
could, and remained a close friend to a few, a familiar name
to many. Toward the end of his life, after the death of his
wife, his own health began to fail; it was a combination of
heart and kidney conditions, complicated by a calcium defi-
ciency. He died of a heart attack the same day that Aldous
Huxley departed in splendid visions from a massive dose of
psychedelics, and President John Kennedy was shot in Dallas.

Looking back at Lewis's life and achievements, one is
struck by their continuity. As a boy, he felt more at home in
the attic where he created worlds of fantasy than downstairs
where his father declaimed on politics at the dinner table.
Years later, at a meeting of the Inklings, Lewis stoutly de-
fended the primacy of imagination. John Wain recalls a time
he and Lewis clashed:

> Lewis considered "fine fabling" an essential part of
> literature, and never lost a chance to push any author, from
> Spenser to Rider Haggard, who could be called a
> romancer. Once, unable to keep silence at what seemed to
> me a monstrous partiality, I attacked the whole basis of his
> view; a writer's task, I maintained, was to lay bare the
> human heart, and this could not be done if he were
> continually taking refuge in the spinning of fanciful webs.
> Lewis retorted with a theory that, since the Creator had seen

---

[5] *Sprightly Running* (New York: St. Martin's Press, 1963), p. 184.

fit to build a universe and set it in motion, it was the
duty of the human artist to create as lavishly as possible in
his turn. The romancer, who invents a whole world, is
worshipping God more effectively than the mere realist
who analyses that which lies about him. Looking back across
fourteen years, I can hardly believe that Lewis said
anything so manifestly absurd as this, and perhaps I
misunderstood him; but that, at any rate, is how my memory
reports the incident.[6]

A careful study of Lewis's letters as well as his books
proves that Wain's memory was not in error. None of Lewis's
narratives is straightforward realism. They may contain
highly realistic elements, like the faculty meeting depicted in
That Hideous Strength, but the mythic, supernatural, or preternatural always figures also. True, he could discipline himself to write expository books like *Mere Christianity* and *The
Abolition of Man,* but these are not his central achievements.
At the heart of his work are the fantasies.

The books that directly influenced Lewis are almost
always those in which imagination creates new worlds. He
was inspired by Bunyan in *The Pilgrim's Regress,* by Dante
in *The Great Divorce,* by Milton in *Perelandra,* by Apuleius
in *Till We Have Faces.* An obscure science fiction writer,
David Lindsay, gave Lewis a new idea of what planets are
good for in *Voyage to Arcturus* and helped prepare the way
for the space trilogy. George MacDonald, whose book *Phantastes* came like a revelation of holiness to Lewis at the age of
sixteen, taught him how fantasy could be the vehicle of serious visions.

The list of authors that he admired, and who may in
some cases have influenced his own work, is almost endless.
It is heavily loaded in favor of the "fine fablers": Edmund
Spenser (perhaps his favorite author), William Blake, Wal-
ter Scott, George Meredith, William Morris, Beatrix Potter,
E. Nesbit, Kenneth Grahame, E. R. Eddison (author of the

---

6 P. 182.

riotously imaginative fantasy, *The Worm Ouroboros*),
Thomas Malory, the whole corpus of European mythology
(especially its northern varieties), and virtually everything
written in Western Europe during the Middle Ages and the
Renaissance. It is true he also admired, for instance, G. K.
Chesterton, whose apologetic writings may have helped teach
Lewis how to turn the tables on sophisticated skeptics. But
the list, taken as a whole, is strong on writers whose most
obvious trait is a soaring imagination.

One particular question is to what extent he was influenced by the writers who were also his close friends. Certainly, he shows the traces of Charles Williams's presence,
sometimes in a diffused way, sometimes specifically, as in his
use of the Arthurian legend in *That Hideous Strength*. Williams's poetry develops the contrast between the ideal England, Logres, and the empirical Britain, and Lewis took
this over. He may also have owed to Williams the insight that
cosmic adventures can take place on earth as well as on
Malacandra and Perelandra. Lewis's psychological and spiritual insights were deepened by Williams; for example, he
learned from the latter that human beings can take upon
themselves each other's burdens, spiritual and even physical.
This theme is dramatized in *Till We Have Faces*.

The name of Tolkien is so linked with Lewis that one
wonders whether he exerted a shaping influence. The similarities in their writing are obvious enough; both are creators
of other worlds. But what different creators they are! Both
men were committed Christians, but Tolkien is as stern in
excluding explicit Christianity from his imagined world as
Lewis is eager to admit it. Tolkien functions more in an archaic world of the sagas; Lewis proclaims a fairy tale that is
also Christian truth. Doubtless the two men stimulated each
other, but one sees little evidence of decisive influence in
either direction.

Another living writer often mentioned in connection
with Lewis is Owen Barfield. Their "great war," a long-time
correspondence on philosophic questions, is fascinating in its

own right, but more relevant to Lewis the philosopher than
to Lewis the storyteller. Perhaps Barfield, with his understanding of imagination as a mode of knowledge, may have
loosened up Lewis and made him more willing to follow his
creative mind and see where it would lead him.

Lewis's highly varied reading gave him a storehouse of
mental pictures, which were reinforced by those that arose
spontaneously in his supremely visual imagination—for instance, a vision of floating islands ultimately launched him on
Perelandra. It is not the primary purpose of this book to
trace his literary sources—a task big enough for another book
by itself—but rather to look at the finished products. And
here a paradox emerges. In his critical writings Lewis
strongly deprecates the modern emphasis on originality. Take
your plots and ideas where you find them, and then do something good with them, is his advice. He was as ready to bor-
row as were Chaucer and Shakespeare. And yet, drawing
upon the common cultural storehouse of ideas and images,
reinforced by his own imagination, he emerged as one of the
most distinctive writers of his time. Who else could have
written *Perelandra?* The Narnia stories? *Till We Have Faces?*

One naturally wonders what kind of man he was in his
private life. I addressed this question to his older stepson,
David Gresham, and received several letters from which he
kindly permits me to quote. David was in his early teens
during the years of Lewis's marriage.

David remembers especially what he sees as contradictions in Lewis's personality: ". . . a humanitarian and anti-
imperialist attitude, and yet an ultra-conservative political
philosophy," and adds, as an indication of Lewis's attitude
toward other countries, "He used to assert that 'in French
hotels, you can smell the plumbing throughout the whole
building,' and he was not impressed by my arguments that
his acquaintance with the most civilized country in Europe
was confined to areas ravaged by the war." But David
Gresham grants that, "In spite of his being bitterly anti-
Socialist, he was glad of the abolition of the more blatant

forms of exploitation which he had seen come about in the course of his lifetime."

About Lewis's general background of knowledge and interest, Gresham says: "Music meant little to him, and painting and sculpture still less. He hardly ever went to the movies, to the theater, or to a concert. He was incredibly ignorant on such things as biology: he thought that a slug was a reptile!"

The picture of the serene Lewis, which often seems to emerge from his books, is contradicted by Gresham's recollections: ". . . in real life [he] was very nervous, not to say irascible—if he dropped or spilt something, he would be very upset, and as you know, he was clumsy with his hands."

Gresham pictures Lewis as completely skeptical of politicians, and in general not particularly interested in keeping up with the latest national or international news. He shunned newspapers except for the book reviews in the *Sunday Times* and the crossword puzzles in the *Daily Telegraph*.

One charming anecdote merits quotation in full:

> Like many former officers in World War I, he had kept his service revolver after having been demobilized. . . . In 1940, he thought that the Germans would conquer England. He had, by the way, volunteered for active service at the outbreak of hostilities, but been turned down, on account of age, I think. He was also convinced that the fascists would murder him, so he threw the gun into the river: he wanted their crime to be without any justification. I can remember that when he told my mother about this episode, she replied: "I would have kept it, so that I could have taken some of the swine with me!" He said that when the Gestapo black list of people to be arrested as soon as the Germans arrived was published after the war, he was disappointed to find that he was not on it.

All in all, the portrait of a very private man. It is true he does briefly develop a political philosophy in *Mere Christianity* when he discusses what a Christian society would be like:

> . . . the New Testament, without going into details, gives
> us a pretty clear hint of what a fully Christian society
> would be like. . . . Every one is to work with his own
> hands, and what is more, every one's work is to produce
> something good: there will be no manufacture of silly
> luxuries and then of sillier advertisements to persuade us to
> buy them. And there is to be no "swank" or "side," no
> putting on airs. To that extent a Christian society would be
> what we now call Leftist. On the other hand, it is
> always insisting on obedience . . . from all of us to
> properly appointed magistrates, from children to parents,
> and (I am afraid this is going to be very unpopular) from
> wives to husbands.[7]

So much for theory. In actual practice, Lewis thought
little about these matters (deeming them the province of
Christian sociologists and economists) and his conditioned
reflexes were more in the Tory direction. I sent him a novel
I had written for teen-agers, *The Rough Years,* in which the
rector of a church was encouraging a youthful gang to meet
there, hoping the environment would have a constructive
influence on them. Lewis was not sympathetic. He wrote to
me:

> Bowman [the rector] is a type we have here with his naif
> conviction of "the spiritual advantages of meeting in a
> parish house" and his certainty that once you get the
> gangsters there "the situation" will "take care of itself." It
> almost sounds as if he thought the Church existed for
> the sake of "togetherness"; never for the knowledge and
> worship of God from which the togetherness will inevitably
> result.

The underlying principle of Lewis's sociology is simply
hierarchy, the Great Chain of Being. The fulfillment of each
creature depends on its proper relation with those above and
below. In terms of marriage, for instance, this does not mean
that the husband simply bosses his wife around and she

---

[7] *Mere Christianity* (New York: Macmillan, 1943, 1960), p. 80.

meekly obeys. His dominion over her, Lewis made clear, carries responsibilities: protection, tenderness, love, respect. The higher one is on the Great Chain the greater his duties.

Was Lewis then a male chauvinist? In an autobiographical sketch he once stated: "There's no sound I like better than adult male laughter." *Current Biography* even asserted he was so shy in the presence of women that he frequently locked himself in his room when women were prowling about the college. I called this story to Lewis's attention and he wrote back:

> The pleasant story about my locking myself in my room when a woman invaded the college precincts is—I regret to say—pure bosh. For one thing, women are wandering through "the college precincts" the whole blessed day. For another, having taken female pupils of all ages, shapes, sizes, and complexions for about twenty years, I am a bit tougher than the story makes out. If I ever fled from a female visitor it was not because she was a woman but because she was a *bore,* or because she was the fifteenth visitor on a busy day.

On the pragmatic level, Lewis maintained that wives should obey their husbands, for otherwise how could a deadlock in family decisions be resolved? Someone must cast the deciding vote, and he argued that neither men nor women seemed eager to place that responsibility in female hands. On a more theoretical level, he argued that male aggressiveness and female submission are needed to make the act of love complete; this is dramatized near the end of *That Hideous Strength* when bluestocking Jane Studdock learns to welcome the advances of her clumsy husband. Masculine and feminine, as Lewis sees them, are more than biological categories. They are metaphysical realities. A man represents the "masculine" to a woman, but God is the ultimate masculine, and the most aggressive man is, so to speak, a woman in the hands of God.

At this point the psychologizers may ask whether his views were colored by a different sexual orientation. However, there seems no indication whatever that this was so. His only close contact with homosexuality was at one of his boarding schools, and his reaction, as recorded in *Surprised by Joy,* is decidedly negative. We know that he experienced heterosexual lusts of the flesh in puberty from contact with his dancing instructress, and he speaks in somewhat vague language of young manhood experiences with women that may have been sexual affairs. At least after his return to Christianity, he seems to have maintained strict chastity, even to the point of refraining from certain foods that he found sexually stimulating.

If Lewis had lived to the present period when the long-deferred women's liberation movement is gathering strength like a colonial insurrection, he might have been compelled to think through his assumptions more thoroughly—but one suspects his final conclusions would not have changed. Certainly there was little in the Oxford of his day to raise his consciousness; Oxford was, and to a large extent remains, a male enclave.

The question has sometimes been raised, Was Lewis's return to Christianity purely an intellectual move, or did it alter his daily life? He endeavored to live by his regained faith and permitted himself remarkably few casuistic escape clauses. For one thing, he was extremely literal about giving to the poor. After he became a prosperous writer he quietly set up a trust fund that dispensed a large part of his extra income to needy individuals. One of his former pupils remarked, "If Lewis had met a man who said, 'I need your coat,' he would unhesitatingly have taken the coat off and handed it over."

Lewis was a man born six hundred years late. The last of the dinosaurs—so he proclaimed himself in his Cambridge inaugural address. And in many ways the self-judgment is valid. He would have been more at home in medieval Paris, engaged in disputations with Abelard, than he was at Oxford, and he was more at home in Oxford than he would have been at an international convention of logical positivists.

When he wrote *The Discarded Image* and lovingly depicted the medieval world view, complete with Ptolemaic astronomy, it was no tour de force for him to speak as though from the inside of that vanished cosmos. Not that he renounced Copernicus, but to him, simply, the older world view as a total way of viewing reality made coherent sense on its own terms. If it was not literally and exclusively true, it was at least a set of poetic symbols that could be used to point toward whatever the ultimate realities may be.

In his expository and argumentative books, Lewis made a great point of emphasizing his own lack of originality; he was, he insisted, simply presenting beliefs that until recently had been taken for granted. The whole trend of his literary criticism was to minimize the importance of originality and to concentrate instead on what the writer had actually set down on paper, perhaps telling a tale he never invented, and using a poetic form inherited from his predecessors.

But a word of warning. A dinosaur surviving by some kind of ecological miracle into the twentieth century is still an inhabitant of that century. For one thing, it may find it must readjust its diet, to compensate for the lack of accustomed foods. It may encounter forms of life it doesn't know and have to study their way of life and how to coexist with them. In the same way, a human dinosaur, living in an age when logical positivists lurk in every senior common room, is not the same as a dinosaur living when every creature of importance was a dinosaur. Lewis's basic philosophy is indeed a vigorous survival and adaptation from earlier times, but the challenge of the twentieth century compelled him to formulate it in ways that would have seemed unusual indeed to his fellow scholars of the Middle Ages. In spite of his protests, Lewis was original.

2

EPISTLES TO A YOUNG TEMPTER

The Screwtape Letters, published near the midpoint of his career, established Lewis's fame in America. It is a good place to begin the examination of his total achievement, though Lewis himself would probably not have approved this priority. The immense popularity of this work on both sides of the Atlantic was an irritation to its author, who was convinced he had written more important books. Indeed, the very writing of it had proved a personal vexation. The idea came to him early one Sunday morning when he was leaving church and suddenly thought, How would it be to present the Christian life from the Devil's viewpoint? This effort of the imagination turned out to be more abrasive than he had anticipated. He was heartily glad when he had composed the last letter.

The epistolary form has its forerunners in the novel, but the unusual thing in *The Screwtape Letters* is the inverted point of view. The Green–Hooper *Biography* suggests that Lewis may have got the idea for this from a book by Valdemar Adolph Thisted, *Letters from Hell,* which he read while at Great Bookham. In the American paperback edition of the *Letters* Lewis mentions the influence of Stephen McKenna's *The Confessions of a Well-Meaning Woman* and the spiritual cannibalism in David Lindsay's *Voyage to Arcturus.* In any case, there was a long gestation period before he set to work on the epistles of Screwtape. In this book, the letters are written not by the young man who is the central human character, but by Screwtape, an Undersecretary of the Infernal Lowerarchy, who is supervising the efforts of his nephew, Wormwood, to bring about the young man's damnation. All the action is seen through the eyes of Screwtape, who prides himself on Hell's peculiar kind of realism.

This literary device has important consequences. The human condition, with its hopes and perils, is filtered through the eyes of a hostile observer. Many details of ordinary life that seem momentous are barely mentioned; seeming trivialities often become the issues on which salvation or damnation depend. Screwtape is a complete supernaturalist. He does not believe; he *knows* from painful experience that Heaven as well as Hell, God, and Christ are the ultimate realities, and that human existence viewed within a purely human framework is not very interesting or enduring. He is enlisted on the demonic side in the cosmic war described in Ephesians 6:12: "For we wrestle not against flesh and blood, but against principalities, against powers, against the rulers of the darkness of this world, against spiritual wickedness in high places." The difference is simply that Screwtape, deep in the diabolic bureaucracy, is one of the rulers of the darkness of this world.

This point of view directs a powerful beam into all sorts of odd corners of human life, revealing issues of life and spiritual death. Newspaper headlines sink in importance. Although the book is set in World War II, Screwtape declares that war is neither favorable nor unfavorable to the purposes of Hell. On the other hand, an aggrieved feeling, "I ought to have some time for myself," may be the thin entering wedge for self-pity and incomplete obedience to God, proving in the long run far more perilous than pulling the trigger on a machine gun. Screwtape's angle of vision has an immense simplicity and clarity. The only question he asks of any human deed is whether it leads the soul closer to God or farther from Him. The deed need not be spectacular:

> . . . the only thing that matters is the extent to which you
> separate the man from the Enemy. It does not matter
> how small the sins are provided that their cumulative effect
> is to edge the man away from the Light and out into the
> Nothing. Murder is no better than cards if cards can do the
> trick. Indeed the safest road to Hell is the gradual one—
> the gentle slope, soft underfoot, without sudden turnings,
> without milestones, without signposts.[1]

One thinks of the insubstantial Ghosts of *The Great Divorce,*
most of whom have found their way to the gray town on the
strength of apparently petty sins, while one of the Solid People turns out to have been a murderer on earth.

The story told in *The Screwtape Letters* is simple. A
young man, unmarried, living with his mother, and apparently employed in a professional or white collar position,
experiences a conversion or reconversion to Christianity.
His guardian devil, Wormwood, also young and inexperi-
enced, and youthfully eager for splendid victories, is given
the task of reversing the conversion and bringing this human
safely to Hell. Wormwood's Uncle, Screwtape, sets about
instructing him, and in the course of commenting on his reports, describes the mortal's life after his conversion. The
story has few moments of high drama. Most of the action is
either mental and invisible to human eyes, or concerns such
minor matters that a human spectator would scarcely notice.
For instance, one of the young man's major spiritual problems lies in his relation with his sharp-tongued and demanding mother, who laments as she grows older that no servant
today knows how to make a proper piece of toast. Mother
and son have developed to perfection the art of saying
things that sound, on paper, perfectly inoffensive, but which
in the context of the moment are infuriating.

After the young man's religious conversion, he tries to
cope with such problems. But his success fluctuates. For one
thing, he strikes up a friendship with a worldly middle-aged

---

[1] *The Screwtape Letters with Screwtape Proposes a Toast* (New
York: Macmillan, 1961), p. 56.

couple and through them meets their whole scoffing "set."
This is a hopeful sign to Screwtape, but he is less pleased
when the man falls in love with a Christian girl, in Screwtape's words, "a vile, sneaking, simpering, demure, monosyl-
labic, mouselike, watery, insignificant, virginal, bread-and-
butter miss," who is "yet ready to fall into this booby's arms
like any other breeding animal."[2] Screwtape's sincere prudery
is genuinely offended.

The young man becomes engaged to the girl described
above, and finds himself accepted by her highly interesting
and intelligent family. Screwtape seeks ways of counterat-
tacking. Meanwhile, World War II has started, and the young
man's present happiness exists against the backdrop of possible conscription and the perils of air raids. The anxieties
produced by fragile happiness and an uncertain future offer
Wormwood many opportunities for eroding the man's religious faith, and these are analyzed in detail by Screwtape.

Finally, the air raids come. The young man is an air
raid warden, exposed to terrifying dangers. During one of
the raids he is killed, and Screwtape's last letter pours forth
his unbearable anguish:

> The howl of sharpened famine for that loss re-echoes at
> this moment through all the levels of the Kingdom of Noise
> down to the very Throne itself. . . . The more one
> thinks about it, the worse it becomes. He got through so
> easily! No gradual misgivings, no doctor's sentence, no
> nursing home, no operating theatre, no false hopes of life:
> sheer, instantaneous liberation.[3]

The plot of the *Letters* is nowhere concerned with magnificent sins or virtues. The young man's final destiny has as
much to do with his facial expressions when he speaks to his
mother as it does with the weighty decrees of the ten commandments. Like so many of Lewis's tales, it is a quest story.
We have an Everyman whose goal is Heaven, but he leads so

---

[2] P. 101.
[3] P. 146.

quiet a life that his pilgrimage is hardly visible except to demonic eyes and their acute vision.

The personality of Screwtape is one of the major literary achievements of this book, and a principal reason the chronicle holds together. One reads on to find out how Screwtape will react to each new situation. He prides himself on his complete lack of sentimentality. Where there are gaps in his theoretical knowledge of mankind he counts on future research, which is being vigorously pursued by Hell, to fill him in. Screwtape, in fact, often talks like a sociologist who understands almost everything about society and some day will understand it completely. (It is interesting that the weak, ambitious young don of *That Hideous Strength* will also be a sociologist. Sociologists were evidently no favorites of Lewis's.) At times, unsolved intellectual problems drive Screwtape into a frenzy. After stating the fundamental philosophy of Hell—". . . one thing is not another thing, and, specially, that one self is not another self. My good is my good and your good is yours. What one gains another loses" — he goes on to recognize with bewilderment that

> . . . the Enemy's philosophy is nothing more nor less
> than one continued attempt to evade this very obvious truth.
> He aims at a contradiction. Things are to be many,
> yet somehow also one. The good of one self is to be the
> good of another. This impossibility He calls *Love,* and this
> same monotonous panacea can be detected under all He
> does and even all He is—or claims to be.[4]

Screwtape tries to deal with spiritual facts as facts, and permits himself no emotion save zeal for his duties. He is, however, a seething caldron of stormy emotions and, when frustrated, can burst out into a torrent of agonized vituperation. At one point, in the midst of his frenzies, he temporarily turns into a large centipede.

Screwtape's emotions are revealed especially in his relation with his nephew. At the beginning, there is a tone of

---

[4] P. 81.

avuncular fondness as he instructs Wormwood in the latest methods of temptation. "Your affectionate uncle" seems appropriate enough at the end of the letters. But by the time the story is over, "affectionate" has taken on sinister connotations, suggesting the delights of eating. In Hell, strong wills literally devour weaker ones. Screwtape and Wormwood provide a dramatic, potentially cannibalistic, subplot while the main story is being acted out.

As early as Chapter II, Screwtape begins to issue stern threats. "I note with grave displeasure that your patient has become a Christian. Do not indulge the hope that you will escape the usual penalties; indeed, in your better moments, I trust you would hardly even wish to do so."[5] By letter IV, a tone of personal irritation and offense creeps in. Apparently Wormwood has criticized some of the advice he received from his uncle.

The tension between uncle and nephew has now been established, and is developed and accentuated by a variety of episodes. Hell, the tale seems to say, is ultimately self-destructive because all the damned have concern only for self. By the time of letter XIX it is clear that neither of the two devils can trust the other. Screwtape has inadvertently written words seeming to suggest that the Enemy really loves humans, and this of course is heresy. He urges Wormwood to keep these incriminating documents under lock and key, and he meanwhile promises to look after his nephew's interests.

Screwtape's letters become grimmer and more threatening as the young man seems to be slipping away from his clutches. During the first air raid, his behavior is, from Hell's viewpoint, extremely discouraging. He does his complete duty, but is frightened, feels like a coward, comes away with no pride.

Finally, in letter XXXI, Screwtape's true affection for his nephew is revealed; it is a glutton's affection for steak. Hearing that the young man has escaped forever, Screwtape speaks plainly:

---

[5] P. 11.

Rest assured, my love for you and your love for me are as
like as two peas. . . . The difference is that I am the
stronger. I think they will give you to me now; or a bit
of you. Love you? Why, yes. As dainty a morsel as
ever I grew fat on.[6]

Screwtape may be incurably bewildered by certain truths,
such as God's genuine love of the bipeds he has created, but
his knowledge of practical psychology is precise, and adequate to bring many platoons of souls into the cattle pens
of Hell. He is also, from the human viewpoint, an effective
satirist. He leads the reader first to laugh at mortal absurdities and finally to question many of his favorite *idées fixes*.
This he does by applying the clear light of Hell to human
nonsense. Screwtape thus unwittingly accomplishes the work
of Christian apologetics, clearing away many of the barriers
to religious commitment.

Screwtape reveals that one of Hell's triumphant strategies has been to inculcate a historical or evolutionary point of
view, with an accompanying horror of the Same Old Thing.
As he explains to Wormwood:

The Enemy loves platitudes. Of a proposed course of
action He wants men, so far as I can see, to ask very simple
questions: Is it righteous? Is it prudent? Is it possible? Now
if we can keep men asking "Is it in accordance with
the general movement of our time? Is it progressive or
reactionary? Is this the way that History is going?" they
will neglect the relevant questions. . . . For the descriptive
adjective "unchanged" we have substituted the emotional
adjective "stagnant."[7]

In another letter (XXVII) Screwtape discusses the Historical Point of View further:

The Historical Point of View, put briefly, means that when
a learned man is presented with any statement in an
ancient author, the one question he never asks is whether ·

─────────
6 P. 145.
7 Pp. 118–19.

it is true. He asks who influenced the ancient writer,
and how far the statement is consistent with what he said
in other books, and what phase in the writer's development,
or in the general history of thought, it illustrates, and
how it affected later writers. . . .[8]

The Philological Arm of Hell has scored triumphs with particular words, such as "real." Here a heads-you-win tails-I-lose psychology has been fostered. If a person has some important spiritual experience, he is reminded by a friend that nothing really happened except he was in a lighted building and heard some music. But someone discussing a high dive will insist that you can't understand it until you climb up and leap into the water. The agents of Hell have taught us to use the word now in one sense, now in the other, the choice being always the one that best destroys belief in transcendent experience. For instance, if you hate another person, you see him as he really is, but if you love him, you are taught that this is nothing but a subjective haze veiling the "real" feeling, which is lust.

Other words that have been transvalued by the Philological Arm include "puritan" and "adolescent"; the most brilliant coup is the replacement of the warm words "charity" and "love" with the passive and cold "unselfishness."

Some of the satire is very simply, but adroitly, accomplished. All Lewis needed to do was have Screwtape describe an exaggerated version of familiar earthly activities. For example, the bureaucratic mentality surely needs no imprimatur from Hell in order to flourish, but the reader becomes more keenly aware of its presence here below when Screwtape pictures it in its final hellish perfection. It sounds as though the central headquarters of "Our Father" is a university research institute and the CIA all under one roof. This research is not, from a terrestrial viewpoint, benign. The purpose is simply and always to understand the Enemy better so as to thwart Him, and to refine the techniques of temptation and damnation.

---

[8] Pp. 128–29.

One useful tool of the devils is the promotion of superficial thought. A man can be led to think that his time is his
own. This is obviously an absurd thought; time is God's invention, and He owns it as surely as He owns the heavenly
bodies. Still, by fuddled thought about time, such a person
can be encouraged to feel personally aggrieved when any
claim is made on a stretch of time that he has earmarked for
his "very own." On the theoretical level such a person, if
religious, readily recognizes that God has a complete claim
on the twenty-four hours, but this fact seldom occurs to him
when he has worked hard at the office, wants to read the
paper after dinner, and sees coming up the street the neighbor
couple whose presence he least enjoys. He rarely remembers
to wonder why these people have been sent to him and what
task he has been appointed to fulfill.

The book is not just about Heaven and Hell, salvation
and damnation. There is the real world of the twentieth century in which this struggle is being waged. Since Lewis found
many things in that world distasteful, he seizes the opportunity to pay his curt respects; this is a habit that carries over
into many of his other books, including those supposedly
written for children. Lewis is, however, clever enough to inte-
grate his personal piques into the framework of *Screwtape*
without violence to the story line. In particular, Screwtape
analyzes at length the experience of "falling in love." He
grants that love of this kind sometimes leads to a marriage
with the intention of fidelity, fertility, and goodwill. On the
other hand, he can speak as soberly as a Chinese marriage
broker when he demythologizes the idea that *only* falling in
love can justify a marriage, and that it alone can sustain one.

Screwtape studies women as a practical psychologist,
though the subject obviously disgusts him. He distinguishes
between "a terrestrial and an infernal Venus." Love for the
former leads to such abominations as charity and marriage
and mutual respect. The more useful woman is the infernal
Venus, most suitable as prostitute or mistress, but also with
interesting possibilities as wife. This Venus attracts by the

tang of evil: "In the face, it is the visible animality, or sulki-
ness, or craft, or cruelty which he likes, and in the body,
something quite different from what he ordinarily calls
Beauty, something he may even, in a sane hour, describe as
ugliness, but which, by our art, can be made to play on the
raw nerve of his private obsession."[9] Thanks to the glorifica-
tion of "Love," men can often be led to marry such a woman,
thus creating a household with infinite possibilities for misery
and eternal damnation.

Screwtape is a very powerful invention to serve the purposes of apologetics. The reader is compelled to rethink his
attitude toward everything from the Historical Point of View
to reductionist theology when he discovers that the demonic
powers thoroughly approve of those trends he has considered
most enlightened. As apologetics, *The Screwtape Letters* are
among Lewis's most effective works. The initial and continuing twist—earth viewed through diabolic eyes—is entertaining, fresh, sometimes startling, sometimes threatening. Gradually, one begins to wonder how much hard thinking he has
ever done. Has he drifted along with the currents of the
times, like the liberal bishop of *The Great Divorce?* Has he
let fashion take the place of real thought? Is he actually a
conformist, instead of an advanced thinker?

As the reader progresses through this short book, his
imagination awakes; he begins to wonder if a strictly human-
istic viewpoint is adequate. Life appears to be set in a supernatural framework. Decisions about the most ordinary things
are no longer purely human decisions. Nothing is *merely*
human.

Lewis does not attempt by formal argument to prove all
this; that is left for books like *Mere Christianity*. He simply
assumes it and dramatizes it through Screwtape's words.
Screwtape does not have to work his way through the collected works of Thomas Aquinas to know that God exists.
God is his daily Enemy; he knows Him face to face, to his

---

[9] P. 93.

terror. The skeptical reader can properly object that Lewis is loading the dice by giving Screwtape the certainties most calculated to shake up an agnostic reader, but the entire book is so logically consistent and imaginatively real that these carping suspicions are constantly submerged by the sheer flow and eddy of a highly entertaining "pilgrim's progress."

For the most part, Screwtape's angle of vision is steadily maintained. Once in a while he forgets his demonic role and seems to put on an Oxford gown. He says, for instance, "In modern Christian writings, though I see much (indeed more than I like) about Mammon, I see few of the old warnings about Worldly Vanities, the Choice of Friends, and the Value of Time."[10] Surely it is the Oxford don speaking directly here. In another letter, Screwtape appears for the moment to feel compassion toward one kind of suffering soul, and shows inadequate delight in the thought of damnation:

> The Christians describe the Enemy as one "without whom Nothing is strong." And Nothing is very strong: strong enough to steal away a man's best years not in sweet sins but in a dreary flickering of the mind over it knows not what and knows not why, in the gratification of curiosities so feeble that the man is only half aware of them, in drumming of fingers and kicking of heels, in whistling tunes that he does not like, or in the long, dim labyrinth of reveries that have not even lust or ambition to give them a relish, but which, once chance association has started them, the creature is too weak and fuddled to shake off.[11]

This is powerful writing, but it would be better suited to *Mere Christianity*. These lapses are rare, and in general Screwtape maintains his distinct tone throughout.

The epistolary form of the book frees it from problems that beset *The Pilgrim's Regress* and *The Great Divorce*. A reader going through a collection of letters does not expect an elaborate system of symbols or allegorical figures. A letter

---

10 P. 47.
11 P. 56.

is a form of exposition. Thus, Lewis can be as expository in *Screwtape* as in *Mere Christianity* or *The Abolition of Man*.

Screwtape is not very visual. Ideas and attitudes are at war, but they are seldom transmuted into symbolic figures. What little visual symbolism there is tends to be of a simple, straightforward kind. There is, for instance, the intense light that pierces the devils: "The humans do not start from that direct perception of Him which we, unhappily, cannot avoid. They have never known that ghastly luminosity, that stabbing and searing glare which makes the background of permanent pain to our lives."[12]

Another simple symbol is the asphyxiating cloud which sometimes surrounds a human and makes a close approach impossible. This apparently occurs at those times when God's grace is directly in operation. Other symbolism is based on the difference between music and noise. Hell prefers noise.

The most consistent symbol, and the one that runs through the book, is that of eating. Satan is looking for food, the strong will consuming lesser wills. God, by contrast, seeks free fellowship with his creatures.

From a purely literary viewpoint, *The Screwtape Letters* is among the most successful of Lewis's fanciful books. Here Lewis avoided the incubus of unwieldy medieval literary forms and hit on a brilliantly simple device that enabled him to express what he wished with a minimum of literary machinery. By having the author of the letters be a highly intellectual devil, indeed a research scholar, Lewis establishes the convention that the book can argue and analyze in a direct way. Since Lewis's expository instincts have a way of overflowing his symbolic containers, this freedom from elaborate symbolism is a liberation. *Screwtape* represents a peculiarly successful blend of approaches used by Lewis in other books. On the one hand, it is as imaginative as *Out of the Silent Planet*. On the other hand, it is written with great directness and clarity, such as one finds in *Mere*

---

[12] P. 21.

Christianity, The Abolition of Man, and *Miracles.* Lewis may have been irritated by the enormous popularity of *Screwtape,* but perhaps his readers recognized in it the potent combination of two of his greatest strengths.

3

THE ALMOST POET

Backtracking now to Lewis's earliest published books, we discover not the famous master of prose, but an ambitious poet. In his teens and into his early thirties, his supreme ambition was to be recognized and remembered as a major poet. He was constantly writing verse, along with prose works. Sometimes he would experiment with a given idea, such as *Dymer,* in both prose and verse. His commitment to poetry was a combative one. Radically out of sympathy with the Eliot–Pound kind of modern verse, he combined with some like-minded friends at Oxford in an abortive plan to publish a traditionalist anthology of modern poetry and sweep the tide back.

In 1919, at the age of twenty, he brought out *Spirits in Bondage* (under the pseudonym of Clive Hamilton) and received some passing recognition as a "war poet." *Dymer,* a long narrative poem, was published seven years later, and while it hardly stemmed the floodtide of modernist verse, it was praised in several reviews. Though Lewis continued to write verse off and on for the rest of his life, he made no serious effort at further publication in book form. Did he recognize that poetic modernism was too strong to be repelled, or was there an inner doubt gnawing away at his self-confidence as a poet?

Spirits in Bondage[1] gives a sampling of the poems Lewis was writing at Oxford, Great Bookham, and even earlier. As a first book by a young college student, it is, of course, uneven—but as instructors of writing workshops are wont to say, "It shows definite promise here and there."

One notices first of all the obvious influences. The language is sometimes reminiscent of Housman, Hardy, the young Yeats, perhaps Keats. The poems are usually direct and easy to understand; they demand no excessive psychologizing. In a loose way, one can say that *Spirits* stands in the broad and ill-defined Romantic tradition, and that only the topical references (as to World War I) anchor them in the twentieth century.

The first poem, "Prologue," sets the tone of escape from the ordinary world. The poet is the quester who brings back news of a land bearing little resemblance to daily life:

So in mighty deeps alone on the chainless breezes blown
In my coracle of verses I will sing of lands unknown,
Flying from the scarlet city where a Lord that knows no pity
Mocks the broken people praying round his iron throne,
—Sing about the Hidden Country fresh and full of quiet green.
Sailing over seas uncharted to a port that none has seen.[2]

The reader is thus invited to escape from the commonplace. The "Lord that knows no pity" is presumably God (or Satan), who figures in a number of these poems, sometimes as an illusion, though often as a Hardy-like impersonal or hostile force.

The basic metaphor in the poem is a comparison between the poet and ancient Phoenicians sailing to the tin isles. The metaphor soon wears thin. This is partly because Lewis in this poem reveals little of the powerful visual imagination that later served him so well in the space trilogy, *The Great Divorce,* and the Narnia tales. The best he can offer is

---

[1] Clive Hamilton, *Spirits in Bondage: A Cycle of Lyrics* (London: William Heinemann, 1919). Available from University Microfilms.
[2] Pp. 7–8.

such prosaic pictures as "legends of their people and the land that gave them birth" and "Sang of all the pride and glory of their hardy enterprise," which rings like chamber of commerce rhetoric.

Since few readers are likely ever to lay hands on a copy of *Spirits,* it may be useful to single out several poems to demonstrate where Lewis stood as a writer while a young student and soldier.

He was, of course, literally a war poet. He had the experiences—stinking trenches, dismembered bodies, a battle wound. The wonder is not that he writes about war, but that he writes about it so rarely. The war must have deepened his already pessimistic vision, but it does not seem to have been a key experience in his life. When conflict is explicitly mentioned, it serves mostly to provide further evidence of mankind's brutish heritage, or to inspire interesting metaphors, as in "French Nocturne":

> Long leagues on either hand the trenches spread
> And all is still; now even this gross line
> Drinks in the frosty silences divine.
> The pale, green moon is riding overhead.

The speaker watches a plane flying toward the moon, and recalls how once he could fantasize about "some harbour of dear dreams." But now he knows the moon is just a big stone, and he has no right to dream beautiful dreams—

> What call have I to dream of anything?
> I am a wolf. Back to the world again,
> And speech of fellow-brutes that once were men.
> Our throats can bark for slaughter: cannot sing.[3]

The trouble with this battle scene is that its peaceful quality does not provide a poetically convincing reason why ordinary men are turned into savage carnivores. It is more like an essay than a poem.

In another poem, "Victory," the indomitable spirit of

———
[3] Pp. 12–13.

man is proclaimed in "Invictus" style. Granting that Roland
is dead, and Iseult's lips are dust, and the faerie people have
gone from the woods, and that poetry itself is not as durable
as brass, the poem yet affirms something in man that transcends even the brutality of war:

> Though often bruised, oft broken by the rod,
> Yet, like the phoenix, from each fiery bed
> Higher the stricken spirit lifts its head
> And higher—till the beast become a god.[4]

One soon notices that in these poems written by an
atheist, God is remarkably alive. No double-talk is necessarily involved; after all, many a devout Christian (including Milton) has written *as though* the whole classical array
of pagan deities actually existed. Poets find their symbols
where they can. Throughout the book Lewis is trying to
decide whether this symbol is friend or foe. More often he is
foe, a Zeus always suppressing Prometheus. One long diatribe against God is "Ode for New Year's Day" with such
lines as "The sky above is sickening, the clouds of God's hate
cover it" . . . "But now one age is ending, and God calls
home the stars / And looses the wheel of the ages and sends
it spinning back / Amid the death of nations, and points a
downward track, / And madness is come over us and great
and little wars." (Note the picture of the stars being called
home, which later is dramatized as part of the "last things"
in *The Last Battle*.) This God is too busy to listen to the
little prayers of humans. "And here he builds a nebula, and
there he slays a sun / And works his own fierce pleasure. All
things he shall fulfil, / And O, my poor Despoina, do you
think he ever hears / The wail of hearts he has broken, the
sound of human ill?" God by this point is no longer an impersonal engineer; he is actively hostile as the poem concludes: "If you could flee away / Into some other country
beyond the rosy West, / To hide in the deep forests and be

---

[4] Pp. 16–17.

for ever at rest / From the rankling hate of God and the outworn world's decay!"[5]

In another poem, "Satan Speaks," it is as though one
hears the future voice of Screwtape, but here speaking in
heroic couplets. Satan refers to the vermin (later Screwtape's
own term) on the face of the earth who try to rise above it.
He hurls his challenge to the rebellious:

> They hate my world! Then let that other God
> Come from the outer spaces glory-shod,
> And from this castle I have built on Night
> Steal forth my own thought's children into light,
> If such an one there be. But far away
> He walks the airy fields of endless day,
> And my rebellious sons have called Him long
> And vainly called. My order still is strong
> And like to me nor second none I know.
> Whither the mammoth went this creature too shall go.[6]

Lewis had a fluctuating philosophy when he wrote
Spirits. He often suspects that the ultimate is malevolent. In
other moods he yearns for transcendent beauty and joy and
fleetingly affirms their possibility. In "Our Daily Bread," a
Platonic angle of vision takes on a Wordsworthian tone:

> Often me too the living voices call
> In many a vulgar and habitual place,
> I catch a sight of lands beyond the wall,
> > I see a strange god's face.
>
> And some day this will work upon me so
> I shall arise and leave both friends and home
> And over many lands a pilgrim go
> > Through alien woods and foam,
>
> Seeking the last steep edges of the earth
> Whence I may leap into that gulf of light
> Wherein, before my narrowing Self had birth,
> > Part of me lived aright.[7]

---

5 Pp. 23–26.
6 Pp. 35–36.
7 Pp. 86–87.

The plot of *The Pilgrim's Regress* is summarized by this poem. There is also a gain in precision here. "Part of me lived aright" has power because there has been a sufficiently exact build-up to justify the subtlety of the line.

On the whole, Lewis was beyond his depth in these early poems that attempted grand philosophic forays or tried to create a second world of the imagination to express the heart's desire. These are apprenticeship pieces, pointing toward magnificent achievements later on, but in prose rather than in verse. Where Lewis succeeded best was where he attempted least. There is, for example, a human realism of a rather poignant kind in "In Praise of Solid People," which moves with something of a Horatian decorum:

> Thank God that there are solid folk
> Who water flowers and roll the lawn,
> And sit and sew and talk and smoke,
> And snore all through the summer dawn.
>
> Who pass untroubled nights and days
> Full-fed and sleepily content,
> Rejoicing in each other's praise,
> Respectable and innocent.
>
> Who feel the things that all men feel,
> And think in well-worn grooves of thought,
> Whose honest spirits never reel
> Before man's mystery, overwrought.

Again, a foreshadowing; the third stanza points toward the praise of the *Tao* in *The Abolition of Man*. But Lewis's main point in this poem is the contrast between practical people and dreamers like himself. He goes on to describe himself sitting alone, yearning for the ineffable, and seeing visions:

> —Then suddenly, again, the room,
> Familiar books about me piled,
> And I alone amid the gloom,
> By one more mocking dream beguiled.

> And still no nearer to the Light,
> And still no further from myself,
> Alone and lost in clinging night
> —(The clock's still ticking on the shelf).[8]

Another poem in which Lewis simply looks at a world he knows well is "Irish Nocturne." It is also one of the most successful from a technical viewpoint. The rhymes are pleasantly unobtrusive. The rhythm has a subdued flexibility and seems to grow from the poem itself.

> But here at the dumb, slow stream where the
>   willows hang,
> With never a wind to blow the mists apart,
> Bitter and bitter it is for thee, O my heart,
> Looking upon this land, where poets sang,
> Thus with the dreary shroud
> Unwholesome, over it spread,
> And knowing the fog and the cloud
> In her people's heart and head
> Even as it lies for ever upon her coasts
> Making them dim and dreamy lest her sons
>   should ever arise
> And remember all their boasts;
> For I know that the colourless skies
> And the blurred horizons breed
> Lonely desire and many words and brooding
>   and never a deed.[9]

In *Spirits* Lewis is bedeviled by the great religious and metaphysical questions, and has no systematic way of dealing with them. It is true that a poet need not have a complete intellectual system, but he does need some central vision as his point of reference. Yeats created his own in *A Vision;* perhaps Frost found one in that clock proclaiming that the time is neither wrong nor right. Dante received one ready-made from Aquinas. Lewis's conversion to Christianity solved an esthetic problem as well as a spiritual one. It gave him his

---

[8] Pp. 62, 65.
[9] Pp. 18–19.

central vision. But by that time, he was already moving away from verse.

In his early poems, when Lewis tries to say weighty things, he often becomes preachy or editorializes, and fails to convert his ideas into effective symbols. At the same time, convinced of the importance of form, he frequently makes a fetish of it and slips into a mechanical quality. In a young poet this dual endeavor can be good in the long run; he learns to weave form and content into a seamless fabric. But at the beginning, he is likely to seem less impressive than his contemporary who concentrates only on technique, or only on content.

The young poet drunk on formal meters is nearly always too perfect, and so it is with Lewis at this stage. His meters have the precisely measured quality of the metronome. Even in so short a poem as "Victory," some occasional variations in meter, some deliberate roughness, would wake it to greater life, but what we get is a succession of oversmooth stanzas like: "The faerie people from our woods are gone, / No Dryads have I found in all our trees. / No Triton blows his horn about our seas / And Arthur sleeps far hence in Avalon."

The same poem illustrates another characteristic found in many of these poems, a cataloguing use of mythological and literary references, instead of organizing them into one dominant symbol through which the poem can speak. The references often have an ornamental or throwaway quality. Some could be added, others omitted, without greatly changing the poem. The reader encounters in quick succession the French hero Roland; the Irish hero Cuchulain; a legendary Greek woman, Helen; then back to the Celts with Iseult; next the assorted fairies, Dryads, Tritons, and King Arthur. They have one thing in common: they are dead. Mention of them prepares the way for ideas stated in almost plain prose: "For these decay: but not for that decays / The yearning, high, rebellious spirit of man / That never rested yet since life began / From striving with red Nature and her ways."

The reader wonders, Would it not be more effective to focus on one mythological allusion, develop it enough so that the idea of death and decay come imaginatively alive, and then set this vivid image in opposition to the concluding and more prosaic part of the poem?

For all his infelicities and failures, the young poet has many things going for him. He is willing to discipline himself to learn the craft. He shows wide reading, and he has a storehouse of allusions that he can learn to use effectively. Most of all, he is a poet determined to settle for nothing short of major poetry. He is wrestling with the eternal questions—life, death, meaning, emptiness, God, Satan, love—toward which great poetry gravitates.

One other book of Lewis's verse was published in his lifetime, again under the protective authorship of Clive Hamilton.[10] *Dymer,* coming out in 1926, disappeared almost without a trace. Lewis, whose confidence in his poetry was never too sturdy though his ambitions were enormous, apparently experienced a failure of nerve and gradually turned to prose as his main medium. It was only after his death, when Walter Hooper searched periodicals and surviving manuscripts, that the substantial bulk of Lewis's poetry came to light. There was enough to fill two considerable volumes: *Narrative Poems* and *Poems* (shorter poems, excluding those found in *Spirits in Bondage*).

During its long period of gestation, *Dymer*—like *Surprised by Joy* and *Till We Have Faces*—vacillated between prose and verse. The form on which Lewis finally settled was rime royal, a stanza used by Chaucer in *Troilus and Criseyde,* by Shakespeare in *Venus and Adonis,* and by countless subsequent poets, usually in narrative poems. A stanza from *Dymer* will illustrate its effect:

---

[10] This was reissued, under Lewis's name, and with a Preface by the author, in 1950. The edition of *Dymer* used here for citation is that in *Narrative Poems* (New York: Harcourt Brace Jovanovich, 1969).

> Remember, yet again, he had grown up
> On rations and on scientific food,
> At common boards, with water in his cup,
> One mess alike for every day and mood:
> But here, at his right hand, a flagon stood.
> He raised it, paused before he drank, and laughed,
> "I'll drown their Perfect City in this draught."[11]

Lewis handles this form well in briskly narrative and satiric passages, and sometimes—though not always—in more descriptive places.

When *Dymer* became available again with the 1950 edition, Lewis's ardent reading public found itself puzzled. This was not the gleaming clarity they expected from him. *Dymer* seems to weave in and out of the light of reason. Some parts, particularly the social satire, are as clear and sharp as though Lord Byron had written them. Other parts are a confused welter of symbolism. Lewis himself acknowledged the reader's problem in his Preface to the new edition, where he describes the genesis of the poem:

> . . . what simply "came to me," was the story of a man
> who, on some mysterious bride, begets a monster: which
> monster, as soon as it has killed its father, becomes a god.
> This story arrived, complete, in my mind somewhere about
> my seventeenth year. To the best of my knowledge I
> did not consciously or voluntarily invent it, nor was it, in
> the plain sense of that word, a dream. All I know about it is
> that there was a time when it was not there, and then
> presently a time when it was. Every one may allegorise it
> or psychoanalyse it as he pleases: and if I did so myself my
> interpretations would have no more authority than
> anyone else's.[12]

Lewis's Preface, with its discussion of the thematic strands in the tale, at least gives some idea of what he intended after the basic symbol came to him. It becomes apparent that the problem is not lack of a theme but an oversupply. It is as

---

[11] P. 20.
[12] P. 3.

though Lewis had three or four passionate convictions which
he jammed together into one long poem by sheer willpower.

The first theme is that a totalitarian utopia and lawless
anarchy are equally undesirable. Though, as Lewis states in
the Preface, he had not at that time read Huxley's *Brave New
World,* the city in which Dymer grows seems a grimmer version of Huxley's overorganized quasi-utopia. Lewis, in some
moods an anarchist, savagely ridicules this kind of society,
but he also recognizes that too complete a revolt can breed
the opposite extreme of savage chaos, symbolized in the
poem by the red-haired hunchback, Bran, who capitalizes
upon the mild liberation movement accidentally begun by
Dymer, when the latter strikes his teacher and sees him top-
ple over dead. Dymer longs for freedom from man-made
shackles, but does not wish to secede from civilization; Bran
is the kind of brute who rises in the second stage of a revolution and exults in the lopping off of hands, torture, and blood.

A second theme is the renunciation of wishful thinking.
In his attempt to be hard-nosed and realistic, Lewis was
obliged, as he put it, to cut down his own former "groves and
high places," repudiating the experiences of "Joy" that had
haunted him since childhood. Dymer renounces the illu-
sions of a friendly universe and recognizes it for the threatening place it is.

Another closely related theme concerns the perils of the
occult. Lewis had been lured to the occult by his reading—
Maeterlinck and Yeats's early poetry—and still more by the
example of Yeats himself, whom he met at several psychic
gatherings. To his amazement he found that Yeats believed
literally in the sort of never-never world that most Romantic
poets celebrated only in a metaphorical way. By the time he
wrote *Dymer,* Lewis had turned against the occult, partly because he had seen a friend sink into madness and ultimately
into death, apparently under the influence of spiritualism.
Dymer's great temptation comes in Canto VII, when a magician (modeled at least in physical appearance on Yeats)
urges him to use otherworldly craft to regain the girl with

whom he had slept the first night of his liberation. At this point, Dymer renounces magic and prepares to face his fate, in the form of the monster he begot with the invisible girl.

The monster episode vibrates with archetypal force, particularly when one bears in mind the Freudian speculation about sons who slay the primal father. Lewis, however, does very little to link it with the rest of the poem. All in all, the various themes twisting through *Dymer* are loosely connected indeed. The resurrection theme at the end of the poem also seems rather an afterthought.

Dymer is a quest tale, and both in its structure and themes points toward *The Pilgrim's Regress,* in which another rebel quester, John, repudiates an oppressive society and sets out to be a free man, seeking whatever meaning there is in life.

Taken as a whole, *Dymer* fails. Considered episode by episode, there is a checkered pattern of failures and successes. Canto I, with its savage satire of pseudo utopianism, effectively pictures the world of virtuous prudes that closed in on Dymer:

> At Dymer's birth no comets scared the nation,
> The public crèche engulfed him with the rest,
> And twenty separate Boards of Education
> Closed round him. He passed through every test,
> Was vaccinated, numbered, washed and dressed,
> Proctored, inspected, whipt, examined weekly,
> And for some nineteen years he bore it meekly.[13]

In the scene with the magician there is a strong evocation of personality:

> It was a mighty man whose beardless face
> Beneath grey hair shone out so large and mild
> It made a sort of moonlight in the place.
> A dreamy desperation, wistful-wild,
> Showed in his glance and gait: yet like a child,

---

[13] P. 8.

An Asian emperor's only child, was he
With his brave looks and bright solemnity.[14]

The magician has no interest in the visible world except
as an entrance into the invisible:

And all his talk was tales of magic words
And of the nations in the clouds above,
Astral and aerish tribes who fish for birds
With angles. And by history he could prove
How chosen spirits from earth had won their love,
As Arthur, or Usheen: and to their isle
Went Helen for the sake of a Greek smile.
. . . .
Dymer was talking now. Now Dymer told
Of his own love and losing, drowsily.
The Master leaned towards him, "Was it cold,
This spirit, to the touch?"—"No, Sir, not she,"
Said Dymer. And his host: "Why this must be
Aethereal, not aerial! O my soul,
Be still . . . but wait. Tell on, Sir, tell the whole."[15]

At other times, as in Canto V, the poem lapses into
passages of generalized description and the drive slackens:

He felt the eternal strength of the silly earth,
The unhastening circuit of the stars and sea,
The business of perpetual death and birth,
The meaningless precision. All must be
The same and still the same in each degree—
Who cared now? And he smiled and could forgive,
Believing that for sure he would not live.[16]

We know that at one time *Dymer* was written in prose,
and the final poem has a quality of *poésie voulue* about it, as
though the author had said, "I'm going to turn this into
poetry," and had set about superimposing lines, rhyme
schemes, and meters on it. There is little distinctively "po-

---

[14] Pp. 56–57.
[15] P. 59.
[16] P. 47.

etic" about the way language is used; the metaphors could equally well have been employed in a prose version. In fact, interest in the poem lies not in how it says things but in what it says.

The confrontation scene is powerful if confusing. Dymer goes bravely into battle and perishes beneath the monster's feet, "broken and bent and white, / The ruined limbs of Dymer." But nature seems to be experiencing a resurrection, ". . . with dancing flowers / Where flower had never grown; and one by one / The splintered woods, as if from April showers, / Were softening into green. . . ." The angel who has been watching is astounded to behold a scene of transformation:

> For when he had gazed hard with steady eyes
> Upon the brute, behold, no brute was there,
> But someone towering large against the skies,
> A wing'd and sworded shape, whose foam-like hair
> Lay white about its shoulders, and the air
> That came from it was burning hot. The whole
> Pure body brimmed with life, as a full bowl.

> And from the distant corner of day's birth
> He heard clear trumpets blowing and bells ring,
> A noise of great good coming into earth
> And such a music as the dumb would sing
> If Balder had led back the blameless spring
> With victory, with the voice of charging spears,
> And in white lands long-lost Saturnian years.[17]

Exactly what does all this mean? Perhaps the only answer is to ask first what Dymer has been doing. He was a conformist in a dull utopian school. He rebelled. He exulted in his new freedom. He was tempted to wishful thinking and magic and rejected the temptations. He came to see the hostility or indifference of the universe. Finally, he resolved to face his own fate in the form of the monster he had begotten. In doing so, he set in motion a cosmic renewal and resurrec-

---

[17] Pp. 90–91.

tion, and the monster is at last revealed as the god he had become. Dymer, however, lies dead.

We know from Lewis's correspondence that he was working on other narrative poems before *Dymer* was published, and for at least a few years afterward. What survives are three narratives (two of which seem incomplete). There is no evidence Lewis ever tried to publish them.

Launcelot was, according to Walter Hooper, probably written in the early 1930's, perhaps half a dozen years after the publication of *Dymer*. The poem has an autumnal and wintry quality to it and the sense of slow changes; the weightiness of the Alexandrine couplets catches this tone well. It is a tale of a world falling into corruption. The Round Table is disintegrating; and old love (Gwinever and Launcelot) grows sad and anxious with time.

Most of the Knights of the Round Table set out in autumn on the quest for the Sangrail. They return more than a year later, remote, defeated, unable to talk of their experience. At last Launcelot himself returns. He goes to Gwinever's chamber and tells the tale of their adventures. They had journeyed through rich country, then come to a wasteland (remarkably like Eliot's). There they encountered a hermit who explained that the sickness of the King Fisherman will not be cured nor the land restored to fertility until a good knight sees the Sangrail and asks whom it served. Launcelot continued his journey, coming to a tomb reserved for the "three best knights of Christendom" but not "For the Knight recreant of the Lake, for Launcelot!"[18]

Launcelot next journeyed into a steamy countryside and met a lady who reminded him of both Gwinever and Morgan the enchantress. She showed him three coffins reserved for "the three best knights—Sir Lamorake, Tristram, and Launcelot du Lake." She explained that the knights would be alive when placed in the coffins, and showed a kind of guillotine resting above. Launcelot was horrified, but she explained:

---

[18] Pp. 100–101.

> . . . for endless love of them I mean to make
> Their sweetness mine beyond recovery and to take
> That joy away from Morgan and from Gwinever
> And Nimue and Isound and Elaine, and here
> Keep those bright heads and comb their hair
>   and make them lie
> Between my breasts and worship them until I die.[19]

The manuscript breaks off at this point. The story itself is much better focused than in *Dymer,* and the central theme is also clear-cut. The fellowship of the Round Table is perishing, poisoned by the sin of Gwinever and Launcelot.

In *Dymer* at its best the language has the crisp precision of good prose. Often, in *Launcelot,* there seems an extra dimension, the peculiar richness and density that poetry can evoke from words. Call it, for lack of a better term, the "music" of words, vibrating in the reader's unconscious and hinting always at more than is literally said.

The evocative quality of the language can be illustrated by the wasteland passages:

> He passes by
> Forsaken wells and sees the buckets red with rust
> Upon the chains. Dry watercourses filled with dust
> He crosses over; and villages on every side
> Ruined he sees, and jaws of houses gaping wide,
> And abbeys showing ruinously the peeling gold
> In roofless choirs and, underneath, the churchyard mould
> Cracking and far subsiding into dusty caves
> That let the pale light in upon the ancient graves.[20]

Launcelot's encounter with the second lady is described in language of an almost Keatsian richness:

> The door was opened, fragrance such as dying men
> Imagine in immortal countries, blown about
> Heaven's meadows from the tree of life, came floating out.
> No man was in the chapel, but he sees a light

---

[19] P. 103.
[20] P. 98–99.

There too of many hundred candles burning bright.
She let him in, and up into the choir, and there
He saw three coffins all of new cut stone, and fair
With flowers and knots, and full of spices to the brim
And from them came the odour that by now makes dim
His sense with deathless sweetness. . . .[21]

In *Launcelot,* Lewis has taken familiar Arthurian material and brought it alive, full of psychological and spiritual nuances, as the great reworkers of the tradition have done: Thomas Malory, Alfred Tennyson, E. A. Robinson. It is a short poem, but it shows an impressive ability to make verse flow and to explore the music possible in combinations of words. It is an impressive advance over *Dymer* in every way.

The Nameless Isle, as Walter Hooper christened it, is a poem fair-copied in 1930. It is a tale of enchantment and the quest for a beautiful maiden, but its main purpose seems to have been an experiment in the Old English alliterative meter. Lewis achieves some striking effects, particularly with descriptions of violent landscapes.

The most interesting narrative poem is *The Queen of Drum.* Lewis mentions it in his diary in early 1927; he appears to have worked on it at least until 1938. It is incomplete and still in rough shape; the work is written in several different meters, one of which, rather oddly, is that of *The Rubaiyat of Omar Khayyam.* The poem is a story of the supernatural or preternatural; we see people venturing out in their dreams to explore fairyland, which lies in the border between Hell and Heaven; its ranks are constantly depleted as a quota of its citizens is periodically yielded to Hell.

The senile king is married to a maenadic young woman, who roams abroad at night on strange adventures. It is later revealed that the general of the king's army is a night rover, too. During the light of day, the prosaic business of government is carried on.

In a number of ways, this is the most impressive of

---

[21] P. 102.

Lewis's narrative poems. He has at last mastered that very difficult art of varying the style of his language while keeping the feel and rhythm of poetry going. This means he can shift from highly colloquial dialogue to elevated descriptive language and back again without jolting. Closely related to this achievement is the ability to have the characters talk in verse and still sound as though they are talking rather than declaiming set speeches. This means that the five main characters—the king, the queen, the chancellor, the general, and the archbishop—can be more sharply delineated. Each of these could be distinguished by his speech alone.

Another achievement is the effortless weaving back and forth between the normal world and the preternatural, without either being subordinated by the other. This is partly due to giving the everyday world its proper respect; it is described with the kind of photographic realism that a naturalistic novelist might employ, and is a perfect foil for the world of nighttime.

Most of all, it is the fluid use of language and meter that impresses the reader, such as the description of the old king waking and being dressed by his servants:

Gentlemen, pages, lords, and flunkey things
In lace who act the nurse to lonely kings,
Tumbled his poor old bones somehow from bed.
Swallowing their yawns, whispering with louted head,
Passed him from hand to hand, tousled and grey
And blinking like an owl surprised by day,
Rubbing his bleary eyes, muttering between dry gums
"Gi' me my teeth . . . dead tired . . . my lords—'t all comes
From living in the valley. Too much wood.
Sleep the clock round in Drum and get no good."[22]

Contrasted with this dreary world are the queen's adventures in the land of night.

And near the parting of three ways
She thought there was a silver haze,

———
[22] Pp. 131–32.

> She thought there was a giant's head
> Pushed from the earth with whiteness spread
> Of beard beneath and from its crown
> Cataracts of whiteness tumbling down.
> Then she drew near, tip-toed in awe,
> And looked again; this time she saw
> It was a thornbush, milky white
> That poured sweet smell upon the night.[23]

The king speaks with the wisdom of one who has learned to
be skeptical about skepticism itself:

> He [the archbishop] guesses well enough
> That back there on the borderline there's stuff
> Not marked on any map their sermons show
> —They keep one eye shut just because they know—
> Don't we all know?
> At bottom?—that this World in which we draw
> Our salaries, make our bows, and keep the law,
> This legible, plain universe we use
> For waking business, is a thing men choose
> By leaving out . . . well, much; our editing,
> (With expurgations) of some larger thing?
> Well, then, it stands to reason; go behind
> To the archetypal scrawl, and there you'll find
> . . . Well . . . variant readings, eh? And it won't do
> Being over-dainty there.[24]

After the general, annoyed by the disintegration of the
kingdom in the hands of its old king, stages a fascist coup
and becomes the duce, he speaks bluntly to the queen in
language that might have come from the pen of Robert
Browning:

> Now listen—for you're neither prude nor dunce
> And I can tell you my whole mind at once;
> First, let me make it absolutely clear
> That nobody has anything to fear

---

[23] P. 171.
[24] P. 145.

From me—provided that I get my way.
I'm always nice to people who obey,
Specially girls: and if you are kind to me
I will repay it double. Try! and see
How much more rich, more splendid and more gay
Your court will be than in the old King's day.[25]

One of the most haunting characterizations is that of the old archbishop, a vague man who has turned his eyes the other way rather than see all the corruption of the court, but who in the crisis turns out to be a real believer and martyr. One thinks of the final glory of Graham Greene's whiskey priest. The duce speaks to the archbishop with the tempter's voice: "Be loyal to the Leader and I'll build / Cathedrals for you, yes, and see them filled, / I'll give you a free hand to bait all Jews / And infidels. You can't mean to refuse?"[26] All he asks is a bit of cooperation—devise some spiritual explanation of the king's disappearance, convert Christianity into a nationalistic religion:

A good old Drummian God who has always some
Peculiar purpose up His sleeve for Drum,
Something that makes the increase of our trade
And territories feel like a Crusade,
Or, even if neither should in fact increase,
Teaches men in my will to find their peace.[27]

The archbishop refuses, and is beaten to death by the duce's thugs:

Ever he calls to Christ to be forgiven
And to come soon into the happy haven.
Horrible dance before his eyes is woven
Of darkened shapes on a red tempest driven.
Unwearyingly the great strokes are given.
He falls. His sides and all his ribs are riven,

[25] P. 159.
[26] P. 163.
[27] P. 162.

His guts are scattered and his skull is cloven,
The man is dead. God has his soul to heaven. Aoi![28]

Thus the poem reaches heights of eloquence, comparable to
the *Song of Roland,* which is being echoed here.

Though he abandoned long poems, Lewis continued to
write shorter ones, many of which he published in periodicals,
usually under a pseudonym. In the early 1950's he made a
start toward putting together a book-length collection but
never completed the task. Using this collection as a starting
point, Walter Hooper rounded up more than a hundred miscellaneous poems and published them as *Poems.*

Many of these poems have wit and almost all are well
constructed so far as formal poetic technique is concerned.
Few are major achievements. They are for the most part
occasional verse, footnotes on ideas Lewis expresses equally
well in prose.

Many of the best poems are satiric, usually good-hu-
mored but not always. Sometimes Lewis uses the sledgeham-
mer, not the rapier, as in "The Genuine Article":

You do not love the Bourgeoisie. Of course: for they
Begot you, bore you, paid for you, and punched your head;
You work with them; they're intimate as board and bed;
How could you love them, meeting them thus every day?
You love the Proletariat, the thin, far-away
Abstraction which resembles any workman fed
On mortal food as closely as the shiny red
Chessknight resembles stallions when they stamp and neigh.[29]

At other times, he is more whimsical, as in his attack on T. S.
Eliot's poetry in "A Confession":

I am so coarse, the things the poets see
Are obstinately invisible to me.
For twenty years I've stared my level best

---

[28] P. 165.
[29] *Poems* (New York: Harcourt, Brace & World, 1965), p. 63.

To see if evening—any evening—would suggest
A patient etherized upon a table;
In vain. I simply wasn't able.[30]

In general, the poems use language as it is employed in
Lewis's best prose. This involves an even pace, neither wordy
nor intricately compressed. There is a certain sameness in the
poetic effect of the poems; they are not full of the linguistic
surprises that poetry frequently offers.

Many of the poems have a historical or mythological
base; in particular, many reveal Lewis's vision of the past. In
"A Cliché Came Out of Its Cage" Lewis quotes someone as
saying, "The world is going back to Paganism," and adds:

Oh bright
Vision! I saw our dynasty in the bar of the House
Spill from their tumblers a libation to the Erinyes,
And Leavis with Lord Russell wreathed in flowers, heralded with
     flutes,
Leading white bulls to the cathedral of the solemn Muses
To pay where due the glory of their latest theorem.[31]

"Evolutionary Hymn" reads as though it were meant to
be sung by the mad Weston when he tries to explain his mission to Oyarsa:

On then! Value means survival—
     Value. If our progeny
Spreads and spawns and licks each rival,
     That will prove its deity
(Far from pleasant, by our present
     Standards, though it well may be).[32]

Sometimes a poem lifts the curtain of privacy a little
and catches Lewis doing what he theoretically thought a
writer had no business doing. He reveals himself in "As the
Ruin Falls" facing Joy's approaching death:

---

30 P. 1.
31 P. 3.
32 Pp. 55–56.

All this is flashy rhetoric about loving you.
I never had a selfless thought since I was born.
I am mercenary and self-seeking through and through:
I want God, you, all friends, merely to serve my turn.
Peace, re-assurance, pleasure, are the goals I seek,
I cannot crawl one inch outside my proper skin:
I talk of love—a scholar's parrot may talk Greek—
But, self-imprisoned, always end where I begin.[33]

Lewis himself reveals uncertainty about his poetry in his correspondence with Ruth Pitter. In one letter to her he confesses, "I meant to send you something of mine but I shan't. It all sounds like a brass band after yours" (July 9, 1946). Miss Pitter jotted down in memo form some of her impressions of Lewis the poet (September 29, 1948):

> Did his great learning, a really staggering skill in verse
> inhibit the poetry? Did he ever (like most of us)
> catch some floating bit of emotional thistledown and go on
> from that, or did he plan on a subject like an
> architect? . . . He had a great stock of the makings of a
> poet: strong visual memory, strong recollections of
> childhood: desperately strong yearnings for lost Paradise
> and hoped Heaven ("sweet desire"): not least a strong
> primitive intuition of the diabolical. . . . In fact his whole
> life was oriented and motivated by an almost uniquely-
> persisting child's sense of glory and of nightmare.
> The adult events were received into a medium still as
> pliable as wax, wide open to the glory, and equally
> vulnerable, with a man's strength to feel it all, and a great
> scholar's and writer's skills to express and to
> interpret. It is almost as though the adult discipline, notably
> the technique of his verse, had largely inhibited his poetry,
> which is perhaps, after all, most evident in his prose.
> I think he wanted to be a poet more than anything. Time
> will show. But if it was *magic* he was after, he achieved
> this sufficiently elsewhere.

I also recall a short letter (May 8, 1950) I received from Lewis. I had written to him about tendencies toward

---

[33] P. 109.

greater clarity I seemed to detect in current American poetry, and he replied by suggesting, perhaps rightly, that the great chasm between himself and the dominant poets was not technique but experience:

> . . . their experience is so very unlike my own. They seem to be constantly writing about the same sort of things that *articles* are written about: e.g., "the present world situation." That means, for me, that they can only write from a top level of the mind, the level on which generalities operate. But even this may be a mistake. At any rate I am sure I *never have* the sort of experiences they express: and I feel most alien when I come nearest to understanding them.

VISIONARY WORLDS

One half of Lewis's mind functions easily within the rational framework of exposition and argument. The other half turns to highly imaginative ways of saying things indirectly. The two halves present the same ultimate intuition of reality, but the strategies by which they storm the reader's guard are very different.

The imaginative Lewis is the older one. His earliest efforts at prose always involved some fanciful convention, no matter how much incidental realism might be scattered through a work. In Animaland the animals talk politics and engage in political intrigues—but they are still talking animals and therefore fanciful. In Lewis's later boyhood experiment with the Arthurian tradition ("Bleheris"), all the liberties of medieval romance attract him—monsters, strange trysts, bewildering quests.

No wonder he became a specialist in medieval literature. But his admiration of medieval literature was selective. One of his early letters mentions his initial encounter with Chaucer, and one is somewhat startled to find a lukewarm reaction:

> I have now read all the Tales of Chaucer which I ever
> expected to read and feel that I may consider the book as
> finished . . . some of them are quite impossible. On

59

the whole, with one or two exceptions, like the Knight's
Tale and the Franklin's, he is disappointing when you
get to know him. He has most of the faults of the Middle
Ages—garrulity and coarseness—without their romantic
charm. . . .[1]

Evidently the realism of Chaucer, with his fornicating students, deceived millers, and untidy villages is not sufficiently
romantic for Lewis's delicate literary stomach. He is more
at ease with worlds located not on a map but in the imagination.

Lewis's imagination peoples many worlds. Two—*The
Pilgrim's Regress* and *The Great Divorce*—are in a typical
medieval form, the dream vision. In each of these an observer (impersonal in the first, slightly individualized in the
second) describes the imaginary world for the benefit of the
reader. *The Pilgrim's Regress* is not only a dream vision but
also (like Bunyan's work) an allegory, the literary form that
Lewis traced through many centuries of literary and psychological history.

Lewis's return to Christianity suggested to him the possibility of *Pilgrim's Regress;* his hostility to the spirit of the
age gave him numerous foes against whom he could tilt his
lance. He would convert his experience into that of an Everyman and trace the path, with all its ambiguities and perils,
that led him back to traditional Christianity in the person of
Mother Kirk.

The book was only moderately successful when it first
appeared in 1933. Many readers found it ill-tempered and
too obscure. When Lewis, now famous, prepared a new edition in 1943, he tried to cope with the latter problem by
providing running heads that interpret the actions taking
place. He also wrote a long Preface in which he explained in
detail what he meant by "Romance"—the sort of momentary
experience that he elsewhere labels "Joy." As for the "un-
charitable temper" of the book, his defense was to point out

---

[1] *Letters of C. S. Lewis,* Edited, with a Memoir, by W. H. Lewis
(New York: Harcourt, Brace & World, 1966), p. 29.

how the world of the twenties looked to one who had followed his particular intellectual path:

> The different intellectual movements of that time were
> hostile to one another; but the one thing that seemed to
> unite them all was their common enmity to "immortal
> longings." The direct attack carried out on them from below
> by those who followed Freud or D. H. Lawrence, I think
> I could have borne with some temper; what put me
> out of patience was the scorn which claimed to be from
> above, and which was voiced by the American
> 'Humanists,' the Neo-Scholastics, and some who wrote for
> *The Criterion*. These people seemed to me to be
> condemning what they did not understand. When they called
> Romanticism "nostalgia" I, who had rejected long ago the
> illusion that the desired object was in the past, felt that
> they had not even crossed the *pons asinorum*. In the end I
> lost my temper.[2]

Lewis states that the book is not strict autobiography, but
certainly the almost anonymous John of the tale confronts
the same dilemmas and experiences that Lewis later pictures
more factually in *Surprised by Joy*. And John's pilgrimage,
guided by Reason and Romance, was also Lewis's.

The book has an elaborate symbolic system. As Lewis
explains in the Preface, the North suggests bitter food and
rigorous doctrines of esthetic purity. The South calls up pictures of excessively fertile land, jellyfish, overly sweet food,
and slovenly artists who indulge every impulse in their work.
Lewis declares one can even recognize "Northern" and
"Southern" types in daily contacts:

> Everyone can pick out among his own acquaintance the
> Northern and Southern types—the high noses, compressed
> lips, pale complexions, dryness and taciturnity of the one,
> the open mouths, the facile laughter and tears, the
> garrulity and (so to speak) general greasiness of the others.
> The Northerners are the men of rigid systems whether

---

[2] *The Pilgrim's Regress* (Grand Rapids, Michigan: Wm. B. Eerdmans, 1933, 1943, 1958), p. 10.

sceptical or dogmatic, Aristocrats, Stoics, Pharisees,
Rigorists, signed and sealed members of highly organized
"Parties." The Southerners are by their very nature less
definable; boneless souls whose doors stand open day and
night to almost every visitant, but always with readiest
welcome for those, whether Maenad or Mystagogue, who
offer some sort of intoxication.[3]

Lewis's model for the book was, of course, Bunyan's *Pilgrim's Progress*. Gunnar Urang's excellent short treatment of
the book explains:

> Some of these differences between the adventures of the two
> pilgrims may be accounted for theologically. As Dorothy
> Sayers has pointed out, the advent of Calvinism brought
> one of those profound changes in psychological outlook
> which tend to be productive of allegory as a literary
> fashion. . . . Bunyan's concern is with the sense of moral
> guilt and helplessness and the need for forgiveness
> and power; and the means for this are all religious, consisting
> of the Bible, preaching and teaching, prayer, and
> Christian companionship. C. S. Lewis, however, stands in
> the Catholic tradition. Created nature can enlist the
> interest of the natural man in a way that is not necessarily
> idolatrous but potentially gracious. Supernatural grace must
> supervene, however, to reveal the true meaning of the
> desire and to reorient it.[4]

The Pilgrim's Regress suffers from vices that also infest
Bunyan's book, and indeed any allegory. If the characters in
a tale exist only to symbolize and embody particular beliefs
and attitudes, they can hardly take on living personality; they
are abstract nouns spelled with capital letters. Thus, the conflicts in the tale are only one step removed from the forms of
public debate. If there is drama, it is in the clash of ideas more
than the wills of vividly conceived persons. The scenes often
become very talky, as though a debate were in progress at the

---

[3] Pp. 11–12.
[4] *Shadows of Heaven* (Philadelphia: A Pilgrim Press Book,
1971), pp. 5–8.

Socratic Club. Add to this a prose style that was not yet fully developed, lacking the grace and sense of the inevitable word that one finds a little later.

The very multiplicity of the ideas that John encounters, and the many false paths he must explore before he finds a true balance between North and South, require a vast number of individual scenes, each with its symbolic setting, all within the framework of Northernness and Southernness. Some are effective, some strained. The movement of the narrative line —from a superficial and misunderstood faith to liberation and, finally, back or onward to faith, now more maturely understood— is clear in general, but the movement is bumpy, with long, undigested passages of exposition and argument.

Yet *Regress* has permanent value. It is, first of all, a spiritual autobiography, no matter how much Lewis may wish to minimize the personal quality of the quest and make his John into a potential Everyman. Combined with *Surprised by Joy,* it records Lewis's intellectual and spiritual history, so far as he could at that time bring it into consciousness.

It is also an important document in intellectual history for anyone wishing to learn and imaginatively experience the currents of thought and feeling in Great Britain and the United States during the 1920's. True, the reader may feel that the book tells more about the intellectual life of college dons than of taxi drivers; on the other hand, the questions with which a don deals may differ more in terminology than in substance from those that any mortal sometimes finds assailing him.

Another value of the book is that though it is full of topical references, it also dramatizes timeless dilemmas of the questing mind and spirit. In any period there are currents of "North" and "South." Today the extremes might be symbolized by linguistic philosophy and cybernetics on one side, and drug-induced mysticism or witchcraft on the other. John's quest for the middle path is not out of date. In the same way, every period has its particular style of reductionism. The great stone head that stared at the captives and

made their intestines visible is not dead; "nothing but" is still
a frequent pair of words in discussing the human condition.
The *Regress* is already taking on a patina of age, a pleasant
chronological quaintness, but time does not render it obso-
lete.

Finally, the *Regress* is of special interest in one other
way. It represents Lewis when he had largely given up hope
of being a major poet, and before he had come into his full
maturity as a prose writer. It is a seminal book in his work.
Many themes that are somewhat oversimply treated in the
Regress reappear in more finely honed form in the later
books.

The tale begins with the boy, John, discovering a beautiful woodland, and being soundly smacked by his mother for
wandering there. Later the cook smacks him for aiming his
sling at a bird. Everything belongs to the Landlord, he is
told, and the Steward—the Landlord's agent—would be very
angry if John touched any of his property. Another year goes
by and we find John putting on ugly and uncomfortable
clothes and going to what seems a Confirmation service. The
Steward hands John a printed card and says, "Here is a list
of all the things the Landlord says you must not do."[5] The
Steward warns him that if he breaks a single rule, the Landlord will "take you and shut you up forever in a black hole
full of snakes and scorpions as large as lobsters—for ever
and ever. And besides that, he is such a kind, good man, so
very, very kind, that I am sure you will never *want* to dis-
please him."

While speaking of holy matters, the Steward wears a
mask with a long white beard attached. He now removes it
and whispers in the lad's ear, "I shouldn't bother about it all
too much if I were you." John returns home, tries (and fails)
to live by all the rules, and is puzzled to find on the reverse
side of the card quite different precepts, such as "Put the
whole thing out of your head / The moment you get into bed"

---

[5] *The Pilgrim's Regress*, pp. 21–23.

and "Unless they saw you do it, / Keep quiet or else you'll rue it."

Finding the comforts of religion confusing, John wanders down the road, and has his first experience of "Romance." There is mysterious music, a voice calling, "Come," a green wood full of primroses, tall enchanters with beards to their feet, a momentary glimpse of a calm sea and an island. The moment quickly fades; John is left with a lifelong desire for the calm sea and the island.

He encounters a naked brown girl in the woods, frequently fornicates with her, and comes to know that sex, though a pleasure, is not another name for the mysterious moments of "Romance." Gradually, he grows up, still haunted by the vanished vision, and sets out on his long quest. At an inn he encounters Mr. Enlightenment (who represents nineteenth-century rationalism). The conversation turns to the Landlord, and Mr. Enlightenment assures John that the Landlord's existence has been definitively disproved. John listens with the will to believe, but is curious to know how the story originated. In a heavily satiric example of sloppy reasoning, Mr. Enlightenment explains:

> "The Landlord is an invention of those Stewards. All made up to keep the rest of us under their thumb: and of course the stewards are hand in glove with the police. They are a shrewd lot, those Stewards. They know which side their bread is buttered on, all right. Clever fellows. Damn me, I can't help admiring them."
>
> "But do you mean that the Stewards don't believe it themselves?"
>
> "I dare say they do. It is just the sort of cock and bull story they would believe. They are simple old souls most of them—just like children. They have no knowledge of modern science and they would believe anything they were told."[6]

John still seeks absolute proof of the nonexistence of the Landlord. Mr. Enlightenment exclaims: "Christopher Colum-

---

[6] Pp. 35–37.

bus, Galileo, the earth is round, invention of printing, gunpowder!!" John is interested in the scientific method as explained by Mr. Enlightenment: ". . . if you make the same guess often enough it ceases to be a guess and becomes a Scientific Fact." Here, as frequently in the book, the satire is so broad and heavy that the reader remains unconvinced. Lewis, through his obedient puppets, is scoring debating points, not exploring an issue in depth.

John next encounters Vertue, a man slightly older than he, who becomes his traveling companion. Vertue seems to symbolize self-reliance, unyielding moral strength, the determination to do not what one likes but what one *chooses*. In modern terms, he could be labeled Mr. Existential. Meanwhile, John has his first explicitly moral experience. No longer inhibited by nightmares of the Landlord, he is free to kill one of the Landlord's robins but decides not to.

They meet an attractive young woman named Media Halfways, who leads John (Vertue temporarily goes a separate way) to the city of Thrill, where esthetic experience, as aroused by romantic poetry, seems for a time the equivalent of "Joy." Media and John kiss and talk "in slow voices, of sad and beautiful things."[7] "This is what I have been looking for all my life," says John. "The brown girls were too gross and the Island was too fine. This is the real thing." Media agrees. "This is Love. This is the way to the *real* Island."

John's approaching amours with Media are interrupted by the sudden appearance of Mr. Halfways' son, Gus, who enters, dressed in a garment made of wire, and reveals that Media is really a brown girl and her father is in the pay of the Brownies. Gus takes John to a shed and shows him an automobile. "She is a poem. She is the daughter of the spirit of the age. What was the speed of Atalanta to her speed? The beauty of Apollo to her beauty?" John's education in the modern arts is further advanced when he arrives at the city of Eschropolis, built all of steel, and attends a recital where a

---

[7] Pp. 42–44.

singer named Glugly intones "Globol obol oogle ogle globol gloogle gloo" and makes a vulgar noise "such as children make in their nurseries." After leaving Eschropolis and its Clevers, John encounters cigar-smoking Mr. Mammon and learns that the Clevers, for all their revolutionary talk, depend on him for their livelihood.

One of the most effective scenes is John's arrest by servants of "the Spirit of the Age" and his confinement in a dungeon. A giant, representing the Spirit, is outside the dungeon, peering at the prisoners within:

> . . . the giant's eyes had this property, that whatever they
> looked on became transparent. Consequently, when John
> looked round into the dungeon, he retreated from his fellow
> prisoners in terror, for the place seemed to be thronged
> with demons. A woman was seated near him, but he did
> not know it was a woman, because, through the face, he
> saw the skull and through that the brains and the passages
> of the nose, and the larynx, and the saliva moving in
> the glands and the blood in the veins: and lower down
> the lungs panting like sponges, and the liver, and the
> intestines like a coil of snakes.[8]

John cries out: "I am mad. I am in hell for ever." At this point Reason, a towering virgin on horseback, appears, and asks three rational riddles of the Giant, who is unable to use the language of Reason. She slays him; the prisoners are freed.

After some instruction in the methods of Reason, John comes to the Grand Canyon, immensely greater than any on earth. He and Vertue, who has now rejoined him, encounter old Mother Kirk, who says she could carry them across to the other side. They are curious about the origin of the canyon, which is called *Peccatum Adae*. Mother Kirk obliges by narrating a vivid version of the story of Adam, Eve, and the forbidden fruit.

The literary and scholarly temper of the age inspires a

---

[8] Pp. 60–61.

set of satiric symbols in the persons of the "Three Pale Men,"
Mr. Neo-Angular, Mr. Neo-Classical, and Mr. Humanist
(transparent disguises of T. S. Eliot, Irving Babbitt, and
George Santayana). They live pale, austere lives and dine on
such delicacies as bully beef and biscuits. Mr. Neo-Classical
concedes: "Our fare is simple . . . And perhaps unwelcome
to palates that have been reared on the kickshaws of lower
countries. But you see the perfection of form. This beef is a
perfect cube: this biscuit a true square."[9]

John eventually begins asking the questions that will
lead him back to Mother Kirk, though he does not know yet
whither he is headed. Several of the chapters center on the
discourses of Wisdom, who is as long-winded as any of the
endlessly verbal characters supplied with words by Bunyan.
As metaphysical questions are debated, the expository writer
in Lewis takes over for a time and the effort to dramatize
ideas in pictorial terms falters.

Still, when John finally submits to the ultimate wisdom
of Mother Kirk (wise beyond mere philosophy) and undergoes baptism, the event is described with majestic symbolism.
On the floor of *Peccatum Adae,* at the command of Mother
Kirk, John strips off his rags and falls into the deep pool
which leads to a tunnel that will bring him out on the other
side. He now learns the true nature of the childhood sea and
island; he has circled the world to return and find them again,
but now with understanding of what they actually signify and
are.

The virtues of the *Regress* are also its problems. It is
marvelously interesting as a young man's perception of the
climate of opinion in the 1920's, but at the same time the
very multiplicity of detail makes for a blunting of dramatic
effect. If it had fewer characters and episodes, it would be
less useful in intellectual history but more effective as literature. And Lewis is not always in complete control of the
allegorical form. Sometimes he is driven to abandon it for

---

9 P. 98.

honest exposition. This partial breakdown of literary structure is especially frequent near the end when what he wants to say overwhelms the form.

Lewis introduces occasional poems and songs into the narrative, and one wishes he had done more of this. They serve something like operatic arias to bring a scene to a focus, and some of them are among Lewis's best poems. Consider, for example, the half-serious, half-playful tone of the song sung by the northern dragon:

> Now I keep watch on the gold in my rock cave
> In a country of stones: old, deplorable dragon,
> Watching my board. In winter night the gold
> Freezes through toughest scales my cold belly.
> The jagged crowns and twisted cruel rings
> Knobbly and icy are old dragon's bed.[10]

Finally, how does Lewis's book compare with Bunyan's? The main difference is in the audience assumed. Bunyan wrote for the common man who might (in the seventeenth century) know the Bible from cover to cover but little else. Lewis's audience is more likely to be familiar with T. S. Eliot than the Bible; they know Freud better than Moses. Though Lewis poses the same eternal questions as Bunyan, these are clothed in very temporal dress. Thus the *Regress* begins to age almost before its print has dried. Doubtless future editions will carry footnotes explaining who the three Pale Young Men are, what political ideologies are represented by the revolutionary dwarfs, and what the currents of contemporary poetry are. But the future soul in distress, fleeing from the prevailing form of the wrath to come, may find a more universal wisdom in Bunyan.

Lewis's other dream vision is *The Great Divorce*, obviously inspired by Dante's *Divine Comedy* but a far freer adaptation of its model than the *Regress* is. The years between the two books had seen a great growth in Lewis's literary confidence. The dreamer here plays a more central

---

[10] Pp. 192–93.

role than in the earlier book; he in fact is Lewis, who wakes
at the end to find it was all a dream.

In one way, Lewis is faithful to the Dante model. The
Florentine needed a guide to escort him through the after-
life, a task undertaken first by Virgil and then by Beatrice.
Lewis's guide is the nineteenth-century clergyman and writer,
George MacDonald, who had baptized his youthful imagi-
nation.

The fundamental assumption of *The Great Divorce* is
a radical either/or. Lewis's mind typically works in this fashion; in book after book he argues that time and change do
not convert evil into good. One must make a conscious choice
at some point, and if this involves backtracking, that is the
way it is; there is no short cut over to the right road:

> Blake wrote the Marriage of Heaven and Hell. If I have
> written of their Divorce, this is not because I think myself
> a fit antagonist for so great a genius, nor even because
> I feel at all sure that I know what he meant. But in some
> sense or other the attempt to make that marriage is
> perennial. The attempt is based on the belief that reality
> never presents us with an absolutely unavoidable
> "either-or"; that, granted skill and patience and (above all)
> time enough, some way of embracing both alternatives
> can always be found; that mere development or
> adjustment or refinement will somehow turn evil into good
> without our being called on for a final and total rejection of
> anything we should like to retain. This belief I take to be
> a disastrous error. You cannot take all luggage with you
> on all journeys; on one journey even your right hand and
> your right eye may be among the things you have to
> leave behind.[11]

The finality of Hell has always been a difficult doctrine, for
infinite pain without any prospect of spiritual and moral
growth seems suspiciously like savage vengeance rather than
the act of a loving God. Medieval thought played with the
idea that even the damned souls had occasional vacations

---

[11] *The Great Divorce* (New York: Macmillan, 1946), p. 5.

from Hell. Later the universalist strand in some kinds of Protestantism held forth the hope that either Hell does not exist or that it is a kind of reform school and of limited duration, preparing its inhabitants for eventual Heaven.

Lewis, with his stern Christian orthodoxy, found a way to solve the dilemma that is esthetically and morally satisfying, whatever theological problems it may pose. The gray town is both Hell and Purgatory. Anyone who chooses to stay there—and most, alas, make this decision—is in Hell. Those who take the supernatural bus to the High Countries and remain now remember the town not as Hell but as Purgatory. Anyone is free to take the bus as many times as he wishes, and each time the gates of Heaven are wide open to him. But the longer one lives in the gray town, the less capable he becomes, psychologically, spiritually, and even physically, of making the liberating choice to stay in Heaven.

The story begins with the narrator experiencing the ominous emptiness of a great city:

> I seemed to be standing in a bus queue by the side of a long,
> mean street. Evening was just closing in and it was
> raining. I had been wandering for hours in similar mean
> streets, always in the rain and always in evening twilight.
> Time seemed to have paused on that dismal moment
> when only a few shops have lit up and it is not yet dark
> enough for their windows to look cheering. And just as the
> evening never advanced to night, so my walking had
> never brought me to the better parts of the town. However
> far I went I found only dingy lodging houses, small
> tobacconists, hoardings from which posters hung in rags,
> windowless warehouses, goods stations without trains,
> and bookshops of the sort that sell *The Works of Aristotle*.
> I never met anyone. But for the little crowd at the bus
> stop, the whole town seemed to be empty. I think that was
> why I attached myself to the queue.[12]

Thus, at the very beginning, one of the dominant symbols of the tale is established. The gray town is not a place

---

[12] P. 11.

of terrifying punishment but simply dull and meaningless, and haunted by the fear that twilight will some day turn into endless night. There is no center; individuals grow weary of their fellow citizens and move to the far outskirts where they can be alone.

While standing in the queue, the narrator observes some of the city's inhabitants and is the spectator of constant, idiotic bickering. The splendid bus finally arrives with a gleaming, presumably angelic, driver. Soon it is soaring over the immense city. The narrator meanwhile is cornered by an unsuccessful poet who produces a pocketful of manuscripts and asks for comments on them.

The futile young poet symbolizes one of the themes dominant in the book, self-pity. He tells how he was shabbily treated by his family and not properly appreciated at any of the five schools he attended. Finally he threw himself beneath a train and then found he was in the gray town, where he obviously did not belong. He is now going where he will be recognized for the genius he is.

At last the bus progresses beyond the gray town. A magnificent landscape, with mountains, rivers, trees, and other earthly and more than earthly features, appears below them. The narrator reflects:

> I had the sense of being in a larger space, perhaps even a larger *sort* of space, than I had ever known before: as if the sky were further off and the extent of the green plain wider than they could be on this little ball of earth. I had got "out" in some sense which made the Solar System itself seem an indoor affair.[13]

When the spirits from the gray town get out of the bus the narrator notices that they are transparent. They look like puffs of smoke. They exist, but barely. The country before them is the opposite; leaves are hard as diamonds and too heavy to be lifted; blades of grass are a torment to the sensitive soles of ghostly feet until they thicken up.

---

[13] P. 27.

This contrast of hardness/brightness with softness/dimness is one of the literary triumphs of *The Great Divorce*. Life beyond death is notoriously difficult to make imaginatively real, and in the great majority of attempts, even the bliss of Heaven seems pale and spooky. The symbolism of the inescapable realness of Heaven plays an important role in the adventures of the ghostly visitors from the gray town. Can their feet endure walking on Heaven's grass?

Those already dwelling in Heaven are the solid people. They have a special duty and privilege. If anyone they knew in the earthly life appears from the bus and seeks knowledge about Heaven, the solid people meet them, answer their questions, encourage them to stay. These solid people may be either clothed or naked, but there is a ceremonial splendor about them in either case.

Heaven is full of revelatory surprises for the visiting spirits. Often they pride themselves on their lofty morality (which usually turns out to be self-indulgence or self-admiration) and are shocked to find how casually the citizens of Heaven can mention the sins of their previous existence. A typical reaction is that of the Big Ghost who avows:

> "I gone straight all my life. I don't say I was a religious man and I don't say I had no faults, far from it. But I done my best all my life, see? I done my best by everyone, that's the sort of chap I was. I never asked for anything that wasn't mine by rights."[14]

This outburst is provoked when he discovers that the Solid Person meeting him is the same man who murdered a mutual acquaintance. The ancient homicide seems not to trouble the Solid Man, but the Big Ghost protests: "What about poor Jack, eh? You look pretty pleased with yourself, but what I say is, What about poor Jack?"

The Big Ghost cannot understand how a murderer is in Heaven, on excellent terms with the man he killed. The Solid

---

[14] Pp. 32–33.

Person, ex-murderer, entreats the Ghost to stay and learn about all these mysteries, but he will have none of it:

> "It's all a clique, all a bloody clique. Tell them I'm not coming, see? I'd rather be damned than go along with you. I came here to get my rights, see? . . . I'll go home. That's what I'll do. Damn and blast the whole pack of you. . . ."[15]

One of the most brilliant chapters concerns an ultra-liberal bishop, complete with ghostly gaiters. Lewis regarded clergymen who watered down the faith as equivalent to soldiers fed by one nation and secretly serving another. Here he pictures a man whose self-love takes the form of intellectual dishonesty. He wants to be modern, up to date, daring, and this is accomplished with great ease—all he has to do is go along with fashionable intellectual currents and be acclaimed for his courage. The ghost in the ghostly gaiters is nice, almost too much so, when he is met at the borders of Heaven by a young man he once knew on earth. He tolerantly recalls their ancient theological debates: "Ah, Dick, I shall never forget some of our talks. I expect you've changed your views a bit since then. You became rather narrow-minded towards the end of your life: but no doubt you've broadened out again."[16]

It is soon clear that the young man has not "broadened out." He still believes in a literal Heaven and Hell. The bishop misunderstands him. "Ah, I see. You mean that the gray town with its continual hope of morning (we must all live by hope, must we not?), with its field for indefinite progress, is, in a sense, Heaven, if only we have eyes to see it? That is a beautiful idea."

The young man explains, "We call it Hell," and shocks the bishop with his irreverence. The latter then asks why he has been in Hell, and is more shocked to learn that he is guilty of apostasy. He insists that honest opinions honestly

---

15 P. 36.
16 Pp. 38–39, 46.

arrived at are not sins. The young man urges the bishop to repent and believe. The bishop insists that he already believes. When the young man shifts the focus and asks simply that the bishop believe in him and accompany him to the mountains, the bishop wants assurances that an atmosphere of free inquiry prevails there. After some more semantic sparring, the bishop conveniently remembers a professional obligation. There is a little Theological Society in the gray town, and he has promised to give a paper on Christology. His new insight is that Jesus "was a comparatively young man when he died. He would have outgrown some of his earlier views, you know, if he'd lived. As he might have done, with a little more tact and patience. I am going to ask my audience to consider what his mature views would have been. . . . I shall end up by pointing out how this deepens the significance of the Crucifixion. . . ."

The Ghost nods its head, beams on the Solid Spirit with a "bright clerical smile" and turns away humming, "City of God, how broad and far."

The bishop is one who has lost the "good of the intellect" by drifting and courting popularity. He does not really merit inclusion with the great heretics who were usually driven by passionate convictions and who were more often rewarded by the stake than by a bishropic. Lewis's satiric portrait gains its power from the accuracy of its small details, all revealing intellectual dishonesty under a shiny finish of modern enlightenment.

In this chapter, one serious problem of the book becomes evident. Though the Solid Spirit who tries to save the bishop represents the redeemed and their concern for visitors from the gray town, there seems no way to dramatize these human saviors without giving them the attributes of a kindly but no-nonsense schoolmarm. The narrative describes one encounter after another in which a Spirit reasons with a Ghost, and in the course of his endeavor really uses the Ghost as an object lesson for the reader. The latter sometimes feels unexpected sympathy for the Ghosts as their defenses are lovingly assaulted. The book, by its very nature, is preachy, and many of the episodes turn into didactic lectures.

The most common reason for residence in the gray town is selfish love masquerading as altruism. In one of the episodes a female Ghost has a long conversation with a female Solid Person, apparently the mother of the Ghost's deceased husband. The Ghost makes it clear she has no intention of meeting Robert; she has forgiven him as a Christian, but "There are some things one can never forget." In a monologue extending over several pages she tells of her life with Robert. She had made a man of him. He had no ambition; she had driven him and he had advanced in the world. She taught him manners and intellectual conversation; picked out suitable friends for him. But he would stare at her with hatred in his eyes. Toward the end she even encouraged him to take up writing again—he had once had ambitions. She wasn't to blame if he had a nervous breakdown. She finally offers to strike a bargain:

> . . . I'll make them a fair offer, Hilda. I will *not* meet him,
> if it means just meeting him and no more. But if I'm
> given a free hand I'll take charge of him again. I will take
> up my burden once more. . . . I know him better than
> you do. What's that? No, give him to me, do you hear?
> Don't consult *him:* just give him to me. I'm his wife, aren't
> I? . . . Please, please! I'm so miserable. I must have
> someone to—to do things to. . . .[17]

The female Ghost towers up for a moment like a dying flame and snaps suddenly; a sour, dry odor quickly vanishes.

By this time the reader beings to wonder what percentage of success the Solid People achieve. Not very high, obviously—but then the more promising souls are already in Heaven. There are, however, occasional victories that trigger cosmic rejoicing. One such has to do with a Ghost whose smoky color is dark and oily. Sitting on his shoulder is a small red lizard, twitching its tail and whispering in the

---

[17] Pp. 84, 89.

Ghost's ear. Presumably the lizard symbolizes the sins of the flesh, which according to traditional Christian teaching are less deep-seated than those of the spirit.

The lizard is noisy and embarrassing. An angel appears and offers to kill it. The Ghost suggests there is no need for hurry; he isn't feeling very well; he ought to consult a physician before undergoing this ordeal. He ponders in an agony of indecision. The lizard whispers in his ear: "He can do what he says. He can kill me. One fatal word from you and he *will!* Then you'll be without me for ever and ever. It's not natural. How could you live? You'd be only a sort of ghost, not a real man as you are now."[18]

The Ghost finally bellows, "Get it over," and whimpers, "God help me." The angel seizes the lizard, breaks its back, hurls it to the ground. Then the transformation begins. An immense man rises from the ground, part by part, quickly whole. The lizard, still alive, struggles, enlarges, grows into a magnificent stallion, the sort of creature on which a god might ride. The newly recreated man leaps on the horse's back, touches the animal with his heels, and they disappear at breakneck speed, scaling the foothills of the distant mountains and vanishing in the brightness of the eternal morning. Nature herself sings a song of welcome:

> The Master says to our master, Come up. Share my rest
> and splendour till all natures that were your enemies
> become slaves to dance before you and backs for you to
> ride, and firmness for your feet to rest on.
> From beyond all place and time, out of the very Place,
> authority will be given you: the strengths that once
> opposed your will will be obedient fire in your blood and
> heavenly thunder in your voice.

The great power of this episode lies partly in the paradox (so it appears to the merely moral) that carnal sins are less mortal than spiritual ones, such as pride. Mainly, however, the episode towers among less intense ones by the vivid

---

[18] Pp. 101, 103–04.

accuracy of its specific symbolism—the lizard as a kind of
Iago, whispering unlawful thoughts, the tormented Ghost
forever dominated (unless he consents to be rescued) by his
natural impulses perverted to base ends—and then the resurrection and redemption of the flesh as the ugly lizard becomes
a heavenly steed.

Even George MacDonald, Lewis's guide through the
afterlife and at times an obsessive talker and explainer, does
not have to give a long explanation of what has happened.
The symbolism says it all.

The Great Divorce gradually sharpens its focus as the
tales unfold. The earlier chapters present a random sample
of Ghosts, most of whom make a definite rejection of Heaven,
though sometimes the issue is left in doubt. Then there is the
key episode of the man with the lizard whose affirmative
decision sets all Nature rejoicing. The next chapter moves to
a vision of salvation achieved on earth. The Solid Person is
Sarah Smith, who had once lived at Golders Green. No
earthly directory of notables lists her, but in Heaven, as
MacDonald puts it, "She is one of the great ones."[19] When
she appears she is preceded by bright Spirits who dance and
strew flowers. Even wild and domestic animals accompany
her, sharing the abundance of life she has received from
Christ. MacDonald concludes: ". . . there is joy enough in
the little finger of a great saint such as yonder lady to waken
all the dead things of the universe into life."

Sarah has come to the fringes of Heaven to talk with
her earthly husband and help him choose Heaven. He appears in the form of a double Ghost. The first shape is that
of a tall, thin Ghost, wearing a soft black hat and looking
like what he had been, an unsuccessful actor. The second is
a tiny Ghost, no bigger than an organ-grinder's monkey. The
dwarf Ghost is holding a chain fastened around the neck of
the tall Ghost.

Sarah addresses the small Ghost and mostly ignores the

---

[19] Pp. 107, 109, 119.

tall wraith. At times the former seems close to responding to Sarah's radiance; he even thickens up a little. But the old patterns of histrionic rhetoric counterattack and claim him. The small Ghost says "You do not love me" in a "thin bat-like voice," and vanishes to his eternity of self-pity. Sarah waits a little, finally walks away, surrounded by Bright Spirits who sing songs of praise.

It is a deeply moving scene, so powerful that the rather long conversation that follows, between MacDonald and the narrator, does not seem tedious. This explores the question of whether the redeemed can be happy when any Spirit chooses to remain outside. MacDonald adroitly avoids giving any firm opinion on whether any souls remain finally lost, but insists that if they do, it would not be tolerable for them to be cosmic dogs in the manger, blighting the happiness of those who have chosen reality. Finally, in a nice touch of symbolism, he reveals that all of Hell, the gray town, actually occupies no more real space than a tiny crack in the ground. It is almost nothing.

There are other transient visitors to Heaven who fill in the picture. A once famous artist arrives and discovers that on earth he is completely forgotten because of changes in artistic fashion; he races back to Hell to launch a counter-movement. Another Ghost thinks that Hell needs real consumer goods to replace the shoddy make-believe articles that are produced merely by thinking them into existence. He struggles unsuccessfully to carry a tiny Heavenly apple back with him; it is too heavy.

Lewis's characters are all generalized types, chosen to give a cross-section of humanity. Dante sought actual models, persons who had lived in reality (or at least in literature) and who could serve as symbols of particular virtues or vices. Most of them would have been familiar to readers of his own time; Dante actually put one pope in the Inferno while he was yet alive. By using real people as symbols, Dante could achieve a variety and specificity of symbol denied to Lewis.

Dante portrays the souls in all provinces of the afterlife

with equal vividness. Hell itself has nothing shadowy about it. Klieg lights seem to shine on all the deceased spirits. Lewis's basic symbolic contrast between bright and dark, hard and soft, opaque and transparent gives him a way to suggest the almost-nonexistence of the damned and the more than mortal reality of the saved.

One test of a book (as Lewis liked to point out) is how frequently it can be reread with increasing pleasure and profit. A reader returning to *The Great Divorce* may have an uneasy feeling that he has squeezed it dry. The long-winded dialogues between Bright Spirits and Ghosts do begin to be tedious; the damned seem created solely in order to be lectured at. The magnificent symbolic framework of the book, with its gray town and the splendor of the frontiers of heaven, creates a soaring sense of divine reality, but the inhabitants of both realms seem interesting not in their own right but because one can point a marker at them and deliver moral homilies. It is a pettier, a more bourgeois book than *The Divine Comedy*. Its moralizing is more compulsive and forced. At the same time, it is one of the closest approaches to Dante's masterpiece that anyone has achieved in this century.

More to the point, perhaps, would be a comparison with Lewis's other dream vision, *The Pilgrim's Regress*. The two books share some of the same problems and defects. Both can be verbose at times as ideas imperfectly converted into symbols are hammered out in pages of exposition. This is more common in the earlier book, though George MacDonald's loquacious ways slow down the action in *The Great Divorce*.

As literary and cultural history, the *Regress* is the more compelling book. A reader with no religious concern at all might still be gripped by its portraits of the intellectual and literary currents of its times. There is much less of this in *Divorce*. The episode of the apostate bishop perhaps echoes current theological controversies, but in general the characters are ordinary people, not shapers of sensibility. There

is little in *The Great Divorce* to compare with the satiric portraits of the Pale Young Men. The later book is also obviously the work of an older man, less exulting in putting his
intellectual enemies down, more filled with a compassionate
(but still stern) concern for those who have taken the wrong
fork in the road and refuse to turn back to where they first
went astray.

The Great Divorce* is clearly superior in its symbolism.
While the *Regress* has individual bits of symbolism that are
highly effective by themselves—one does not quickly forget
the giant whose eyes make the intestines visible—the overall
symbolic system, based on the distinction between North and
South, seems to come alive by fits and starts. *The Great Divorce* has a firmer symbolic framework, which builds up
chapter by chapter. Thus, while one may more vividly remember characters and episodes from the *Regress, The Great
Divorce* offers not so much a gallery of clearly etched characters as a total mood and vision of what is most real, and
what is so insubstantial as to be hardly more than a puff of
smoke.

THE WOMB OF SPACE

Lewis at last found a literary genre ample enough to accommodate his profligate imagination when he chose a form that has been brought to its mature development in the last two centuries—science fiction or space fiction as it is sometimes called. In this one way, at least, he was thoroughly twentieth century and modern. He selected for three of his novels a literary form as characteristic of our times as the rhymed romance was of the Middle Ages.[1]

Lewis's interest in space fiction was deep and ardent, but not indiscriminate. Many space tales are nothing more than cowboy stories transplanted to another planet. What interested Lewis and ultimately set his imagination to work was the kind of tale that uses space adventure as the medium for metaphysical, philosophic, religious, and psychological themes. *Childhood's End,* by Arthur Clarke, would be an example. It depicts a universe in which mankind is in process of merging with total cosmic being. Another such epic is W. O. Stapledon's *Last and First Men,* again using an evolutionary framework, and tracing the rise and fall of eighteen civilizations until humanity's culmination and destruction in Eighteenth Man.

---

[1] Portions of this chapter previously appeared in slightly different form as "The Reeducation of the Fearful Pilgrim" in *The Longing for a Form: Essays on the Fiction of C. S. Lewis,* Peter J. Schakel, ed. (Kent, Ohio: The Kent State University Press, 1977).

Lewis paid particular tribute to two authors who taught him "what other planets are good for." One was H. G. Wells. It would be difficult to think of a writer whose habits of thought were more antithetical to Lewis's. Wells was—at least in his more cheerful phases—an apostle of the carefully planned scientific state. But Lewis learned from him that space adventures can be philosophic adventures, and not mere cosmic horseplay.

The book that Lewis most often mentioned as a model is *A Voyage to Arcturus,* by David Lindsay. It is awkwardly written by its young author, and save for its impact on Lewis, might be completely forgotten. It deals with a voyage to a planet circling the star Arcturus. There are fantastic adventures in abundance, but they are all set in the framework of metaphysical and moral challenges. The sun itself is a set of twins, one blue and one yellow. Two forces seem to be struggling on the planet for dominance, perhaps good and evil, though it is difficult to know which is which. Human wills come into conflict, the stronger sucking in the strength of the weaker. Every action in this world takes on the character of exploration into the soul, and no absolutely clear vision ever emerges, but the reader has journeyed far into the terror of being a human being before he ends the book.

Space fiction has its own set of literary conventions, gradually evolved by a multitude of authors, and usually based on the science of their times, plus extrapolations. Lewis, at least as long as he confined himself to the solar system, would deal with a universe that had already been mapped out, often by authors now obscure or forgotten. For example, a writer does not need to create a new Mars; he already knows from his science fiction reading that Mars is an old planet, chilly, with thin atmosphere, and of course a low gravity that might encourage things to grow slender and tall. Its scanty water supply is nearly always dependent on artificial channels. When Lewis set about writing *Out of the Silent Planet,* he was able to exploit these traditions without being constricted by them.

As so often happened with Lewis, the impetus for the book was a jumble of colors and pictures in his imagination. He first saw the surface of Mars, and from there his imagination evolved the tale. Before he was done with the solar system, he had explored it in two other novels, *Perelandra* and *That Hideous Strength,* but there is no evidence whatever that this grand design was in his mind at the beginning.

As any space fiction reader would expect, the kidnapped Ransom finds himself on a Mars which maintains an archaic civilization, depends heavily on "canals" for water, and has so thin an atmosphere that the actual surface of the planet cannot support life. The very colors that gently engage his eyes—lavender and pale green and pale rose—have a subdued quality, as though anything flamboyant would be out of place on a planet which passed through the stages of its youth long before life existed on the earth. So far, orthodox space fiction. But Lewis gives it a new twist. He pictures the desiccation of the planet and the loss of most of its atmosphere not as an inevitable geophysical process, but as the doing of the "bent" Oyarsa, the angelic viceroy who had once been God's appointed governor to rule the earth.

The book is replete with visual symbolism, and at times it is difficult to know what is symbol and what is a logical extrapolation of scientific knowledge. Take, for instance, the peculiar vertical quality of Malacandra—the mountains rising at impossible angles, the vegetables taller than earthly trees, the elongated figures of the *hrossa* and *séroni.* Some readers have seen in all these a deliberate symbology of spiritual aspiration. Possibly. But an author may perfectly well end up with apparent symbolism (readily recognized by a clever literary critic) that he has not consciously inserted. The particular question—the verticality of Mars—can be interpreted only in the light of the entire book. Is there something peculiarly spiritual about life on Mars? Here each reader must judge for himself. He may find himself more impressed by the matter-of-fact presentation of the religious situation. The three varieties of rational species (*hnau*) are not much given to mystical ecstasies. Rather, the truths of religion are ordinary common sense to them. Simple obedience to Maleldil is the keynote.

Out of the Silent Planet is the novel that shows most clearly its space fiction ancestry. As the story opens Malacandra (Mars) is threatened by a greedy gold seeker, Devine, and a half-demented scientist, Weston. Ransom,[2] a Cambridge philologist with an evocative name, is kidnapped by the unholy pair, who have previously traveled to Mars and mistakenly believe that the residents of that planet want a human sacrifice.

When we first meet Ransom, he is a bachelor don, in early middle age. He is pious in a quiet way; when expecting death on Malacandra he says his prayers, and at one point he worries about whether he should impart some elements of revealed religion to the Martians, who turn out to be troubled by the same question in reverse. Ransom's one begetting sin is anxiety. He doubts his own uncertain courage, and his mind is filled with an appalling vision of space as void, dead, threatening. When he does think about the possibility of life on Mars, his science fiction reading and fearful imagination conjure up "various incompatible monstrosities—bulbous eyes, grinning jaws, horns, stings, mandibles. Loathing of insects, loathing of snakes, loathing of things that squashed and squelched, all played their horrible symphonies over his nerves. But the reality would be worse: it would be an extraterrestrial Otherness—something one had never thought of, never could have thought of."[3] For his perfection and fulfillment he needs merely to lose his fears, which stem from an imperfectly vivid awareness that the cosmos belongs to God (because He made it) and is therefore not to be feared.

One explicit symbol that figures prominently is that of birth or rebirth. At the beginning, Ransom is hiking a lonely

---

2 I am indebted to Peter J. Schakel for suggesting to me the centrality of Ransom's reeducation.

3 *Out of the Silent Planet* (New York: Macmillan, 1943, 1965), p. 35.

English road, seeking a place to lay his head, but the hotel in the little village is full. After he is kidnapped by Weston and Devine and taken into their spacecraft, the birth images multiply. The inside of the craft is remarkably like a womb. The cloying heat compels him to strip himself naked. He is within a local, man-made womb, but all around him is the creative womb of space:

> . . . the very name "Space" seemed a blasphemous libel
> for this empyrean ocean of radiance in which they swam.
> He could not call it "dead"; he felt life pouring into him
> from it every moment. How indeed should it be otherwise,
> since out of this ocean the worlds and all their life had
> come? He had thought it barren: he saw now that
> it was the womb of worlds. . . .[4]

He suffers like a pregnant woman when the spacecraft approaches Mars: "It was explained to him that their bodies, in response to the planet that had caught them in its field, were actually gaining weight every minute and doubling in weight with every twenty-four hours. They had the experience of a pregnant woman, but magnified almost beyond endurance."[5]

Finally, the spacecraft lands on Malacandra, and the three men emerge head and shoulders first through the "manhole." A newborn uncertainty of vision afflicts Ransom: "He saw nothing but colours—colours that refused to form themselves into things. Moreover, he knew nothing yet well enough to see it: you cannot see things till you know roughly what they are. His first impression was of a bright, pale world—a water-colour world out of a child's paintbox. . . ."[6]

Even before he leaves the spacecraft, Ransom has experienced some important reeducation. As we saw, he comes to a new vision of space, and recognizes that the planets are

---

[4] P. 32.
[5] P. 38.
[6] P. 42.

dark spots in the teeming splendor of space. Also, while yet
inside the craft, he begins to lose a little of his fearfulness.
For one thing, he takes time out from observing his twitching nerves, and makes practical preparations for life on the
planet. Specifically, he conceals a knife and resolves to commit suicide rather than be turned over to the fearsome *sorns*.

This initial step toward conquest of fear proves fragile.
Soon after their landing, Ransom catches his first glimpse of
the *sorns,* and in terror struggles to escape from Devine's
clutch. During their combat, they suddenly sight a *hnakra,*
and in the confusion Ransom makes his escape, without
having resolved his horror of the *sorns*. He still believes he
will be sacrificed by the half-manlike creatures.

The tale now becomes "The Reeducation of the Fearful
Pilgrim." Step by step, as Ransom perforce explores the
planet in his flight from Weston and Devine, he comes to
grip with his terrors, and with many sidesteps and backward
steps, gradually overcomes them.

The most important part of his reeducation begins when
he encounters a *hross* and they become friends across the
linguistic and biological barriers. He is made welcome in the
hrossa village. Gradually, he learns their language. Their way
of life clarifies his own thinking, the very set of his emotions.
He learns, for example, that the *hrossa* do not fear death. It
comes at its appointed time, the age of 160; it is as though a
senior were looking forward to the special day when he will
graduate. Death is predictable, and to be desired; any *hross*
knows it is the door of rebirth into a spiritual existence with
Maleldil. All this is explained matter-of-factly by the *hrossa*
who marvel that any *hnau* should not know it already.

The religious faith that Ransom brought with him, including trust in God, is everyday folk wisdom on Malacandra,
not a conviction arrived at with great spiritual toil and in
conflict with the practical assumptions by which life is lived
on Tellus. Another startling bit of wisdom Ransom learns is
that *hnau* can actually live by reason, day in and day out.
Malacandra might easily have a population problem, but

does not; the *hrossa,* by continence, voluntarily limit themselves to a couple of offspring. They cannot think of sex apart
from procreation; it is all one totality. When they bring their
breeding days to an end, they compose songs about the experience and spend their years reliving in memory the
moments of love, but the thought of actually repeating the
act horrifies them.

Ransom spends much of his time trying to understand the
relation of the three rational species: *hrossa, séroni,* and the
froglike *pfiffltriggi.* Who rules whom? He comes to realize
that only his experience on the fallen and silent planet, Thulcandra, made him ask the question. No *hnau* rules other
species of *hnau.* Maleldil benignly rules them all, functioning
through Oyarsa, his viceroy; in turn Oyarsa supervises the
planet through the *eldila,* almost invisible pulses of light that
are roughly equivalent to earthly angels. It is a thoroughly
hierarchical world with the chain of command starting at the
top and descending rank by rank. Any human quibbling is
simply silly; those of high rank know best.

Ransom notices a great stir in the *hrossa* village. Word
has reached them that *hnakra* are swimming down from the
melting polar ice cap. As the esteemed visitor from another
handra, Ransom is given the place of honor, at the front of
the fleet. "A short time ago, in England, nothing would have
seemed more impossible to Ransom than to accept the post
of honour and danger in an attack upon an unknown but
certainly deadly aquatic monster," but Malacandra is making
a new man of him. "Whatever happened, he must show that
the human species also were *hnau.* . . . he felt an unwonted
assurance that somehow or other he would be able to go
through with it. It was necessary, and the necessary was
always possible."[7]

When Ransom strikes the mortal blow and is acclaimed
as *hnakrapunt* (*hnakra*-slayer) he enters a new spiritual and
psychological state, though he does not put it that way to

---

[7] P. 81.

himself. By braving the monster, he has passed through death and beyond, and can now act with freedom and spontaneity. He also begins to be released from constant, subjective misgivings. He learns, with some help from the *hrossa,* to disregard the state of his emotions. It is not a once-and-for-all victory. His old fears still leap out of the storehouse of archetypes once in a while as he travels toward the land of the *sorns,* on the way to Meldilorn, but he now knows that he can brush the horrors aside. The important thing is simply to keep going, to accomplish his task. He will be given the strength to do this. So we find Ransom, summoned by Oyarsa, steadfastly seeking the very *sorns* he had so frantically tried to avoid. He finds them, and eventually, in a flash of true vision, recognizes that their elongated faces are not frightful nor spooky but "august."

His final education occurs when, with the help of the *sorns,* he reaches holy Meldilorn, the island where Oyarsa receives *hnau* who journey there. As Ransom serves as interpreter for Weston and Devine, and later has a private audience with Oyarsa, it is no longer a question of faith but of knowledge. Though Oyarsa seems as unsubstantial as pulsing light, he is unquestionably *there,* and is the undoubted viceroy of Maleldil Himself.

Malacandra is a very archaic planet. Indeed, the fallen Oyarsa of the earth (commonly called the Devil) struck at Malacandra long before the simplest life appeared on Tellus, and brought about desiccation, cold, and shortage of oxygen. The Martians could have migrated to earth and established their own forms of life there, but they decided instead to leave earth to its own evolution, and to make Mars habitable even after the bent Oyarsa's heavy blows. They created the system of great channels and waterways, so that part of the planet could support life. But it is a slowly dying world, a prospect that does not trouble the Martians. They know that Maleldil endures for ever, but that stars and planets and species do not. Death is as much a theme of the book as birth and rebirth. It is all part of the divine plan.

Ransom, citizen of a distant and fallen planet, where truth can proclaim itself only by such costly bridgeheads as a Socrates drinking hemlock or a Jesus on the cross, has seen spiritual reality as it is, without the obscuring pollution of sin. On Malacandra all is clarity and charity. Like a well-organized, self-motivated army, physical and spiritual beings exist in harmony, all under the guiding love of Maleldil.

True, this sweetness and light exacts a penalty. Malacandra is a planned society, with the virtues and maybe the defects of a well-run preparatory school. Its safeguards against the fallen powers of the universe are so systematically worked out that neither an individual nor society as a whole has much chance to launch a rebellion. Oyarsa's unbodying rod is at the ready, to deal with any major challenge to the Martian way of life. To phrase these demurrers is perhaps merely to demonstrate the fallen nature of the human animal, and its insistence upon the freedom to be unhappy. Doubtless Ransom learned the inner meaning of the old prayer, "whose service is perfect freedom," and in happily conforming to the Martian mores and morals found his deepest freedom and fulfillment.

Ransom's companions are ordered back to earth; he himself is given the option of staying. He finally decides to rejoin his own species on earth, but enters the spacecraft with a heavy heart. Invisible *eldila* share the voyage to protect him, and the craft barely reaches earth before a Malacandran self-destruct device reduces it to nothing visible. As Ransom emerges and walks (presumably naked) into a British pub to order a pint of bitter, he is inwardly a far different man from the one who had been kidnapped and sent on the terrifying voyage to Mars. He now *knows,* face to face, the truths that he once believed as through a glass darkly. Never again will he listen to the Enemy's chatter about "cold, dead space."

This discussion has concentrated heavily on Ransom's reeducation, which consists essentially of exchanging faith for knowledge, and thereby learning to live without fear. But if the novel is approached without any presuppositions, the first level on which it operates is simply that of a good adventure story, set in a space fiction framework. There must be readers who could not care less about Ransom's soul, but who thrill to the appearance of a *sorn* or *hnakra*, and who avidly follow Ransom's adventures among the *hrossa*.

Apart from serving as a vehicle for Ransom's reeducation, the adventures lead him over a large part of the planet, enabling him to learn about the peculiarities which distinguish it from life on Tellus. He comes to think of the solar system as a commonwealth of planets, all but one of which (Tellus) are in easy communication with the others. God is not absent from space; indeed, if the mode of His presence varies from one place to another, he is especially present in "empty space." The reader also recognizes that the war between good and evil is cosmic. Mars is merely one battlefront.

Another theme of the novel is the relation between earthly mythology and interplanetary reality. Ransom studies an ancient carved stone and deduces that it is a map of the solar system. Suddenly he notices that the symbol representing the planet Venus is a female form with the shape of breasts clearly evident. It appears that mythology is not just earthly fancy but has some kind of universality. The very *eldila* seem like legends of angels or "airy folk." The young *sorns* herding domesticated animals recall Homer's Cyclopes, who also were shepherds. Perhaps, Ransom speculates, the rigid distinction between myth and fact may be an interim category of man's Thulcandran thinking, and will be corrected as a by-product of his redemption from sin.

Lewis's symbolism is not a private system. One cannot imagine him creating and publishing anything like Yeats's *Vision*. But the traditional symbols serve him well and he renews them with astonishing vigor. Take, for instance, the symbolism of light. It may have originated as the first caveman looked about at his darkness and gave thanks for the outer sun and that little domestic sun of fire on the floor of his dwelling. The meaning of light was life and relative freedom from carnivorous teeth; the meaning of darkness was menacing shapes circling about. Lewis does not alter this symbolism but simply uses it to such good effect that the book seems aglow with light. There is first of all the brightness of space, the great womb of life. The gleaming stars proclaim the glory of God. The spiritual powers that control the destiny of Malacandra are (to human eyes at least) pulses of light.

Some readers of *Out of the Silent Planet* have reasonably wondered why the aquatic monster, the *hnakra,* lives in a world where all species of *hnau* and animals coexist peacefully. The *hnakra* does indeed seem out of place in this peaceable kingdom. Is he a symbol of evil? Not in the eyes of the *hrossa.* They love him dearly even though in the heat of combat they may momentarily hate him. Ransom's *hross* friend explains:

> . . . it is not a few deaths roving the world around him
> that make a *hnau* miserable. It is a bent *hnau* that would
> blacken the world. And I say also this. I do not think the
> forest would be so bright, nor the water so warm,
> nor love so sweet, if there were no danger in the lakes.[8]

The *hnakra* thus seems to supply an element of menace that makes every day more significant because a shade less certain. And of course, a Martian really has nothing to lose, for if he perishes in a *hnakra* combat he not only arrives early in the realm of Maleldil's immediate presence, but he is also remembered forever in heroic ballads.

Each variety of Martian *hnau* seems lopsided by human standards. The *hrossa* farm, fish, and live by the words of their poets. The *séroni* are intellectuals, with a dry, ironic way of viewing life, and much preoccupied with scientific research. The *pfifltriggi* are the miners, craftsmen, and artisans, busy little fellows, henpecked, and always bustling about. Combine the three species into one bodily form and merge their special gifts, and you would have the ideal of a well-

———
8 P. 75.

balanced *hnau*. What is Lewis saying by this trifurcation? Perhaps, as the *hrossa* suggest, that human sympathies and thoughts are limited or one-sided because we cannot compare them with those of other kinds of *hnau*. It seems natural to the Malacandrans that rational beings can exist in a variety of forms and temperaments; it is up to Maleldil to determine these particulars. What one species cannot do, another can do for it; the harmony and cooperation that prevail on Malacandra make it unnecessary for each species to be self-sufficient. The Martians have, in addition, an advantage over us. They cannot associate rational life exclusively with one bodily form, as we are tempted to do. If they found a spider speaking a language and talking sense, they would recognize in him a fellow *hnau*. As an added bonus, they are freed from the need for pets. Each kind of *hnau* regards the two other kinds not precisely as pets, but as having some of the endearing (and absurd) qualities of pets. A vast amount of "ethnic humor" of a harmless kind arises from the interaction of the three species.

The theme of fallenness runs through the novel, as Ransom, an exile from the "silent planet," explores a world in which sin has never taken root. He learns that fallenness is a matter of degree. He himself is lightly tainted. Devine is not merely bent; he is broken. He exists only for greed. Weston is somewhere in between, but closer to Devine. Oyarsa rather wistfully remarks that if Weston were his *hnau,* he would set about to reeducate him. Badly bent as Weston is, he retains one trace of moral understanding—his perverted but still real sense of identification with his own species.

Out of the Silent Planet is an extraordinarily compelling tale; it wins and carries its readers along, however little they believe in the literal reality of Maleldil and his angelic ranks. Partly this is because Lewis has a highly visual imagination and can create unforgettable landscapes. In addition, Lewis is well aware of one of the first principles of science fiction: the more fantastic the setting and events, the more essential it is to include familiar, everyday details. This he does with great skill. The opening scene where Ransom meets Weston and Devine in their sinister house is a model of psychological accuracy. How precisely Lewis pictures Ransom's ambivalent feelings toward his old schoolmate! Life inside the spacecraft is described with a good eye to scientific factors such as changing gravity, and is remarkably similar to the actual experience a few years later when space travel left the science fiction bookshelf and became real. On Malacandra, boats are like boats; alcohol is esteemed; the angular landscape bears semblances to earthly scenes. And Ransom's changing emotions are sensitively portrayed as he wanders the planet.

Devine, though a one-dimensional character, is still convincing as the kind of man who would cheerfully murder for gain. The flashbacks to his school days, when his cynical wit made him a hero of his fellow students, creates a plausible backdrop for his present stage. Though Weston is presented as a scientist on the way toward mania, he occasionally reveals touches almost of human understanding, as when he remarks, in connection with their plans to offer Ransom as a human sacrifice, "I dare say . . . he would consent if he could be made to understand."[9]

Despite a wealth of concrete details enough mystery and uncertainty are left to give the feeling of a unfamiliar reality. For example, Ransom learns from Oyarsa that *eldila* are not quite equivalent to angels, but never discovers just what the difference is. The *eldila* are much wiser than mortals, yet they are not omniscient; they do not automatically understand a foreign language, and Ransom knows more about the earth's spiritual history than the Martian Oyarsa does.

The principal reason for the story's success lies in the author's creation of the character Ransom. Not particularly complex, Ransom is a Cambridge don, a philologist, a bachelor, a Christian. Whatever happens on Malacandra is seen as Ransom sees it, and his Martian education is gradual

---

[9] P. 19.

enough, and plausible enough, so that the reader enters into the experience step by step.

When Lewis began this novel, there is no evidence that he had a trilogy in view or was in process of evolving a cosmic (or at least solar) mythology. By the time he wrote the last chapter he knew that more had to come. At the end of *Out of the Silent Planet* is a letter from "the original of Dr. Ransom" to Lewis in which he says: "Now that 'Weston' has shut the door, the way to the planets lies through the past; if there is to be any more space-travelling, it will have to be time-travelling as well. . . ."[10]

This statement has direct bearing on an odd bit of literary history. Lewis and his brother had agreed that his miscellaneous manuscripts should be destroyed, and after Lewis's death, Warnie assembled bushels of such leavings, and put them to the torch. The bonfire lasted three days. During this time, he instructed the gardener to add a vast quantity of Lewis's notebooks and papers to the pyre. As Walter Hooper recounts the story in his Preface to *The Dark Tower,* the gardener prevailed on Warnie to wait. Hooper happened to come by and gained permission to take the material home. When he went through it, he came on an incomplete handwritten manuscript, which began: "Of course," said Orfieu, "the sort of time-travelling you read about in books—time-travelling in the body—is absolutely impossible."[11] Hooper read on and soon came to the name of Ransom. This was evidently the follow-up book to *Out of the Silent Planet,* but apparently never revised, and certainly never finished. When eventually brought out in book form, it filled about eighty pages.

The Dark Tower includes some mention of Ransom's earlier adventures, and hints that good and malevolent forces are locked in combat. But it is difficult to imagine a book less like its predecessor. *Out of the Silent Planet* is alive with color and brilliantly realized scenes, and goodness shares equal time with evil. Its characters, also, while not invaded by deep psychological probes, are plausible. The characters in *The Dark Tower* are dull to read about. The scientist Orfieu and his assistant Scudamour are colorless, the fictional Lewis hardly opens his mouth, Ransom is subdued and uninteresting, and the MacPhee of this book is nothing like as strong as the skeptic of the same name in the later book, *That Hideous Strength*.

It is a terribly talky story. Much of the space is devoted to long paragraphs of pseudoscientific jargon, debating the possibility of time travel. The slight plot revolves around the invention of a chronoscope, a machine that projects pictures of other times on a screen. The main picture that comes through is of a sinister dark tower. It is never clear whether it exists in the past, the future, or some other dimension of time for which we have no name. Most of the scenes deal with what seems a hideous religious rite. Certain men go through great physical agony and emerge with a sting on their forehead. Ordinary folk are then led in, stung, and turned into zombies, the "Jerkies."

Toward the end of the manuscript, Scadamour sees his sweetheart on the screen, and in a rage smashes the equipment. He then lands in Othertime; evidently the two times are not totally separated. Soon thereafter he grows a sting, and when he talks with Camilla is barely able to resist the urge to sting her into becoming one of the automata. The story breaks off before anything is resolved.

It is a curious, unpleasant, rather morbid tale, more gothic than anything else by Lewis. It has its quota of marvels, but they do not seem to *mean* anything. It may be—one can only speculate—that Lewis sensed this was a rather routine horror story compared to what he was capable of doing.

One might object, of course, that we have here perhaps a fourth of a book. But there seems no foreshadowing of greatness in chapters yet to come. Perhaps Lewis simply lost interest, as he did with many other abortive literary projects.

He probably never read the manuscript once he had cast it aside. By this time he knew that *Out of the Silent Planet* called for one or more sequels, but he had to bide his time until a mental picture came to him, in the form of floating islands, to set him on the road to *Perelandra*. This did not occur until in the interim he had written *The Problem of Pain, The Screwtape Letters,* and his radio talks.

When Lewis began *Perelandra* he was careful to shun the problems encountered by Milton. He avoided the depiction of unfallen sexuality and denied the demonic (in the person of Weston) any glamour or dignity. No future critic can argue that the Devil is really the hero of the tale. He also took his Eve far more seriously, and gave her chapter after chapter of stage center when she wrestles with the question of whether to obey God or defy Him.

In *Perelandra,* Ransom is supernaturally summoned to Venus and transported in a kind of celestial coffin. He suspects, rightly, that he is being called to battle principalities and powers. The coffin deposits him on a surging ocean and quickly melts away. He is alone, from all appearances, on *Perelandra*. Unthinkingly, he starts swimming. And now he begins to experience the sensuous delights of Perelandra, which proves to be a planet like one's visions of a Polynesian world, minus sin.

> He was riding the foamless swell of an ocean, fresh and cool after the fierce temperatures of Heaven, but warm by earthly standards—as warm as a shallow bay with sandy botton in a sub-tropical climate. As he rushed smoothly up the great convex hillside of the next wave he got a mouthful of the water. It was hardly at all flavoured with salt; it was drinkable—like fresh water and only, by an infinitesimal degree, less insipid. Though he had not been aware of thirst till now, his drink gave him a quite astonishing pleasure. It was almost like meeting Pleasure itself for the first time.
>
> There was no land in sight. The sky was pure, flat gold like the background of a medieval picture. It looked

very distant—as far off as a cirrus cloud looks from
earth. The ocean was gold too, in the offing, flecked with
innumerable shadows. The nearer waves, though
golden where their summits caught the light, were green on
their slopes: first emerald, and lower down a lustrous
bottle green, deepening to blue where they passed beneath
the shadow of other waves.[12]

He discovers that floating islands dot the surging ocean
and swims to one of them. It consists of matted vegetation
held together by a network of roots and creepers. It takes on
the shape of the waves, and thus is in constant motion and
ever changing in form. All the time he has the most delicious
sensations of pleasure. Yet this paradise has its restraint and
sobriety. He comes on a gourdlike fruit so delicious that "It
was like the discovery of a totally new *genus* of pleasures,
something unheard of among men, out of all reckoning, beyond all covenant. For one draught of this on earth wars
would be fought and nations betrayed."[13] He is about to con-
sume a second one when it occurs to him that he is now
neither hungry nor thirsty. Some inner voice advises him to
let well enough alone. Another time he discovers some green
berries that are good to eat but produce no ecstatic new
pleasure. Occasionally there is a variant with a red center so
delicious he is tempted to seek them out and scorn the prosaic
berries. But again an inner voice tells him to take his food as
it comes, and not to seek only the special delights.

By this point, something of the basic contrast between
Malacandra and Perelandra has been established. Both are
beautiful worlds, but Malacandra is a planet long past its
youth and middle age, and life can exist only in special places.
Its history stretches longer than its future will. There is something melancholy about this archaic planet. By contrast,
Perelandra is a planet in its youth, warmer, more luxuriant,
just at the point (as Ransom soon discovers) when its own

---

[12] *Perelandra* (New York: Macmillan, 1944, 1968), p. 35.
[13] P. 42.

kind of *hnau* are being brought into existence. Its past has been the time of preparation for this moment, and its future (if sin does not enter and take root) is a fresh beginning for the solar system.

All this is not clear in Ransom's mind at first, but he begins to understand this new world after he meets its queen, the Green Lady. He sees her on a neighboring island. She is "green like the beautifully coloured green beetle in an English garden,"[14] and is surrounded by stylized ranks of animals and birds.

At first, the Green Lady smiles with excited pleasure; she thinks her husband, King Tor, has returned from an exploring expedition. Then, seeing the visitor from earth at closer range, her face drops. Neither of them is embarrassed by their own nudity as such, though Ransom realizes that his blotches of sunburn make him a ridiculous sight. He clambers up on her island, and thanks to the fact that both speak Old Solar, they are able to communicate. At first she assumes that he is *the* father of Tellus, i.e., Adam. When she discovers he is a commoner she treats him with noblesse oblige.

The plot of the novel is as simple as that of *Out of the Silent Planet* is complex. The latter novel has something of a picaresque structure, though it has firmness of theme—the education of Ransom. In *Out of the Silent Planet,* Ransom comes to know God's reality more unquestionably than he had on earth, and also aids in frustrating the designs of Weston and Devine. In *Perelandra,* heavenly powers have assigned him a specific job: to journey to Venus and take whatever steps are needed to avert the fall of that planet.

This soon becomes evident when. Weston lands in a spacecraft and seeks out the Green Lady. Weston has deteriorated since he and Ransom were on Malacandra. He is now intermittently possessed by demonic powers. This takes the form of a surprising religious conversion. Weston assures Ransom:

---

14 P. 53.

. . . nothing now divides you and me except a few
outworn theological technicalities with which organized
religion has unhappily allowed itself to get incrusted. But I
have penetrated that crust. The Meaning beneath it
is as true and living as ever. If you will excuse me for
putting it that way, the essential truth of the religious view
of life finds a remarkable witness in the fact that it
enabled you, on Malacandra, to grasp, in your own mythical
and imaginative fashion, a truth which was hidden
from me.[15]

Now a disciple of the *élan vital,* Weston no longer has
a provincial partiality for *homo sapiens.* He advocates the
spread and ultimate fulfillment of Spirit, whatever forms it
may take. Indeed, he assures Ransom, he is now "guided."
He has been taught Old Solar through supernatural channels. He has abandoned dualistic thinking. With his voice
rising to a howl, he proclaims:

. . . There is no possible distinction in concrete thought
between me and the universe. In so far as I am the
conductor of the central forward pressure of the universe, I
am it. Do you see, you timid, scruple-mongering fool?
I *am* the Universe. I, Weston, am your God and your
Devil.[16]

At this point, Weston has a demonic seizure. For an instant,
the scientist stares with horrified eyes and screams for help.
Immediately his body spins round and he falls to the ground,
speaking incoherently and tearing up handfuls of moss.
Terrifying as this is, Weston is merely at the beginning of his
career as a host to the Devil; the spirit who now possesses
him will drive him into greater agony and idiocy before the
story is over.

The middle stretch of the novel is almost a continuous
three-sided debate. To achieve his goal, Weston—or the
Unman as he is called by Ransom—must persuade the Green

---

15 P. 91.
16 P. 96.

Lady to undertake the one specific action God has forbidden: stay overnight on any of the fixed lands of Perelandra. Perhaps God has arbitrarily chosen to forbid this particular act simply so that the new Eve and Adam can make conscious moral decisions. Or perhaps life on a floating island which constantly changes shape is a better parable of the religious life than life on *terra firma*. The king and queen of Perelandra have not been told a reason for God's edict. All they need to do is obey it.

Weston takes a psychological approach combined with high idealism. He implies that God has issued an unreasonable prohibition precisely in the hope that the inhabitants of the new paradise will show some spirit and disobey it. Then God's joy will be supreme, for he will recognize that His creatures have fully come of age. His other approach is more subtle. He tells the Green Lady many tales about the tragic heroines of earthly history. These were women who were ready to disregard the dictates of society or God and run uncalculated risks for the sake of the men they loved. Weston insinuates that men are cautious, unimaginative, not given to ultimate deeds, and they must be redeemed by the daring of their women, whose glorious exploits and self-sacrifices are sung from generation to generation. So effectively does Weston present the picture of the tragic heroine that the Green Lady begins to take on some of the associated mannerisms, and even shows an alarming interest in covering her perfect body with clothes.

During this time, Ransom tries to counter Weston's arguments, though handicapped by the fact that he must stick to plain truth. He points out that the pitiful condition of earthlings resulted from the willingness of Eve to listen to similar logic from the mouth of the serpent. He tries to demythologize the glory of tragic heroines. But on the whole, Weston is the better debater, and it gradually becomes clear that the woman is close to the ultimate disaster. She is already imagining with what eyes of love and admiration her husband will gaze upon her when he realizes how bravely she has acted in order to grow up and be one whom God secretly and the king openly will approve.

Finally, Ransom sees that he is losing the debate and must find other ways of prevailing. In a night where he feels the presence of Maleldil, he goes through his agony of soul, crying out for a miracle. Then he realizes that his presence on Perelandra *is* the miracle. Slowly, the knowledge pushes against his consciousness; this is not just a struggle to be fought by competitive brains. If debate will not work, then he must attempt the physical destruction of the Unman. This decision leads to a direct conflict that involves hand-to-hand grappling, a pursuit on enormous fish, and finally the climactic struggle in an underwater cave, where Ransom at last destroys what remains of the original Weston. He is the savior of Perelandra.

Ransom beholds Malacandra and Perelandra face to face, and is in their presence when they celebrate the transfer of their guardian duties to the king and queen of the planet.

> "The world is born to-day," said Malacandra. "To-day
> for the first time two creatures of the low worlds, two
> images of Maleldil that breathe and breed like the beasts,
> step up that step at which your parents fell, and sit
> in the throne of what they were meant to be. It was never
> seen before. Because it did not happen in your world a
> greater thing happened, but not this. Because the greater
> thing happened in Thulcandra, this and not the greater
> thing happens here."[17]

There follows an epiphany in which he beholds the Great Dance. It is an infinitely weaving and pulsing pattern. He comes to recognize different kinds of realities, ranging from civilizations and arts (shortlived) to universal truths and, most of all, individual beings, the most enduring realities of all. The vision modulates into dimension upon dimension, and he enters a state of inner privacy and renewal as the manifestation comes to an end. He has looked into the heart

---

[17] P. 197.

of reality, short of gazing directly upon Maleldil. Finally, back in a celestial coffin and covered with red flowers, he leaves Paradise Retained and journeys home to sad Thulcandra.

The Green Lady is a tour de force character sketch. She is at once regal, wise and realistic (so God has made her) and young and naïve. She finds it almost impossible to doubt anything that anyone says to her, for in her life there have been no lies and deceptions. Her great desire is to please Maleldil and her husband. In her innocence she will listen to any suggestion. Ransom is constantly forced into the position of sounding like a cautious uncle whose main arguments are vignettes of earth's corrupted mode of existence. Though he is arguing for plain obedience to God, his advice is not as exciting and alluring as that of the Unman. All in all, she is surprisingly real—sheer goodness but with an imagination that can play with other possibilities.

The picture of Weston is one of the most convincing dramatizations of demonic possession in literature. His state of consciousness fluctuates. Sometimes the "real Weston" seems to speak a few words; at other times his mortal body is nothing more than a shell within which the Devil actuates his muscles and makes him speak, move, or fight. Having abandoned the gift of reason, he is often like an idiotic little boy. Ransom learns this when he comes on a trail of frogs that have been hideously mutilated so that they can no longer hop. The trail leads him to Weston:

> . . . He did not look like a sick man: but he looked very like a dead one. The face which he raised from torturing the frog had that terrible power which the face of a corpse sometimes has of simply rebuffing every conceivable human attitude one can adopt toward it.[18]

Their eyes meet, and Weston smiles with a devilish smile, as though inviting Ransom into an inner circle of hideous

---

18 P. 110.

pleasures. Yet, in the verbal battle for the soul of the Green Lady, the Unman can appear reason personified.

At times he acts like a desperate human being and even arouses Ransom's momentary sympathy, but there is no way of telling whether such brief interludes are genuine, or a diabolic stratagem to put Ransom off his guard. During a lull in their physical combat, when they are riding enormous fish, Weston pleads for Ransom to speak to him, and launches into a pitiful harangue about the finality and ugliness of death:

> "That's why it's so important to live as long as you can. All the good things are now—a thin little rind of what we call life, put on for show, and then—the *real* universe for ever and ever. . . .
>
> ". . . Homer knew—that *all* the dead have sunk down into the inner darkness: under the rind. All witless, all twittering, gibbering, decaying. Bogeymen."[19]

In his terror (or is it a stratagem?) the Unman cries: "Oh, Ransom, Ransom! We shall be killed. Killed and put back under the rind. Ransom, you promised to help me. Don't let them get me again."[20] They are about to smash against a rocky coast. Ransom urges the Unman to repent, to say his prayers. Suddenly the Unman wraps him in an iron embrace and the struggle resumes.

The sensuousness of the book is such that the earth by comparison seems a pale planet, with muted colors, smells, and tastes. The most ordinary experiences are highlighted and intensified on Perelandra. A drink of water is like the taste of some exotic vintage; plants and trees vie to produce the most delectable fruit, and eating becomes something midway between a sacrament and a Bacchic celebration. Long after a reader has forgotten most of the debating points scored by Ransom and Weston he will remember, with his senses, the innocent pleasures of an unfallen paradise.

The relation of myth to fact and truth, already dramatized in *Out of the Silent Planet,* is explored further in this
book. When Malacandra and Perelandra reveal themselves
to Ransom near the end, he sees with his own eyes the divinities that the ancient classical world, by an understandable
confusion, elevated to a status higher than God intended them
to occupy. But the Greeks and Romans were not entirely
wrong. Mars and Venus indeed exist, but not as independent
gods. They are more like the highest rank of created spirits.

When Ransom, victim of a body-soul dualism, stands in
the invisible presence of Maleldil, and struggles against the
thought of physical combat with the Unman, he comes to
understand that truth, fact, and myth are not ultimate dis-
tinctions:

> . . . It would degrade the spiritual warfare to the condition
> of mere mythology. But here he got another check.
> Long since on Mars, and more strongly since he came to
> Perelandra, Ransom had been perceiving that the triple
> distinction of truth from myth and of both from fact was
> purely terrestrial—was part and parcel of that unhappy
> division between soul and body which resulted from the
> Fall. Even on earth the sacraments existed as a permanent
> reminder that the division was neither wholesome nor
> final. The Incarnation had been the beginning of its
> disappearance. In Perelandra it would have no meaning at
> all. Whatever happened here would be of such a nature
> that earth-men would call it mythological.[21]

Mars and Venus explain to him how his Silent Planet
has received news of them. There is not only an environment
of space; there is one of minds. The universe is a great whispering gallery "where (save for the direct action of Maleldil)
though no news travels unchanged yet no secret can be
rigorously kept." In fact

> . . . in the very matter of our world, the traces of the
> celestial commonwealth are not quite lost. Memory passes

---

[21] Pp. 143–44.

through the womb and hovers in the air. The Muse is a
real thing. A faint breath, as Virgil says, reaches the
late generations. Our mythology is based on a solider reality
than we dream: but it is also at an almost infinite
distance from that base. And when they told him this,
Ransom at last understood why mythology was what it
was—gleams of celestial strength and beauty falling
on a jungle of filth and imbecility.[22]

Perelandra is in many ways the fulfillment of *Out of the
Silent Planet*. Ransom loses any planetary provinciality remaining in him. He begins to think in terms of the solar system, even the cosmos, and though earth is quarantined and
besieged, its isolation seems a little less than he had previously thought. He sees that the stakes are doubled and re-
doubled. On Malacandra life exists at a low level of moral
risk; no serious rebellion against Oyarsa has any chance of
success. By contrast, Perelandra is as vulnerable to ruin as it
is beautiful; there are no angelic powers instructed to save it
from itself.

Most important of all, *Perelandra* is far more archetypal
than the previous novel. In *Out of the Silent Planet,* the
Martian way of life, its inhabitants, its rules and regulations
are as quaint as they are archetypal. One can read the book
solely for odd landscapes and odd encounters. But on Perelandra a daring new beginning has been made. Paradise is
created anew, and despite the doleful results of the earthly
experiment, God dares yet again to set a man and a woman
in paradise and give them freedom to obey or rebel.

Paradise is one of the most persistent universal myths,
always cropping up in our minds when we least anticipate
it. It can be as naïve as the Big Rock Candy Mountain with
its little streams of alcohol, as sophisticated as the Marxist
dream of a prehistorical communist paradise. Lewis's enormous achievement in *Perelandra* was to present a paradise
come of age, a planet which in all its details is a sacrament
of God's creative goodness.

———————
[22] P. 201.

The Green Lady and her husband are as archetypal as the biblical Adam and Eve, and the Unman is the ultimate revelation of that mysterious intelligence called the Enemy or Devil. The cave where Ransom slays the Unman evokes all our inherited terrors of the Underground world and its alien sights and horrors. Ransom's return to the surface of the planet is a kind of resurrection, and he arrives back on earth renewed and younger-looking than when he left. Still another universal theme is the yang and yin of those metaphysical absolutes, the masculine and the feminine. This is dramatized on one level in the green pair, on another in the epiphany of Mars and Venus.

Perelandra, more insistently theological than *Out of the Silent Planet,* is a story of creation with a happy ending. At times the theology is a little tedious, as Ransom and Weston debate for chapter upon chapter. And yet, it is significant that the reader's attention rarely wavers. With a sure intuition he recognizes that his own identity and destiny are at stake; this controversy is not carried on for the sake merely of scoring points.

Like the earlier book, *Perelandra* has little touches of everyday realism to make the reader more willing to accept the vision dramatized by the book as a whole. Ransom's desperate effort to convince himself (and Maleldil) that the struggle with Weston should remain spiritual is an example; who would not try to avoid physical combat with the Unman's long nails, so suitable for ripping skin? The temptation toward greed, familiar enough on earth, assails Ransom when he discovers that if he searches hard enough he could eat only the specially delicious fruits and berries. Ransom's irritation when he begins to lose the debate with Weston reveals the frustration of an academic when his tool, language, begins to fail him.

While Malacandra is a cautious experiment, quietly but constantly supervised by Oyarsa and the *eldila,* Perelandra presents Maleldil subjecting Himself to a kind of kenosis, deliberately withholding his decisive power and leaving the

Green Lady and her husband free to say yes or no to Him. Thus goodness has a more absolute quality on Perelandra than on Malacandra, and individual decisions become the moments that will shape the history of the solar system, for good or ill.

Perelandra is, in sum, an astonishing achievement, and of a high mythic order. By an act of imagination, both probing and soaring, Lewis has created a world in which goodness is at least as convincing as evil, and where the very taste of water and fruits is the objective correlative of the newly minted goodness of the planet. To read the book and then return in thought and activity to this planet is to see the familiar world in a very unfamiliar light. *Perelandra* leaves one the taste of sheer goodness, and that it is a rare and unsettling flavor.

We come therefore to the inevitable novel set on the sinful Earth, *That Hideous Strength*. The tone is established by the epigraph, a quotation from *Ane Dialog* by the medieval Scottish poet, David Lindsay:

> The shadow of that hyddeous strength
> Sax myle and more it is of length.

The lines refer, of course, to the Tower of Babel story in Genesis 11:1–9. Few myths are more haunting than this one. In it the built-in price of human consciousness is dramatized. Mankind, knowing that individuals perish, clutches at some kind of collective immortality. An individual's name may be forgotten, but France, China, or America can strive to live forever. The catch is that eternal life, whether for the individual or his collectivities, is the gift of God, not something to be achieved by building a fortress against death. In the myth, the tower builders seek to live on in the memory of future generations. Ironically, they already have the most essential human continuity, that of speech and collective memory. What need is there for more? Humanity will carry on their memory. But this is not enough. They must make sure. They try too hard, and a "law of reverse effect"[23] comes into play. God sees this bustling scene as a challenge to His authority. These people will come to think of themselves as autonomous, creating their own goals, disregardful of God who is the setter of limits. He abruptly interrupts the project and subjects the builders to the very fate they have striven to avoid: they are scattered all about on the face of the earth. In addition, their speech is spilt into hundreds of languages, so that they can only with extreme difficulty organize themselves into rivals to God.

In the first two novels, the theme of man's attempt to become God is dramatized through Weston's cosmic pretensions. The theme becomes most clearly focused in *That Hideous Strength*. Here the biblical tower, symbolizing man's arrogance, is represented by the National Institute of Coordinated Experiments (N.I.C.E. for short) which exists ostensibly to solve all humanity's problems by social, scientific, and technological research. The Institute is actually a front for the "macrobes" (demonic powers) whose ultimate goals have nothing to do with curing diseases, reforming the legal system, or finding a remedy for insanity. The macrobes, in cooperation with their human allies, are aiming at making hell incarnate on earth. At the beginning, *That Hideous Strength* appears to be a perfectly normal story of academic life and its urbane intrigues, but gradually the cosmic conflicts become apparent.

Lewis subtitled the book "A Modern Fairy-Tale for Grown-Ups." His Preface explains why, and points out the reason for the realistic tone of the opening chapters:

> I have called this a fairy-tale in the hope that no one who
> dislikes fantasy may be misled by the first two chapters
> into reading further, and then complain of his
> disappointment. If you ask why—intending to write about
> magicians, devils, pantomime animals, and planetary

---

[23] For a discussion of this concept, see my book *From Utopia to Nightmare* (New York: Harper & Row, 1962), pp. 151ff.

angels—I nevertheless begin with such hum-drum scenes
and persons, I reply that I am following the traditional
fairy-tale. We do not always notice its method, because the
cottages, castles, woodcutters, and petty kings with which a
fairy-tale opens have become for us as remote as the
witches and ogres to which it proceeds. But they were
not remote at all to the men who made and first enjoyed
the stories.[24]

The opening chapter introduces Jane, the wife of Mark
Studdock, a young fellow of sociology. Jane is meditating
about her marriage, and wryly contrasting it with the words of
the marriage service—"Matrimony was ordained, thirdly, for
the mutual society, help, and comfort that the one ought to
have of the other." She is getting very little of these in her
drab marriage. To add a touch of terror to the boredom of
her life, Jane is subject to recurrent nightmares. Or so she
takes them to be. Later it turns out that they are instances of
clairvoyance. Her most recent vision has been of a strange
head which another person screws off from a human trunk.
This head merges with another—an old man who is being
dug up in a cemetery, and who is clad in a long mantle like a
druid. He gradually wakes up and speaks in a language
vaguely resembling Spanish.

The dream in itself could be dismissed as a nightmare,
but next morning Jane picks up the paper and reads about
the execution of Alcasan, the "scientist bluebeard." The
photo is exactly the first face she saw the night before. At this
point the basic realism of the story begins to be infiltrated by
hints of magic and the preternatural. Meanwhile, Mark is
busy with university politics. During his five years at the
university he has gradually been accepted by that inner circle,
the progressive element. To be an insider is a hunger and passion for him; he will almost sell his soul in order to be where
the wheels are turned.

On a particular day, the drab Studdocks go their sepa-

---

[24] *That Hideous Strength: A Modern Fairy-Tale for Grown-Ups*
(New York: Macmillan, 1946, 1965), p. 7.

rate ways. Jane runs into plump and motherly Mrs. Dimble, wife of Cecil Dimble, a fellow of Northumberland College. Suddenly Mrs. Dimble, with a flash of insight, asks whether there is anything wrong. Jane tries to keep her poise, but bursts into tears, and seeks the comfort of Mrs. Dimble's cuddly arms.

During lunch Dr. Dimble talks about Arthurian England and the strange character of Merlin, who, although a magician, is also a Christian. Legend has it that he was buried in nearby Bragdon Wood and will one day return to active life. The N.I.C.E. wants to purchase the wood, ostensibly for building space, and Dr. Dimble wonders what they will find when they start digging. At the mention of Merlin and his possible resuscitation, Jane nearly faints. Embarrassed and confused, she describes her dream of the night before. Dr. Dimble is extremely interested, but before he can question her further, one of his pupils arrives.

Meanwhile, Mark is conferring with members of the progressive element and enjoying the delicious sense of being an insider. All this is in preparation for a faculty meeting at which a decision must be made whether to sell Bragdon Wood to the N.I.C.E. One of the group is Lord Feverstone, fellow of Bracton, who is none other than the Devine of *Out of the Silent Planet*. Time has not improved or even changed him.

The faculty meeting is a model of political maneuvering. Most of the members are not aware that the question of selling Bragdon Wood is on the agenda. When the matter is proposed, the debate is sidetracked to the bad condition of the wall surrounding the wood and the prohibitive cost of rebuilding it. Before long, the junior faculty are sure that the choice will be between their salaries and a fancy new wall. The opposition, the traditionalists who simply love the wood as it is, have no chance. Mark and his friends bring the meeting to its programmed conclusion.

By this time the stage is set for the story of deviltry trying to take over the earth. The N.I.C.E. must have Bragdon

Wood because they must have Merlin. The latter's powers of magic can tip the scales in the cosmic conflicts now shaping up in the quiet university town.

As part of its devious plans, the N.I.C.E. courts Mark, flattering his professional ego and simultaneously dealing with him in a frighteningly absent-minded way. What he does not know is that they have no interest whatever in his sociological expertise. All they really want is Jane and her gift of clairvoyance, so she can alert them to the resuscitation of Merlin when that event occurs.

The nominal head of the N.I.C.E. is Jules, a novelist and scientific popularizer who seems to bear some resemblance to H. G. Wells. He refutes religion by pointing out that the average village church is larger than Solomon's temple. The real head is the Deputy Director, John Wither:

> Wither was a white-haired old man with a courtly manner.
> His face was clean shaven and very large indeed, with
> watery blue eyes and something rather vague and chaotic
> about it. He did not appear to be giving them his whole
> attention and this impression must, I think, have been due
> to the eyes, for his actual words and gestures were
> polite to the point of effusiveness.[25]

Wither is so far gone in service to the macrobes that he is spiritually dwelling with them while leading a ghostly life on earth. He wanders about like an apparition, observing everything and everybody, and changing from one mood to another with a terrifying unpredictability.

N.I.C.E. headquarters are filled with ghastly people. One is the physiologist, Professor Filostrato, whose great ambition is to *clean* the planet. Real trees will be cut down and replaced by metal ones, which will never drop leaves. Another memorable character is Professor Frost, with pointed beard and pince-nez. Later he is in charge of the attempt to brainwash Mark into the complete loss of all moral absolutes. Still another frightening character is Straik, a religious fanatic

---

[25] P. 52.

who counts on the N.I.C.E. to usher in the Kingdom of God. Finally, there is the Fairy, the woman heading the special, autonomous police force of the Institute, and much given to grisly jokes about the physiological aspects of hangings; she can be crudely jolly or vicious by turn. All in all, the N.I.C.E. is a display case for hideous human beings. Those who have gone farthest in service of the macrobes are a little like Weston in *Perelandra*. They seem not so much to act as to be acted through.

Mark, always unsure of his status at the N.I.C.E. and kept in a state of constant anxiety, has little time to think about Jane, who meanwhile has taken refuge in a country house called St. Anne's on the Hill. Here a small group of people, mostly Christians, quietly wait for supernatural instructions on how they must counteract the evil brewing at Belbury, the temporary center of the N.I.C.E. Ransom, now eternally young from his stay on Perelandra, is there. So is the resident skeptic, MacPhee, modeled on the Great Knock and serving the valuable function of challenging the ideas of the believers as they try to make sense of the strange events happening in the area. Another inhabitant is Mr. Bultitude, the bear, whose gentle life stands in symbolic contrast to the tormented beasts vivisected at Belbury. The Dimbles, evicted from their home when its lease is not renewed, are also at St. Anne's. The little group seems a forlorn army to repel the organized evil of the N.I.C.E., but they have on their side the support of supernatural legions as well as Jane, who by her visions can track the movements of Merlin and make it possible to enlist his white magic on their side. Meanwhile, Belbury has its holy of holies, the room where the guillotined head of Alcasan is wired and tubed up so that a kind of life remains in it; it serves as a medium of communication between the macrobes and their earthly servants.

The narrative line gradually becomes very complicated. The central thread is the competition to find Merlin and press him into service on one side or the other. This leads to night-time searches when Jane reports that he has risen from his comatose centuries. There is much comic confusion when the N.I.C.E. seizes an innocent tramp and questions him in exotic languages. Another theme is the reeducation of Jane, who in the absence of her husband is taught that wifely obedience is not just a male chauvinist ideal but an erotic necessity. Along with her acceptance of wifehood is her eventual conversion to the Christianity that she has so long dismissed as a medieval superstition.

Back at Belbury, Mark also is undergoing reeducation. He is falsely accused of murder and is subjected to a process of objectification, the object being to destroy all concepts of normality. Here the tale draws heavily on *The Abolition of Man,* with its insistence that certain emotions are proper for given situations: e.g., righteous anger is a proper feeling when confronted by cruelty; and approval, when goodness is seen in action. In a terrifying scene Mark is confined in a room where a pattern of dots, not quite symmetrical, confronts him on the ceiling, subtly eroding his sense of normality. The climax of his reeducation comes when he is commanded by Professor Frost to trample a crucifix. Mark has never had any religion, and it suddenly occurs to him that just possibly this crucifix might symbolize something real and meaningful. Some instinct, some trace of plain goodness and decency, inwardly forbids him to obey the command.

Meanwhile, the quiet people at St. Anne's have made contact with the awakened Merlin, and he, recognizing in Ransom the Pendragon of Logres, commits his white magic to their use. Merlin is a marvel of historical imagination. His magic is not quite what modern magic would be; it dates from a time when nature and man were less sharply sundered, and magic could be neutral rather than definitely good or evil. Merlin, speaking a strange Latin and primitive Celtic, finds the twentieth century difficult to cope with. He is amazed at the luxury of his accommodations while offended that no attendants sleep in his chamber as would befit his dignity. Though a Christian, he casually suggests that Ransom decapitate Jane, who with her birth control has passed by the opportunity to conceive a Pendragon who would reign for a thousand years. All these differences wrought by the passage of time make communication with Merlin difficult, but there is no question where his loyalty lies: he is with St. Anne's. There he receives from the assembled *oyéresu* their powers, and goes forth to battle Belbury.

Belbury is preparing for a visit by its nominal director, Jules, who believes he is really the intellectual foundation of the entire project. As described in the book,

> Jules was a cockney. He was a very little man, whose
> legs were so short that he had unkindly been compared with
> a duck. He had a turned up nose and a face in which
> some original *bonhomie* had been much interfered with by
> years of good living and conceit. His novels had first
> raised him to fame and affluence; later, as editor of the
> weekly called *We Want to Know,* he had become such a
> power in the country that his name was really necessary to
> the N.I.C.E.[26]

Jules talks compulsively while sipping sherry, and the power structure of the N.I.C.E. nervously attends him. He impatiently awaits the banquet and the chance to deliver a formal address. At last the banquet is out of the way, the king's health is drunk, and Jules rises to speak. All is normal at first, then strange slips of speech begin occurring. Jules seems to be saying that something was "as gross an anachronism as to trust to Calvary for salvation in modern war." Soon he is saying, with the clearest possible enunciation, that "The madrigore of verjuice must be talthibianised."[27]

The guests, not being biblical scholars, do not recognize that Merlin, drawing on preternatural powers, is confounding their language so they can no longer communicate with one another. Jules is puzzled by the bewildered expressions everywhere around him. All civil cooperation breaks down. Jules is shot by the Fairy; the company panics; men and women

---

26 P. 338.
27 Pp. 343–44.

are trampled underfoot as they attempt to flee. The destruction of the N.I.C.E. is climaxed when the tortured animals break loose and roam the banquet room with bloody jaws and flashing teeth.

Wither and Straik survive. They seize Filostrato and take him to the head room, where they guillotine him in a ceremony suggesting a pagan sacrifice. Wither then kills Straik, and in turn is disposed of by Bultitude the bear. Meanwhile, Frost sets himself on fire. A suspicion that he has been wrong all along comes to him in his agony. "He half saw: he wholly hated. The physical torture of the burning was not fiercer than his hatred of that. With one supreme effort he flung himself back into his illusion. In that attitude eternity overtook him as sunrise in old tales overtakes trolls and turns them into unchangeable stone."[28]

The destruction of Belbury is followed by a series of severe earthquakes. All in all the forces of the bent Oyarsa have suffered a disastrous defeat. There is no hint that this is for all time; Belbury is not the "last things" of biblical prophecy but a dress rehearsal. Meanwhile, the quiet folk at St. Anne's are busy preparing a marriage chamber for their servant, Mrs. Maggs, whose husband—imprisoned for theft— is due to be released. Even this humble task is invaded by mythological manifestations. When Jane is alone in the bridal chamber she suddenly notices an archaic figure sharing the room with her. This is a woman dressed in a flame-colored robe in the style of a Minoan priestess. With her are many dwarfs, intent on tearing the room apart. But the mysterious goddess of the marriage bed puts a torch to the objects in the room and instead of flames, flowers begin to entwine everything. Janes realizes that the archaic quality she has detected in Mother Dimble is now here in full strength, without the humanization of Christianity.

The visit of the preternatural woman is only a first manifestation of the temporary breakdown of categories like

---

[28] P. 358.

natural, preternatural, and supernatural. Before the story ends, the *oyéresu* of the solar system or their earthly duplicates invade St. Anne's. There is a special epiphany as Aphrodite reveals herself, and animals modestly wander off into darkness to consummate their love. And Jane, now a Christian wife, prepares to receive Mark when at last they meet again. She is even willing to obey.

That Hideous Strength is, for a literary critic, a more troubling book than the two other space fantasies. The fundamental question is whether Lewis tried to pack too much into it, and whether the final chapters lose strength and cogency because of this. The problem is perhaps one of pacing. How much intensity and catastrophe can a reader absorb before his capacity to respond is dulled? The book is also intellectually overstuffed. It is as though Lewis has taken a series of convictions dear to his heart, and forced them between the covers of one book. There is the whole solar mythology, as developed in the two earlier works and now amplified. There is his particular concept of myth, and the relation of myth to Christianity. There is the dramatization and vindication of the traditional Christian doctrine, dear to Lewis, that women should be subordinate to men; Lewis even convinces us, for a moment at least, that this is not mere custom but the reflection of metaphysical realities, and indeed necessary for a meaningful sex life on the part of both partners.

Most of all, there is the Arthurian material and the key role of Merlin. One senses here the strong influence of Charles Williams, whose poetry is based so largely on the Arthurian legend; the distinction between the eternal England (Logres) and the empirical Britain is clearly borrowed from Williams. Lewis has combined Merlin and the Arthurian legends with apocalyptic passages from Scripture. The question is how well does Merlin fit into the total book. Certainly, his presence requires a vast amount of discussion and explanation during the course of the story.

In Merlin, Lewis brilliantly conceives a half-barbarian, half-Christian magician at the end of the Romano-Celtic period in England. Lewis's sense of history, of how men, for all their common nature (the *Tao*), are shaped and colored by their times, gives a peculiar reality to the magician who was so close to nature that it was not impious for him to use his white powers of magic; he was a part of the world he manipulated.

The more troubling aspect of Merlin is that he comes close to being a deus ex machina. The conflict between macrobes and *eldila* hinges on who will capture Merlin first and put his magic powers to work for the destruction of the other side. What would have happened if Belbury had gained control of Merlin? Would the *eldila* have intervened more directly in mortal affairs to ensure the victory of St. Anne's? Was the victory of the good people a lucky accident?

These questions arise because the more realistic sections of the novel are extremely well done. Lewis knew the academic animal and his penchant for inner circles and conspiratorial preparations. Few academic novels have presented a faculty meeting with greater sardonic insight than *That Hideous Strength* in its opening scenes.

Lewis may not probe psychoanalytic depths in his portrayal of the sad sociologist, Mark Studdock, and his equally sad wife, Jane, but the twin pictures are real and convincing. Who on any campus has not met the anxious young instructor who sniffs the air to find which way the wind is blowing, and nervously nuzzles up to the power centers? Who has not met his intellectual wife, who wants to be admired for her brains and is disconcerted to find that males (perhaps even God, she finally concludes) admire her because she is a cute little thing? For a bachelor author, Lewis gives a remarkably accurate picture of two people in an increasingly boring marriage. Neither, at the beginning, has enough identity to bring the other alive. Only the experiences generated by Belbury can make them wake up into full life and the ability to rediscover each other.

Many of the other characters are thoroughly convincing —some quite minor, like the servant Maggs, and the anonymous tramp. Lewis had a sympathetic insight that extended beyond the academic world, and indeed he often handles his humbler characters with a gentler touch than he bestows upon the principals. Of the major characters, only Ransom himself, now revealed as the Pendragon, is a shade ghostly, almost as though he were pure spirit temporarily caught in the confines of a body. The denizens of Belbury are particularly well done, ranging from the bawderies of the Fairy to the haziness of Wither and the cold objectivity of Frost.

The realistic elements in the narration are invariably successful. The fantasy gives rise to problems. The final triumph of goodness and God's forces leaves a number of troubling questions in the reader's mind. The two earlier space novels did not do this; the victories achieved in them were clear and imaginatively compelling.

It might be argued that since *That Hideous Strength* takes place on this fallen earth, nothing is likely to be as neat and precise as on Mars, which has never had a fall, and Venus, where a fall is averted. Still, one finds the thought recurring, What would the book have been like if the whole Merlin theme had been eliminated, and the victory of the good forces had to be achieved by more direct methods, analogous to Ransom's triumph on Venus? It would have been a much shorter book; but possibly a stronger one.

Looking at the three books as one total work, it is evident that certain themes underlie all of them. One is that of moral reeducation. In *Out of the Silent Planet* Ransom undergoes a quest that gradually frees him of his neurotic fears and strengthens the religion that he already professes but is not able, at first, to rely on without misgiving. In *Perelandra,* Ransom is further educated. He comes to see that the conflict between God and Satan is not a purely "spiritual" one but may require a wrestling match with the Unman. In *That Hideous Strength* Ransom requires no further education, but Mark and Jane do; they stand for Everyman and Everywoman of the modern, enlightened sort, who need to have all their easy, rationalistic assumptions destroyed so that they can see the world, with its demonic and divine dimensions, as it actually is.

Lewis's theory that everything in the universe is coming to a point—good is becoming better, evil worse—is dramatized by the way the stakes are raised in the three novels. In the first, Devine and Weston are rather pathetic figures; their grandiose plans for spoiling Malacandra are doomed from the beginning. In the second novel, Weston has a more realistic chance of wrecking the newly created paradise. His rhetoric outdoes Ransom's in the debate before the Green Lady, and in physical combat with Ransom they are about equally matched. So the odds are one in two that Venus will repeat the history of Tellus and become a fallen planet.

The third novel pictures a still more ghastly possibility. Tellus is already fallen, but it is filled with enclaves of resistance against the demonic powers. These enclaves are the work of Christ, who has planted redemption in the very midst of the enemy's camp. If Belbury succeeds, it will wipe out these divine pockets of holy resistance, and the work of Christ will be undone. Thus the stakes are highest in *That Hideous Strength,* and it is no wonder that the *eldila* and *oyéresu* reveal themselves most openly in this final novel of the trilogy, where the need for them is greatest.

It is Ransom, however, who provides the strongest unifying element of the three books. We see him entering into progressively deeper experience and knowledge. By the last book, he is a "little Christ," far removed from the timid academic of the Martian tale.

W. D. Norwood, Jr., in his essay, "C. S. Lewis, Owen Barfield, and the Modern Myth," expresses this another way:

> . . . a reader can see the archetypal theme: *Out of the Silent Planet* is Ransom's confirmation in Christian knowledge and a study in faith, reason, and death; *Perelandra* is his baptism and a study in hope, romance, and birth; *That Hideous Strength* is his new life and a study in love, mystery, and choice. . . . The reader who sees the books in this light recognizes an organic unity to the

trilogy which makes it an artwork in its own right, separate
from, although composed of, the individual novels.[29]

The trilogy is indeed a quest story, and the emphasis
moves from faith to hope to the supreme virtue, love, as Ransom's reeducation proceeds from book to book. There is no
reason to suppose that Lewis plotted out this thematic triad
at the start, but the attempt to explore at increasing depth the
meaning of existence quite naturally evokes and dramatizes
these central themes.[30]

---

[29] *The Midwest Quarterly* (Spring 1967), pp. 279–91.

[30] *The Dark Tower* also includes four short fantasies, three of
which are competent and one, "Forms of Things Unknown," remarkable for its creation of foreboding and horror. In addition, there are
the few fragments of what Lewis intended to be a novel about Helen
of Troy after the destruction of Troy. So little was written that one
cannot be sure how it would have turned out, but at places there is a
mythic aliveness, and it is just possible that if Lewis's health had permitted, this novel would have taken its place alongside *Till We Have
Faces*.

6

THE PARALLEL WORLD
OF NARNIA

Lewis's first book for children, *The Lion, the Witch and the Wardrobe,* was published in his early fifties. For seven years, at the rate of one a year, the Narnia books came off the presses. Readers accustomed to adult fare found themselves puzzled by this sudden alteration in his focus.

The shift is easier to comprehend if one takes a second look at Lewis's childhood, when he and Warnie played in the roomy attic. Their principal activity was composing adventure tales set in such imaginary locales as Animaland, India, or Boxen. Lewis continued this activity up to his early teens, as in a story probably written around 1912—"Boxen: or Scenes from Boxonian City Life."[1] This tale, never published in book form, begins as follows:

I

Night was falling on the Bosphorus as the town guardsman sighted a small but tidy schooner tacking up to Fortessa. Forward stood a young Fracity Chessary Pawn and at the tiller a sturdy thickset knight stolidly smoking his pipe. With a little deft maneuvering he brought

---

[1] Quotations from Lewis's juvenilia ("Boxen" and "Bleheris") are courtesy of The Trustees of the Estate of C. S. Lewis, and are copyrighted by the Estate.

her up a secluded, rocky creek and dropped anchor about
200 yards from the shingle. He called the assistance of
the Pawn to lower his solitary boat, which soon was
lying under the schooner's counter, and several vigorous
strokes sent him to the beach. Mooring the boat he stepped
out and in the dusk descried two athletic figures
walking along a short distance away.

"Why! Your Majesties!"

They turned. "Macgoullah."

"At your service. What are you doing here?"

"Oh," said the 'Jah. "Learning Turkish."

"Alone?" inquired the knight.

"No. Big's here," answered Buny.

"At the inn?"

"Yes."

The three friends walked together to the postern
gate, where the guard admitted them for a small fee. A few
hundred yards brought them to the inn. Through the
door into the dinner room Macgoullah caught sight of a
stout frog in evening dress.

"I'll stay in the Outer," he observed.

The boys walked into the Inner. It was a small room
crowded to overflowing. Round the table sat Puddiphat,
Goose, Quicksteppe, and the Little Master.

"Boys, where have you been?" asked the Frog.

"Oh, nowhere special," returned the 'Jah with
characteristic vagueness. Big gulped and continued bisecting
a portion of cod. All present were Boxonians except one
Prussian who sat in a far corner silent and morose,
unnoticed by all: true, there was a cautious look in
Quicksteppe's grey eyes, but no one observed it. The
company bent over their meal and conversation and quietly
the Prussian slipped into a curtained cupboard. Big
looked up.

"Are we alone?"

"Yes, my dear little Master," said Goose.

"Now Goose, tell your tale."

"Yes. Gentlemen, I have just found that the whole
Clique is threatened by Orring, one of the members for 'the
aquanium—' "

"Come, my good bird," cried Big. "What does that
mean?"

"For Piscia, my good Frog," Big gulped, "has determined to throw all the present clique out of office, and
is bribing right and left."

One touch of the future scholar is seen in the story's
footnotes. Two occur in the passages just quoted. The first
explains that "The kingdoms of Boxen, although united in
Parliament, retain their monarchs, the Rajah of India and
the King of Animaland." The other fills in background:
" 'Little Master' was the speaker of the Parliament, and had
many powers, including that of being the constant guardian
and adviser of the Kings. The present one, Lord Big, exercised much influence over King Benjamin and the Rajah, as
he had been their tutor in their youth: in private he neg-
lected all the usual formulae of address to a prince. . . ."

One hopes that some day a selection of Lewis's juvenilia
will be published, both for scholars and the simply curious.
Meanwhile, the portions quoted from "Boxen" give some
idea of Lewis's writing as he entered his teens.

A reader coming on "Boxen" might first leap to the conclusion that here is the ancestry of the Narnia tales, but he
would quickly learn that the resemblance is superficial,
amounting to little more than a cast that includes talking animals. These characters seem like normal men dressed up for
a masquerade. The profound difference is in atmosphere.
Narnia is a kind of fairyland, and even its political and military events have an otherworld quality. In "Boxen," one is
plunged into a tale of cliques and conspiracies and counter-
measures. The everyday Tellurian world is very much with
us. One seems to hear in the background the voice of Lewis's
father, declaiming political opinions. Or one senses the influence of cheap adventure and mystery books in which such
sinister characters as a Prussian lurk in curtained cupboards.

In short, "Boxen," despite its vocal animals, represents
one side of Lewis: the realist. From this book he *could* have

evolved into a realistic novelist, determined to present the earthly condition in all its photographic concreteness.

This was not the road he took, and yet in minor ways "Boxen" foreshadows things to come. Even if the animals act completely human, still they are animals and they do talk. The theme of inner and outer circles, so important in Lewis's later work, is already here, as is the conviction that government must function as a kind of conspiracy. There is a keen eye for small, specific details. Most of all, perhaps, even at this early age we have a smooth narrative style.

More typical of the later Lewis is "The Quest of Bleheris," written two or three years later after he had fallen under the magic spell of the Arthurian legends. Here instead of talking animals there are knights and fair ladies. It begins:

THE QUEST OF BLEHERIS

CHAPTER I—Of the City of Nesses and of certain that dwelt therein

As I sate in the garden in summer time, when the sun had set and the first stars were trembling into light, and while the ghostly, little bats were bleating above me, it came to me in mind to write for you, Galahad, somewhat of the life and dealings of this Bleheris; for—in my conceit— since he was surely not unlike yourself, it seemed that you might have pleasure in hearing of his life and his death, that fell so many years ago. Know then, that in the old days, when this world was still young and full of wonders, there lay a little country that men called The Land of Two Nesses: for there was a wide bay, and on either side of it stood great, bold nesses where the rocky hills sank down into the sea, and between them was a beach of fair, golden sand. . . . Now from out of the heights that were thereabouts came a swift and deep stream, called Coldriver, that ran through the valley-land, and out into the bay beyond, on the which stood the City of the Nesses: the same was a very fair city of stones, with five

bridges over that stream, and good wharves for many ships
of the merchants that lay by them, and towers and
palaces and rich halls as fair as might be. . . .

For in that city was a rich old knight, a worthy man
who had done great deeds of arms in his day, driving back
rovers that came to harry them from over the seas, and
riding at all adventure in the ill lands beyond the pass of
which I told you. . . . Now the whole prop and stay of
this old knight, and all his pride and glory was [his daughter]
for she was the fairest and most virtuous maiden as at
that time alive: and her hair was more yellow than corn
and her feet and her breasts more white than—But, in
truth, my friend, there is little need to tell of such matters:
for I believe well that you, who have read so deep in
old books, must have heard this same lady spoken of
ere now. . . .

Now the fame of this lady was very great in the land,
inasmuch as all squires and knights, yea and barons and
great kings wooed her to wife: but she would have
none of them. . . . But though many said that they would,
yet it is not known that any man died for love of her:
nay, some even were so ungentle that they went afterwards
and wed others, and lived merrily all their life days.
. . . But let us go forward: now, as might be looked for,
this young knight [Bleheris] would be no worse than his
fellows either in love or in war or in any other thing, so that
he too sought the favour of Alice the Saint, and wrote
verses upon her and jousted for her, and sighed piteously
and altogether deemed that he was no less sorely
smitten in love than Lancelot or Palomides or any of
the knights of old song. None the less, he forebore not to
eat lustily, to ride to the chase with a good heart, and to
sleep sound of nights.

So far the tale shows Lewis wavering between complete
commitment to his story and a schoolboyish debunking tone.
He makes Alice the Saint a frigid maid, and as we have seen,
comments on her conventional beauty with tongue in cheek.
As the story goes on, Lewis falls more under its spell and
develops a series of visionary scenes, some of which are

powerful. For instance, the death of Wan Jadis, a companion of Bleheris (Chapter XI):

> . . . now nothing was left of Wan Jadis, above the marish,
> but only his head and his arms stretched out desperately
> to the landwards. And, whereas his helmet was off (for in his
> haste he had left it hanging by the saddle), Bleheris
> could see the beautiful, sad face strained and drawn with
> loathing and the agony of death: it seemed that he
> strove to speak, but in that moment the slime and mud
> rose to his white lips, and the evil creeping things crawled
> over the fair skin, more delicate than porcelain. His
> eyes cast one more look upon Bleheris: and then the marish
> closed over his head, and thus Wan Jadis died.

"Bleheris" is full to overflowing with marvelous sights and strange adventures. It is that form so beloved of Lewis, the quest story, but not a Christian one; indeed there is an antichurch tone and Christianity is treated as a superstition. At times the description of scenery reminds one of *The Great Divorce* and the variety of symbolic episodes suggests *The Pilgrim's Regress*. The turning point in Bleheris's quest is the death of Wan Jadis, which is one event he cannot take half frivolously.

Lewis's mature talent represents a merger of the fanciful and the realistic, the quest and the intrigue. In "Boxen," despite its talking animals, one sees the realist at work, and there is even a foreshadowing of the future logician and satirist. "Bleheris," by contrast, explores mysterious landscapes where the soul is challenged to know itself; realms of deadly perils but also occasional hints of "Joy."

Lewis was not a man who consorted much with children. Then how did he learn to depict them so well? The answer may be the obvious one, that like almost all effective writers, he both grew up and stubbornly refused to grow up. As a small boy he was fascinated by never-never lands. He never lost this interest. Advancing years merely gave him the

courage and skill to exploit the abiding dreams of childhood.[2]

Though Lewis speaks of the influence of Beatrix Potter,
he seems to have been more familiar with the stories of
E. Nesbit. On the whole, however, he appears not to have
read vast quantities of children's stories in his early boyhood
but he devoted a good deal of time to producing his own.

The adult Lewis was haunted by a mental picture of a
faun carrying parcels in a snowy wood, a picture that went
back to about the age of sixteen. Eventually, when around
forty, his imagination began to play with the recurrent picture. This appears to have coincided with the arrival at
Lewis's home of some schoolgirls who had been evacuated
from London in fear of air raids. Perhaps, one can speculate,
their presence aroused and intensified his long-standing interest in children's stories. It is not certain that he did much
actual writing on the project at the time. I recall that in 1948
when I first met Lewis, I asked him what he intended to
write next, and he said something rather vague about com-
pleting a children's book he had begun "in the tradition of
E. Nesbit." By this time he was beginning to see more pictures, including a "queen on a sledge" and perhaps Aslan.

Another catalyst may have been a still unpublished tale
by his former pupil, Roger Lancelyn Green, *The Wood That
Time Forgot.* A reader coming on it today would be sure it
derived heavily from *The Lion,* but the truth is if anything the
opposite. Green told Lewis about the fantasy he was writing;
Lewis asked to read it and tried, unsuccessfully, to find a
publisher for it. The tale concerns three children and an
undergraduate friend who stumble into a wood where time is
suspended. There they find a girl who is a kind of succuba;
she is pursued by a bad angel. With the aid of the children,
she and the undergraduate finally meet, and by saving each

---

[2] Anyone wishing a fuller account of the genesis of Narnia should
consult Chapter X of Green and Hooper's *C. S. Lewis: A Biography,*
which lays out the background in great detail. In the present book I
am concerned more with the finished works than with their evolution.

other, save themselves. Several parts of the story have a strong Narnia flavor. When the children visit Agares in his home, he seems a jolly and innocent old man, and they do not suspect the drink, a sort of raspberry cordial, which lures one of the children to side with the forces of evil. This instantly brings to mind the White Witch's temptation of Edmund by the use of magic Turkish Delight. It is, however, not so much individual episodes as the total feeling of the wood that brings most strongly to mind the enchanted world of Narnia. Lewis's cavalier disposal of his own manuscripts makes it impossible to determine how detailed an impact Green's book had on him but, at the very least, we know he was greatly excited about it.

As Clyde Kilby has pointed out in his excellent discussion of the Narnia tales in *The Christian World of C. S. Lewis,* the order of publication of the tales does not correspond to the chronology of events inside the sequence. *The Magician's Nephew* should come first, *The Lion, the Witch and the Wardrobe* next, and *The Last Battle* of course last.

All seven of the stories are rich in Christian symbolism. Three, however, carry major themes. *The Magician's Nephew* presents the creative act by which the divine Aslan sings Narnia into existence. *The Lion, the Witch and the Wardrobe* dramatizes the crucifixion and the resurrection, as Aslan first dies at the hands of the White Witch and then triumphs over the bonds of death. *The Last Battle* is, as its title indicates, the account of how the earthly Narnia comes to an end and the heavenly Narnia takes its place.

The remaining four stories are by no means lacking in theological themes, but they are less conspicuous. It is as though these books correspond not to the key events in the Bible but the quieter events and dimensions of everyday life. Aslan, it is true, weaves in and out of the four books, but not as centrally as in the three key tales. The chapter in Kilby's book, "The Kingdom of Narnia," points out the many ways that these four other stories embody Christian themes: In *The Silver Chair* Jill must pass close to Aslan in order to drink of the sparkling water she craves. Aslan will not promise to leave her untouched if she moves toward the water; at the same time He tells her there is no other source for the kind of water she seeks. In *The Voyage of the "Dawn Treader"* a lamb gives the children fish, an ancient Christian symbol, and then reveals Himself as Aslan. In *The Horse and His Boy,* which Kilby rightly singles out as the tale having the fewest explicit Christian echoes, we find Aslan insisting that the skeptic Bree touch Him and know from experience that Aslan actually exists.

Some critics have asked whether the symbolic dimensions of the seven tales are handled in such a way as to make the stories more effective works of literature. Or rather, do Christian doctrines seem dragged in by their heels, converting the stories at their most theological moments into sugarcoated Sunday school instruction? Perhaps those best able to answer this question are the people who read Narnia as children. I have had the chance to talk with many of them, particularly as they move on into college and perhaps seek counsel on additional Lewis books they might read. I find two things: the first is that children almost always recognize a second level in the tales. This in no way obstructs or engulfs the primary level, which is simply a series of good stories. But they become alert to characters and events operating on two levels. This is rarely taken as the sly attempt of an older and pious man to sneak in religious propaganda. Children know from fairy tales and science fiction all about "willing suspension of disbelief." They enter into the game. They welcome Aslan as a special kind of talking animal and the focus of luminous meaning. Second, this acceptance of Aslan and the whole other level of the stories may or may not take an explicitly Christian form, depending on what sort of religious background the young reader has. The one who has been brought up as a Christian instantly recognizes Aslan as a kind of Christ for the talking animals and begins to see parallels with specific events in the life of Christ. The child lacking this background sees in Aslan something awesome and compelling, however he may put it in words. It is interesting that often readers of both backgrounds single out the most theological events of the tales as the most effective episodes. This suggests that the firm theological themes running through the tales may be a literary asset rather than otherwise.

Another factor is at work here. If the Chronicles of Narnia were a straight allegory, in the manner of *The Pilgrim's Progress* (or *The Pilgrim's Regress*) the reader would expect every event to have a precise correspondence with some proclamation of Christian doctrine. In Narnia, life simply goes on. It has its occasional epiphanies and revelations, but it also has long stretches in which the characters have interesting but rarely definitive adventures. The realism and detail of these routine experiences help to make the high points stand out more sharply.

Since a full treatment of Narnia would require a book the length of this one,[3] I shall concentrate on the three major tales which are central from both a literary and a religious viewpoint.

In *The Magician's Nephew,* the land of Narnia is sung into existence by Aslan. The actual creation comes rather late in the book. This is partly a way of building toward a climax, but it also represents a way of dealing with fantastic material. We saw the same strategy earlier in the interplanetary tales, all of which commence with realistic, indeed prosaic details, thereby winning the reader's confidence, and preparing him for a gradual movement toward the unexpected and incredible.

The earthly setting is a line of Victorian row houses in the time of Sherlock Holmes. Polly, a young girl living in one of the houses, gets acquainted with Digory, who later—in *The Lion*—reappears as an adult, Professor Kirke. Digory lives in the adjoining house; his father is away in India on

---

[3] An interesting start, mainly theological in emphasis, is provided by Kathryn Ann Lindskoog, *The Lion of Judah in Never-Never Land* (Grand Rapids, Michigan: W. B. Eerdmans, 1973).

some imperial mission; his Aunt Letty and eccentric Uncle Andrew Ketterley are more or less taking care of him, while concentrating their attention on his gravely ill mother. The uncle is something of an amateur magician, and is perfectly ready to use the children as guinea pigs in his experiments.

Digory and Polly play in the connected attics and explore Uncle Andrew's study. There they find yellow rings and green ones, which—they accidentally discover—have the power to transport them to other worlds and to bring them back.

The uncle has the trademark of Lewis upon him. He is a little like Weston, a little like Devine, but more absurd than either. Andrew defends the practice of magic as a prerogative of superior persons. He recalls how his godmother, Mrs. Lefay, who helped inspire his passion for magic, had given him a box of magic before her death and instructed him to burn it unopened; he did not carry out her instructions. Digory is shocked at this betrayal, but his uncle explains:

> . . . Oh, I see. You mean that little boys ought to keep their promises. Very true: most right and proper, I'm sure, and I'm very glad you have been taught to do it. But of course you must understand that rules of that sort, however excellent they may be for little boys—and servants— and women—and even people in general, can't possibly be expected to apply to profound students and great thinkers and sages. No, Digory. Men like me who possess hidden wisdom, are freed from common rules just as we are cut off from common pleasures. Ours, my boy, is a high and lonely destiny.[4]

This sounds like Weston proclaiming the higher morality that could justify the extinction of the Malacandrans if the deed would advance the Tellurian destiny. Later, in a conversation with Jadis the Witch, Digory hears her make exactly the same defense of her destruction of the city of Charn. "You must learn, child, that what would be wrong for you or for any of

---

[4] *The Magician's Nephew* (New York: Collier Books, 1955, 1970), p. 18.

the common people is not wrong in a great Queen such as I.
The weight of the world is on our shoulders. We must be
freed from all rules. Ours is a high and lonely destiny."[5]

If the White Witch, alias Queen Jadis, represents pure,
metaphysical evil, Uncle Andrew in his eager and bumbling
way is trying hard to catch up with her but will never make it.
She attracts; she terrifies; she never amuses. Uncle Andrew's
grand gestures are more often comic than lordly in their consequences.

The plot of the tale is built around a series of adventures
in other worlds with return visits to the earth. Digory and
Polly travel by means of the magic rings. One world they
visit is Charn, obviously the victim of some vast destructive
force. Here they first encounter Queen Jadis. She discovers
the children are from a newer world and instantly resolves to
conquer it. The children hastily touch their rings to return to
London, but Jadis goes along by touching the children. The
queen and Uncle Andrew meet in London and he finds himself spending his last penny to entertain her in proper queenly
style. Their night on the city ends in a wild hansom cab ride
and the beginnings of a local riot, with Uncle Andrew humili-
ated almost to the point of losing his elevated dignity.[6] The
children manage to touch the queen with their rings and
then find themselves in the Wood between the Worlds, from
which they enter the world of nothing. With them are Jadis,
Uncle Andrew, the cabbie, and his horse.

Up to this point the story has been a rather relaxed
adventure tale, spiced with magic. The one serious metaphysical theme is the nature of good and evil, simplified and indeed
almost oversimplified into the contrast between the Witch and
the naturally good and kind cabdriver. Another theme running through the story is health and illness, life and death.

---

[5] P. 62.
[6] As Clyde Kilby points out, this is one place where a direct
literary influence is obvious; the ride and near-riot are inspired by a
similar scene near the end of G. K. Chesterton's *The Man Who Was
Thursday*.

One gets the impression that Digory's mother has some lingering and probably fatal illness. She is constantly on his mind, and he yearns to find, perhaps in "another world," a cure for her.

These themes begin to draw together when Aslan starts singing. High, heavenly voices join in harmony with His deep notes; the black heavens suddenly gleam with countless stars. Out of nothing, hills emerge and take shape. Grass springs up and trees grow tall before their eyes. Flowers pierce the air. A new earth stands in its first perfection. Animals now appear. Aslan wanders among them, picking out certain ones and giving them the gift of speech, almost as though the image of God were being planted in them. The Witch futilely opposes him. The evil she represents may have eventual consequences in Narnia and require strange and even hideous remedies, but for the moment she is defeated.

The great lion sends Digory to the mountains of the Western Wild to pluck a particular kind of apple and bring it back uneaten. The cab horse, now turned into a winged Pegasus, carries the two children on his back. Arrived there, they discover Jadis eating an apple, and she almost persuades him to follow her example. Obedient to Aslan, Digory resists the temptation, and he brings the apple back intact. A new tree springs up from its seeds and Aslan gives Digory an apple to take back for the healing of his mother. Meanwhile, the new tree will protect Narnia from the Witch for many years, though not forever.

Back on earth, Digory buries the core of the apple that cured his mother in his back yard, and with it the magical rings, to prevent future harm. What he does not know is that the tree that grows from the core still has some of the magic of Narnia, and that when later he fashions its wood into a wardrobe, it will prove an entryway to Narnia.

These magic apple trees seem to serve a double role in the story. Depending on who uses them and under what circumstances, they can be trees of the knowledge of good and evil (with all those fateful possibilities) or trees of life, incarnating in their quieter way the overwhelming abundance of life that Aslan has sung into beautiful existence.

The Magician's Nephew provides a theological and metaphysical background for the other tales. The theme of the apple trees is less convincingly depicted than that of creation. It is almost as though Lewis were here guided more by theological necessities than literary imperatives. This episode lacks the freshness, the sense of "So this is what the legend is all about," that a reader of *Perelandra* experiences when he suddenly realizes what the fixed land symbolizes.

The Magician's Nephew has relatively few clanging swords and bloody tumults compared to some of the other tales. With the exception of climactic moments, it moves quietly, as one adventure fades into another. Thus, even the creation of Narnia has a more lyric and less epic tone than one might expect. Aslan quietly goes about His business, and His fullness of life, expressed through His singing, brings forth a universe and its inhabitants. For all its quietness, it is one of the great creation myths. Few readers will quickly forget the rapid stages of Narnia's creation, and such startlingly effective pictures as the little hillocks out of which all varieties of animal burst forth into the splendor of existence. Abundance is the word for all Aslan's creative deeds; He has come into the world of nothing and made it something, gloriously alive and fertile.

The distinction between good and evil, as has been suggested, is brought to a point in the contrast between Queen Jadis and the cabbie and his wife. No explanation is ever offered of why the Witch is evil. After all, who can give a genealogy for a metaphysical absolute? It is not that she is filled with evil. She *is* evil, and anyone who is locked in combat with her is battling demonic forces. The cabbie and his wife are simply plain, good people. They have come from the innocence of the countryside into teeming London, driven by the necessity to earn a living. When Aslan names Frank and his wife the first king and queen of Narnia, they represent everything that is lacking in the glittering but utterly evil Witch.

Aslan's song, to Uncle Andrew, is unrecognizable as song; His attempts to communicate with animals fail. They are puzzled by Him—is He an animal, a tree, or what? In a scene reminiscent of the dunking in cold water that Weston endures at the court of Oyarsa, the animals decide He is a tree and try to plant Him in the soil, with great squirts of river water delivered from an elephant's capacious trunk.

In Aslan, Lewis has created a highly effective objective correlative to Christ. Bestiaries are not a favored literary form today, but popular assumptions about the nature of animals still color metaphorical speech. A fox is automatically assumed to be clever and crafty, a snake is sneaky, a wolf (despite all the zoologists may say) is bloodthirsty, and so it goes. The lion is the noblest of the beasts, formidable in his power to destroy but regal in that very power. At the same time, a lion looks remarkably like a magnified kitten. The lion, Aslan, can roar with the authority of the universe and advance into battle with fierce face and gleaming teeth. But at other times, and with no loss of leonine dignity, He takes children riding on His back, or tussles with them in a montage of flailing limbs and teeth. He is ultimate power, ultimate gentleness, ultimate goodness, even ultimate cuddlesomeness. Without Aslan, we would have simply stories of cute talking animals with a few human beings scattered in. They would be superior tales, more vivid and convincing than most in their genre, but not fundamentally different. The presence of Aslan introduces and sustains the additional dimension that makes the Chronicles of Narnia more than a series of adventures and marvels; Lewis infuses them with the spirit of great myth. One suspects this is the largest element in the near-universal appeal of these stories, which introduce the reader not merely to strange lands and odd creatures, but into that holy land of the unconscious where the mighty archetypes dwell, and both sacred and demonic figures act out their ritual dramas.

These archetypes never die in our consciousness, no matter how rigidly modern and reductionist the mind may fancy itself. They are waiting in the shadows, to transform a familiar landscape. Lewis, through Aslan and the events he sets in motion, challenges the reader to say yes or no to what is already affirmed in his innermost soul. Thus it is that the religious (or mythological) strand of the tales is the source of their greatest power, and that the three most theological (or mythic) stories are the ones that last longest in the memory and reverberate with the most resonance. They take us to where we already are in our inwardness.

The relatively quiet tone of *The Magician's Nephew* helps make it a good contrast to the tale immediately following in the Narnian chronology. In this story the dark prophecies of Aslan come true, and He plays a more central role, acting out his passion and resurrection. Once again, Lewis is careful to create a matter-of-fact, prosaic setting for the beginning of the tale:

> Once there were four children whose names were Peter,
> Susan, Edmund and Lucy. This story is about something
> that happened to them when they were sent away from
> London during the war because of the air-raids. They
> were sent to the house of an old Professor who lived in
> the heart of the country, ten miles from the nearest
> railway station and two miles from the nearest post office.
> He had no wife and he lived in a very large house with a
> housekeeper called Mrs. Macready and three servants.[7]

Like Polly and Digory in *The Magician's Nephew,* they set out to explore the more than ample house. Lucy, more curious and venturesome than the others, goes into a huge wardrobe, not knowing it is built of magic wood from the

---

[7] *The Lion, the Witch and the Wardrobe: A Story for Children* (New York: Collier Books, 1950, 1970), p. 1.

apple tree that Digory (now Professor) Kirke planted many years ago. Suddenly, she finds that the coats hanging there have disappeared, and she is standing in a dark woods with snow falling. As she looks around she notices a faun carrying an umbrella and some brown-paper parcels. He is described in realistic detail, as though it were important to distinguish one faun from another. The meeting of beings from two worlds is initiated courteously; the faun exclaims a conventional "Good gracious me!" and well-bred Lucy says, "Good evening." The faun picks up the packages he has dropped, makes a belated bow and tactfully inquires whether she is a "Daughter of Eve." When she looks puzzled, he explains, "a girl." She accepts the label. He then asks how she got into Narnia and where she is from, but their lack of geographical knowledge about the other's country makes communication vague and unclear. Finally, he suggests a cup of hot tea to ward off the winter chills, and Lucy—worried about what people will be thinking back at the professor's house—agrees, but says she can't stay long. He takes her arm and holds the umbrella over both of them, and they walk to his tidy cave, inside of which a wood fire is cheerfully burning. He lights a lamp with a piece of blazing wood, and puts the tea kettle on to boil. Something of a "beauty and the beast" intuition stirs her in a gentle way—the meeting of the human and the nonhuman.

Tumnus the faun is a troubled soul. He bursts out sobbing and disjointedly reveals that he is in the pay of the White Witch. Then he escorts Lucy as far as the wood from which she can see the wardrobe door, and in fear and trembling says goodbye to her. She soon finds the other children in the old house and is astounded to learn that no time has elapsed. Her story of strange adventures falls on deaf ears; they think she is attempting an obvious hoax.

Tumnus is destined to reappear in the tale. When the children finally enter Narnia as a group, they go to his cave and find a notice nailed to the floor proclaiming that "The former occupant of these premises, Faun Tumnus, is under arrest and awaiting his trial on a charge of High Treason against her Imperial Majesty Jadis . . . also of comforting her said Majesty's enemies, harbouring spies and fraternising with Humans."[8] Later they learn that he has been taken to the queen's house, where doubtless he will join the group of stone statues she has created by her magic of ossification. Mere human power cannot save him; only Aslan is equal to that task.

In the group of four brothers and sisters there is a Judas, by name Edmund. At first, his leaning toward the side of the enemy seems trivial, almost harmless. It begins with his passion for Turkish Delight. The Witch lures him by promising an infinity of this delicacy. What he does not know is that the confection is habit-forming. The witch offers to bring him up as a prince, and when she is gone, he will reign with a golden crown on his head and eat Turkish Delight from morning to night. He is still not a complete scoundrel in his heart, but he is weak and unable to resist temptation. The plight of the repentant Tumnus and the traitorous Edmund both cry out for supernatural rescue. The case of Edmund is particularly grave, for by the rules of the Deep Magic of Narnia, traitors belong to the White Witch, and only a terrible deeper magic can release them.

The movement of the story is a leisurely progress from yearning for Aslan to rumors of His return and His actual appearance. Some of the episodes, such as the visit with the cozy beaver family, seem deliberately prolonged for perhaps two purposes: to create a sense of ordinary life in Narnia going on as best it can, and to allow sufficient time for tension to build up as the world turns more and more demonic. Long before Aslan appears, He is firmly planted in the reader's imagination as a messiah, the only one who can save the suffering folk of Narnia.

The White Witch's downfall comes about very gradually —as two things happen, closely connected. Rumors of As-

---

[8] P. 55.

lan's return combine with the empirical fact that in the south
a thaw is setting in and there are signs that the long winter is
drawing to an end. Lucy asks if Aslan is a man. Mr. Beaver
emphatically replies in words that suggest the Divine becoming incarnate: . . . "Certainly not. I tell you he is the King
of the wood and the son of the great Emperor-Beyond-the-
Sea. Don't you know who is the King of Beasts? Aslan is a
lion—*the* Lion, the great Lion."[9]

Further conversation makes it clear that Aslan is good
but not safe—as one person after another in the tales puts it,
"He is not a tame lion." Mr. Beaver also explains that the
four children are the first humans to come to Narnia, and that
their arrival and the simultaneous arrival of Aslan is no co-
incidence. An old Narnian saying has it that when the four
thrones at the palace of Cair Paravel are occupied by two Sons
of Adam and two Daughters of Eve, it will mean the end not
only of the White Witch's reign; it will also mean her death.
No wonder, then, that the Witch is implacably pursuing the
earthly visitors, whose survival can mean her destruction.
Through Mr. Beaver, the children learn that Aslan has summoned them to meet Him at the ancient Stone Table. Aslan
is on the move, Aslan is on the move. The phrase begins to
be a kind of drumbeat, building up in intensity each time it is
uttered. Some revelation is at hand.

Mr. and Mrs. Beaver and the three children continue
their journey to the Stone Table, as commanded by Aslan's
message, and come to the top of a long hill. In the middle of
the open hilltop is the Stone Table. A great crowd of creatures is assembled, among them Tree-Women and Well-
Women (Dryads and Naiads) who are playing stringed in-
struments. In the center of the throng stands Aslan. It is an
overwhelming experience of the numinous. Aslan is both ultimate good—the goal of all truly seeking hearts—and awesome. No one is willing to approach him. Finally, Peter advances, salutes with his sword, and says, "We have come—

———

[9] P. 75.

Aslan."[10] Lucy begs Aslan to do something to rescue Edmund, and Aslan promises all possible help, but explains that the task may be more difficult than they think.

The climax of the book, the Passion and Resurrection of Aslan, now approaches. Here Lewis achieves one of his most remarkable reimaginings of a familiar biblical theme. He undertakes a thorough process of translation. The human figure of Christ is replaced by the noblest of the animals. A Witch becomes the concentrated embodiment of all the converging forces of evil that brought Christ to His death. In Edmund is symbolized the self-serving self-deceptions of ordinary life, which have their inevitable consequences and can be redeemed only by the deepest magic of all.

It is not enough, in the economy of the divine Magic, to slay the Witch and rescue Edmund. A price must be paid for the affront to the *Tao* (the term Lewis uses in *The Abolition of Man*). The moral foundations of the Narnian universe have been undermined. Mere fleshly strength cannot rebuild them. But what Lewis dramatizes is not simply the price but the glory of the price, as new life is released into a redeemed world.

Despite the profound theological overtones at this point, the reader does not find the story heavy. Aslan catches us with our guard down. And He is not merely an animal objective correlative to Christ. He is, in some ways, a vegetation god in addition to all else; where He stands, there is abounding life, not just of the spirit but also of the very earth with its teeming manifestations of vitality.

The action of the tale speeds up once Aslan appears. The desperation of the Witch increases. She is frantic to accomplish the death of Edmund, to make sure only three children are left to reign at Cair Paravel. What the Witch does not know is that in her own completely evil way she is moving the course of Narnian history toward a good greater than any the land has ever known.

Later, Aslan and Edmund have a private, heart-to-heart

---

[10] P. 123.

talk. Edmund goes to his brother and two sisters and tells
each of them, "I'm sorry," and they all reply, "That's all
right."[11] Meanwhile, the Witch's Dwarf approaches and
arranges a conference between Aslan and the Witch. She
soon appears in an eddy of cold air and takes her place face
to face with Aslan. The two confer with a circle of humans
and talking animals eavesdropping as best they can. The
Witch summarizes the Deep Magic that is written on the
Stone Table. All traitors belong to her and death is her prerogative. The fact that no treason was committed against her
personally is irrelevant. Unless she has blood as the law commands, Narnia will perish in fire and water.

The great Lion denies none of this. He orders the group
to fall back while He and the Witch continue talking in low
voices. Finally, He summons the multitude and tells them
the Witch has renounced all claims to Edmund's life. What
he does not reveal is that Aslan has agreed to take Edmund's
place. This is the deepest magic of all.

The climactic moment is near. The death of Aslan at
the hands of the Witch is one of the most compelling Passion
stories. It achieves its power partly by a process of selection.
Many events from the biblical story are repeated here, suit-
ably modified for a Narnian setting. Jesus had a large and
loyal following of women; likewise, on Aslan's last night it
is the two girls who accompany Him to the Stone Table and
try to comfort Him. The tone of this scene is like that on the
Mount of Olives; Aslan, the very channel through whom
God's creative energy has brought Narnia into being, is
weary, sad, desolate.

When they reach the Stone Table, a vast concourse is
there:[12] the Witch, of course, and multitudes of "Ogres with
monstrous teeth, and wolves, and bull-headed men; spirits of
evil trees and poisonous plants," not to mention "Cruels and
Hags and Incubuses, Wraiths, Horrors, Efreets, Sprites, Ork-
nies, Wooses, and Ettins." Aslan is spat upon, and His mane

---

[11] P. 136.
[12] Pp. 148, 150, 152.

shaved off. The hideous creatures pluck up courage to mock him: " 'Puss, Puss! Poor Pussy,' and 'How many mice have you caught to-day, Cat?' and 'Would you like a saucer of milk, Pussums?' " The Witch whets her knife, as Aslan—quiet but unafraid—looks up at the sky. Then, before she stabs him to death, she bends down and speaks her words of triumph into His ear:

> "And now, who has won? Fool, did you think by all this
> you would save the human traitor? Now I will kill you
> instead of him as our pact was and so the Deep Magic will
> be appeased. But when you are dead what will prevent
> me from killing him as well? And who will take him out of
> my hand *then?* Understand that you have given me
> Narnia forever, you have lost your own life and you have
> not saved his. In that knowledge, despair and die."

It is a moment when Aslan might well cry out, "My God, my God, why hast Thou forsaken me?" But Lewis knew better than to overwork the parallel.

At dawn the children discover that Aslan is gone and the Stone Table is cracked in two. A mighty voice calls from behind them. They turn. There, gleaming in the sunrise, even larger than they remember him, stands Aslan, shaking His mane, which is now fully restored in all its splendor. The risen Lion explains that the Witch's magic goes back only to the dawn of time. If it had extended farther back, she would have known that when an innocent victim took a traitor's place on the Stone Table, the table itself would crack, and Death would begin working backward. Moment by moment, new life flows into Aslan. He then commands the girls to climb on His back and they begin the most glorious of bareback rides, lasting almost till noon, when they come to the Witch's castle. With His breath Aslan restores the stone statues to life. He then organizes a search of the castle to find any more prisoners, and in the course of this operation liberates the poor faun, who is none the worse for having been a statue. After a pitched battle, Aslan slays the Witch. He then knights Edmund, who has behaved with great heroism.

The children gradually signalize their new adult and royal status by adopting a style of speech reminiscent of *Bleheris*—for example, King Peter to Queen Susan:

> . . . never since we four were Kings and Queens in
> Narnia have we set our hands to any high matter, as battles,
> quests, feats of arms, acts of justice, and the like, and
> then given over; but always what we have taken in hand,
> the same we have achieved.[13]

The purpose is obviously to dramatize their metamorphosis from ordinary British school children to monarchs with golden crowns. Some critics, including the author of children's books Jacqueline Jackson, have found this sudden linguistic shift jolting. Perhaps it is a little too cute, seeming to introduce a note of condescension toward the young which is otherwise blessedly lacking in the book.

The rest of the story moves swiftly. The four children are solemnly installed on the four thrones of Cair Paravel. Great multitudes cheer, and there is the sound of mermen and mermaids singing close to the castle in honor of the new queens and kings. Aslan quietly slips away; no one knows when He will return, but that is His way. The children grow up, prove excellent rulers.

The Magician's Nephew and *The Lion* have some elements in common. Each is full of talking animals acting remarkably like ordinary children and adults. Each has Aslan as the central character. Each succeeds in making a never-never land convincing. Where they differ is in intensity. Aslan's supreme deed in the earlier book is that of creation, which He accomplishes so easily that it seems the by-product of a song. But in *The Lion,* His great deed is one that Christians refer to with such words as propitiation, redemption, and salvation. The whole moral landscape darkens from one tale to the other. Uncle Andrew fraternizes with evil; Edmund is shown moving steadily toward absolute complicity. When in *The Lion* Aslan pays the price to rescue Edmund, there is a depth of feeling that one does not find in *The Ma-*

---

[13] P. 184.

gician's Nephew. At the same time, Aslan's resurrection evokes deeper joys and more spontaneous gaiety.

The Magician's Nephew has the more casual structure. It moves along from one adventure to another. When the great act of creation comes, it appears almost as offhand as the other marvels of the tale, suggesting that the creation of a world, while impressive to mortals, is all in a day's work for the Aslans of this universe.

The Lion has a more tightly organized structure, built around the Witch–Edmund relation, and the coming of Aslan. These two strands interweave and finally coalesce. The tempo of the tale is carefully controlled, so as to move from faint rumors of Aslan to signs of his activity (like the melting snow) to his final manifestation. In the same way, by slow and measured stages, Edmund gives himself into the hands of the Witch. With the intersection of these two strands, there is the image of the cross. Only by Aslan's sacrifice can Edmund the traitor be saved.

The firm framework of the three key Narnia tales is theological, reaching from the creation of Narnia to last things, when the old Narnia ceases to exist. If one thinks of the biblical perspective as involving a cosmic five-act drama, the parallel becomes clear:

	BIBLE	NARNIA
I	Creation of universe	Creation of Narnia
II	Struggle of good and evil	Aslan vs. the Witch
III	Death and resurrection of Christ	Death and resurrection of Aslan
IV	The present world, with its confused struggle of good and evil, though good has already triumphed in principle	Aslan intermittently reappears
V	The "end of the world" and the emergence of a new world	The end of the old Narnia and the coming of the new Narnia

The four tales that, by Narnian chronology, belong between *The Magician's Nephew* and *The Lion* at one end, and *The Last Battle* at the other, are episodes from Act IV of the Narnian drama. Lewis's fantastically fertile imagination, so well stocked with all the conventions and traditions of fairy tales, and so free in reshaping them and supplementing them by pure products of his own imagination, pours forth one set of adventures after another. We see earthly children restoring Prince Caspian to his throne. We experience one of the most haunting of myths, the land of eternal youth, when a group of children sail into clear seas and find the water is fresh and filled with white waterlilies, while the sun is much larger than they remember. In another story we encounter a prince always in danger of turning into a serpent. In yet another, a queen must be rescued before she is compelled to marry a man she detests. In all these tales, Aslan weaves in and out, supplies advice, sometimes crucial aid, but does not perform any of the grand, cosmic deeds such as those in *The Magician's Nephew* and *The Lion*.

Although relatively marginal, the role of Aslan in the four tales critically affects the reader's response to the total myth of the seven chronicles. If Lewis had written only the three most theological stories—or if he had contrived to pack more theology into the other four—there might have been a stronger sense of the swift rush of divine events. But at the same time, the portrayal of daily life would have been out of balance; Heaven, so to speak, would have engulfed earth.

Finally comes *The Last Battle*. This is surely one of the most astounding children's stories ever written. Such tales do not ordinarily end with the death of all the characters. But as Ransom was told in *Out of the Silent Planet*, Maleldil creates new worlds but not one of them is meant to last for ever. So it is with Narnia. It has served its purpose; it is time now for the heavenly Narnia, on the other side of death, to take its place.

The Last Battle begins quietly. There is first of all Shift, an old ape, clever, selfish, malicious. He notices a strange object in the water and commands his companion, the dull-witted donkey, Puzzle, to pull it out. It is a lion's skin. Always eager for mischief, especially when it can advance his own comfort and power, Shift makes a garment to put on Puzzle so that he will look, more or less, like a lion. He wants Puzzle to pass himself off as Aslan and thus gain control over the inhabitants of Narnia, who desire nothing so much as the return of their leonine ruler. Poor Puzzle is pushed into the role of being a fake messiah, receiving the adoration of the people. Shift promises Puzzle that he will tell him what to say. The donkey, dim-witted but right-minded, protests.[14] "It would be wrong, Shift. I may be not very clever but I know that much. What would become of us if the real Aslan turned up?" Shift has an answer for every objection: "Probably he sent us the lion skin on purpose, so that we could set things to right. Anyway, he never *does* turn up, you know. Not now-a-days." As usual, Lewis does little to reshape the traditional symbolism associated with animals. Apes are clever and crafty, donkeys are stubborn but not intellectual giants.

After the prologue of the ape and donkey, the scene quietly shifts to King Tirian at his hunting lodge, in conversation with his beloved friend, Jewel the Unicorn. The king is in a state of euphoria as he recounts all the reports he has heard of Aslan's return. They are joined by Roonwit the Centaur, who bluntly tries to destroy their dream. No matter what gossip-mongers may report, the message of the constellations is a clear negative. Not only do they deny the rumors about Aslan's return; they prophesy' unspecified but terrible events for Narnia. The tone of the story, still very quiet, is becoming more somber and foreboding. Next they hear a voice, Cassandra-like, crying out, "Woe for my brothers and sisters! Woe for the holy trees! The woods are laid waste. The

---

14 *The Last Battle* (New York: Collier Books, 1956, 1970), p. 10.

axe is loosed against us."[15] The speaker appears, a tall tree-spirit or Dryad. She explains that the talking trees are being felled. In his fury, the king and Jewel rashly set out to find the axemen and stop them. Soon they encounter a Water Rat on a raft and he explains that Aslan has given orders to fell the trees and sell them to the barbaric, dark-skinned Calormenes. The king and Jewel are bewildered. Could this be possible? After all, as Jewel points out, Aslan is not a *tame* Lion. Presumably his thoughts are not always their thoughts. A terrible ambiguity has entered their lives. They want to serve and obey Aslan, but first they must find out if this rumored lion *is* Aslan. Uncertain whether they are doing the right thing, and heavy-hearted, they continue on their way and soon hear the sound of axes on tree trunks. A great crowd of talking animals and human beings is at work. The men were ". . . not the fair-haired men of Narnia: they were dark, bearded men from Calormen, that great and cruel country that lies beyond Archenland across the desert to the south."[16]

The mention of the Calormenes and their complexion is worth a moment's pause, as an indication of how readily Lewis accepted conventional symbolism. In the space tales he uses the contrast of light and darkness for good and evil. To anyone ever caught in a cave, it might perhaps seem an inevitable association. The reference to the dark skins of the Calormenes evokes the British Empire at the height of its civilizing zeal when clean-cut blond young men went to darkest Africa to suppress the Fuzzy Wuzzies. Darkness (to blond people) suggests aliens, probably dark within as well as without. European fairy tales and romances of the Middle Ages prefer blonds.

Lewis was less bothered by these matters than a modern liberal would be. He simply took his symbols where he found them. And as we will see later, Lewis could depict a noble, dark-skinned Calormene who turned out to be a true servant

---

[15] P. 16.
[16] P. 21.

of Aslan without knowing it. This, however, is a cause for much astonishment as well as rejoicing.

When Tirian and Jewel the Unicorn discover two Calormenes savagely whipping a Narnian talking horse as he strains at a heavy log, their fury knows no bounds. They plunge in and slay the aliens. The king leaps on the unicorn's back and they quickly make their escape. Tirian is then smitten by pangs of conscience. They have slain two men without challenging them—and furthermore, can they be sure that the felling of the trees is *not* being done at the command of Aslan? More by tone than explicit exposition, the story increasingly conveys the feeling of a moral order falling apart; no one is any longer sure what is right and what is wrong. If Aslan has become an ambiguity, then the center cannot hold.

Tirian and Jewel walk back and give themselves up to the Calormenes. "Then the dark men came round them in a thick crowd, smelling of garlic and onions, their white eyes flashing dreadfully in their brown faces."[17] The captors lead them to a small stable, outside of which Shift the ape is eating. He is dressed in odds and ends of fancy clothing like some savage who has raided a wrecked passenger ship, and the main thing on his mind is nuts. In the name of Aslan he commands the squirrels to bring a better supply. From the ape's rambling oration it becomes clear that he is in alliance with the king of Calormen and is using the prestige of the false Aslan to sanctify such activities as the felling of talking trees.

The general situation is like a fairy-tale version of the opening of *That Hideous Strength*, when the forces of progress, represented by the N.I.C.E., move in on the university. The land of the Calormenes is a modern results-oriented society advancing and taking over. Most of the Narnians are uneasy and miserable, but they believe, more or less, that everything is at the will of Aslan—though Aslan seems to have changed His values since the Narnians last saw Him. The Ape

---

17 P. 25.

assures the talking animals that they will learn the value of
hard work, dragging things and working in mines. All in all,
the Ape's rambling discourse is a classical description of imperialist capitalism on the march, spreading civilization and
gaining profit. This is accompanied by theological warfare, as
the invaders coin the portmanteau word, Tashlan, to express
the belief that Tash and Aslan are really the same god.

King Tirian finds himself thinking about the long history of Narnia, and how when things are at their worst, a
rescue expedition is always mounted by earthly children in
alliance with Aslan. In despair he cries out the name of Aslan
and asks that Narnia be saved though its king may die.

His prayer is answered by a vivid dream in which he
makes spectral contact with seven humans in a lighted room.
Two of them, a man and a woman, are very old; the others
are children. They see him faintly and exclaim. One of the
children is Peter the High King, who commands Tirian to
explain his mission. Tirian tries to, but his lips make no
sound. The vision fades, but not until some sort of contact
has been made with earthlings who may prove of help.

In fact, two children shortly appear from nowhere. They
are Eustace Scrubb and Jill Pole, who in an earlier adventure
had rescued a Narnian king from a long enchantment. They
cut the king's bonds and sate his hunger with six sandwiches.
The children, back on earth, had been traveling on a train
when there was a terrible crash, and immediately thereafter
they found themselves talking with King Tirian. What they
do not know until later is that they are dead. From this point
on, the distinction between the living and the dead becomes
blurred.

It is not necessary to follow the military operations in
detail. The king and his little following of children and talking animals put up valiant rearguard resistance to the massed
forces under the Calormene banner, but it is almost as though
this struggle were being fought to keep the record clean
rather than in any real hope of victory. The basic problem is
not a military one; rather, a question of morale. The lies

about the false Aslan and the new doctrine of the universal god, Tashlan, have eaten away at the moral and psychological integrity of the Narnians. Even when the fakery of the false Aslan is finally revealed, many of the Dwarfs draw the conclusion that everything, including also the real Aslan, is propaganda, and impartially fight both the Calormenes and the Narnians.

King Tirian now has another vision—or is it simple reality? He sees seven kings and queens in their crowns and glittering garments. One of them is Jill, another is Eustace, both fresh and clean and splendid in their attire. Tirian himself is no longer battle-stained; he is dressed as though for a great feast at Cair Paravel. The other monarchs all turn out to be previous participants in the annals of Narnia.

Soon the air turns sweeter and a brightness flashes. Aslan, the true Aslan, has returned. Tirian flings himself at the divine feet, and the great Lion commends him for standing firm at Narnia's darkest hour. From now on, it becomes harder and harder to say who is living and who has passed through death. All this is eloquently dramatized in Chapter XIV, "Night Falls on Narnia." Father Time wakes from his long sleep and blows a strangely beautiful melody on his horn. At once, the stars of the sky begin to fall by the hundreds, and soon not a star is left. Great companies of living beings, both animals and humans, begin streaming through the stable door. They are being called home. As each comes close to Aslan he is impelled to look Him straight in the eye. Those whose faces mirror fear and hatred disappear to the left of the doorway. Those who gaze upon Him with love do not disappear. In the mirror of Aslan's eye, each creature finds out what he is.

Dragons and giant lizards denude the landscape; the sun enlarges and begins to die. As Jewel the Unicorn said earlier in the tales, all worlds draw to an end. This one ends with a surrealist landscape: enormous red sun, the moon in the wrong position, a great tide of water that washes away the mountains. The moon and sun come together; masses of fire

drop into the sea; steam rises. The giant reaches out one arm
and squeezes the Sun as though it were an orange. Utter
blackness everywhere. The story of Narnia is over. Aslan
commands Peter the High King to shut the door.

But the new Narnia is beginning. The children find blue
sky now above them, flowers, and laughter in Aslan's eyes.
While they yet mourn for all that was good and beautiful in
the old Narnia, Aslan summons them to come further in,
come further up. It is while exploring the paradise in which
they now find themselves that they meet a wandering Calormene, Emeth, who tells his story. He has long been a true
devotee of Tash, and has yearned to meet him face to face.
He was one of the disguised soldiers sent into Narnia. This
pleased him, for he hated Aslan and felt that by defeating
the Narnians he would be striking a blow against a false god.
When the Ape had invited people to enter the stable to meet
Tashlan, Emeth accepted the invitation, hoping the true Tash
would be there. Once through the door, he found himself in
a land of grass and flowers, and set out to find Tash. Suddenly, Aslan appeared in his path, terrible in His gleaming
beauty. Then followed a dialogue in which Aslan explained
that Emeth had sought Him all along.

> . . . the Glorious One bent down his golden head and
> touched my forehead with his tongue and said, Son, thou
> art welcome. But I said, Alas, Lord, I am no son of Thine
> but the servant of Tash. He answered, Child, all the
> service thou hast done to Tash, I account as service done
> to me. . . . Therefore if any man swear by Tash and keep
> his oath for the oath's sake, it is by me that he has
> truly sworn, though he know it not, and it is I who reward
> him. And if any man do a cruelty in my name, then,
> though he says the name Aslan, it is Tash whom he serves and
> by Tash his deed is accepted. Dost thou understand,
> Child? I said, Lord, thou knowest how much I understand.
> But I said also (for the truth constrained me), Yet have
> I been seeking Tash all my days. Beloved, said the Glorious
> One, unless thy desire had been for me thou wouldst

not have sought so long and so truly. For all find what they truly seek.[18]

The episode of Emeth is one of the few places where one may feel that for the sake of theological completeness Lewis has inserted what is more an essay than part of a story. It is disproportionately long for the pace of the narrative, but its beauty is so great one cannot really regret that it is included. In fact, as *The Last Battle* ends, it is on the verge of bursting the narrative bonds and becoming a great hymn of praise. Narnia, which in book after book has dramatized the ways of God with man, is pointing beyond all symbols and allegories to Him who is not a symbol but sheer being.

The Last Battle has a particular wealth of symbolism which serves not merely to convey ideas but to create moods. It is a darkening world; the human enemies ranged against the world of Aslan show it in the very color of their skin. Ordinary, decent life itself is under attack. The talking trees are being felled, the talking beasts whipped into slavery. The gift of speech that many of the animals possess seems to be a symbol of "the image of God" (or image of Aslan) that was originally breathed into them, for when any of them reject Aslan at the end they simply lose this gift and become ordinary animals. The god Tash is not an illusion. He symbolizes brute evil and thus is the opposite of Aslan. The one is like a hideous vulture with cruel beak and flailing arms to grasp and tear, the other glorious in his golden mane and justly hailed as the king of the beasts. The remaining characters are the spectrum of mortal possibilities in between, pulled this way and that, but in the long run making their choice between the two absolute alternatives. That choice is made as they pass through the narrow door of the stable and read in Aslan's eyes their decision.

All this vast cosmological drama is firmly buttressed by details of ordinary realism. The Ape is real as any selfish schemer. The Donkey reacts in a dim-witted way human

───────

18 Pp. 164–65.

readers can consider plausible. King Tirian is believable as one who has lost hope but finds honor still worth dying for. The invasion of the Calormenes is as carefully organized as any imperialist expedition, complete with psychological warfare and the manipulation of religion. Much of the action and many of the incidental details in *The Last Battle* are perfectly convincing from the purely terrestrial viewpoint; at the same time the reader never forgets that eternal and ultimate forces are locked in conflict, and that, as Lewis liked to say, things are coming to a point.

The charge most frequently leveled against the Narnia tales is that they cash in on "stock responses," particularly to the high points of the Christian tale. Nearly two thousand years of psychic history have engraved these pictures in our imagination. Thus—so the criticism runs—Lewis could achieve an easy victory by presenting this cultural heritage under a transparent disguise. A half-truth is involved here. Western man does indeed carry within himself this storehouse of significant images, but they would not have gripped him so powerfully in the first place if they had not seemed the fulfillment of still older images living immortally in the unconscious mind. The earliest converts to Christianity already knew that a self-sacrificing God is needed to resolve the contradictions of existence. When Lewis evokes Christian parallels, he is at the same time profiting by racial memories older than Christianity.

Tolkien, a devout Roman Catholic, was himself troubled by the Narnia stories. In part, it may have been a feeling that the stories came too easily. Lewis could write seven books quicker than Tolkien could write one. But he also disapproved of the obvious Christian correspondences. He was attempting a different kind of imaginary world, one overwhelming in its own integrity and relying less on resemblances to the earth and its familiar beliefs. Where Lewis redramatizes the decisive moments of the Christian story, Tolkien slowly, stroke by stroke, builds up a world that is heroic and tragic, more akin perhaps to *Beowulf* and the Icelandic sagas

than to the relative cheerfulness and hopefulness of a believing world that beholds its salvation in a Christ or an
Aslan.[19]

By the time Lewis began writing Narnia, his mind was
uniquely filled with usable images and symbols. He knew his
Germanic, Celtic, and classical mythology. He commanded
the literature of Western Europe, at least through the Renaissance period. He had already created many symbols in his
own writing, particularly in *The Pilgrim's Regress* and the
space tales. With the freedom that seems to characterize a
major writer, he was willing to draw on his own private store
as well as from the public symbology that he shared. He used
talking animals in *Out of the Silent Planet* and used them
again in Narnia. His Weston corresponds in his early stages
to a more impressive Uncle Andrew, and in his later Unman
stages he would be a suitable mate for the White Witch. As
early as *The Pilgrim's Regress,* varied landscapes of mountains, hills, and well-watered valleys had been symbols of the
heart's desire, paradise, the new Narnia, Heaven. Symbolism
of light and dark runs through his books. Speech itself is a
symbol of rationality and the kind of relation with God that
only rational beings can experience. In his use of animals,
Lewis was like the author of a medieval bestiary. Of a given
animal, he is less interested in "What is this animal good for?"
(still less its exact biological classification) than in "What
does this animal stand for?" Thus, it is no surprise when
Lewis chose a Lion for his central character; the bestiaries
would have certified the choice. Even Lewis's use of cold as
a symbol of evil has its precedent in the bottom circle of *The
Inferno* where the worst of sinners lie perpetually congealed.

In a way, the mature Lewis (maybe apart from his lit-

---

19 A short but valuable comparison of Tolkien's and Lewis's imaginary worlds is contained in Charles Moorman, " 'Now Entertain Con-
jecture of a Time'—The Fictive Worlds of C. S. Lewis and J. R. R.
Tolkien," published in Mark R. Hillegas, editor, *Shadows of Imagination* (Carbondale, Illinois: Southern Illinois University Press, 1969),
pp. 59–69. See also Richard Purtill, *Lord of the Elves and Eldils*
(Grand Rapids, Michigan: Zondervan, 1974).

erary criticism) had one main theme, which is to reveal and justify the ways of God to man. This did not prevent him from writing books which can be thoroughly enjoyed by a reader as atheistic as the Great Knock. It emphatically does not mean that the literary merit of his books is a kind of disguised religiosity. No, from a literary viewpoint, the religious themes of his books are like the moral themes of Dickens or the sociological themes of Ibsen. They are part of the structure of a given book, and must be evaluated not by whether they will get you to Heaven, but by whether they are doing their literary job.

It is an irony of literary history. This man, who wrote the most glittering religious apologetics of his time, and who was a major literary historian, may well have created his most lasting work in seven fairy tales nominally for children. All theories of literary determinism and influence falter at the thought. He had no children of his own; the tales were launched before he acquired stepsons. It is said that a fetal ape looks more human than a mature one, and some have suggested that humanity arose through a process of arrested development. A writer sometimes succeeds as much from his limits as from his unlimited outreach. By remaining a boy as well as becoming a man, Lewis was able to speak in a language which is simultaneously the tongue of the fairy tale and the epic; he speaks to the adult, the child, and the child within the adult. He speaks to everyone, except to those ossified grown-ups who have stifled the child within.

7

THE ROAD TAKEN TOO LATE

Ever since his undergraduate days, Lewis had been haunted by the story of Cupid and Psyche. Time after time he wrestled with it, sometimes in prose, sometimes in verse. The tale proved singularly recalcitrant. What he wanted to do with it was quite different from the original clear-cut philosophical allegory of classical antiquity. Lewis's version did not see print until 1956, and the reception of *Till We Have Faces* was a major disappointment to him. The sales were modest; reviewers seemed more bewildered than impressed. Perhaps Lewis's previous reputation for overwhelming clarity had left his public unprepared for a novel in which ambiguities abound.

The tale on which the novel is based is one of the few surviving prose narratives from its period. It comes from *The Golden Ass,* a collection of stories composed—or perhaps revised from earlier versions—by Apuleius, a second-century Latin writer whose career was a multiple one: wandering philosopher, lawyer and magistrate, mystery cult priest, professional storyteller.

The story of Cupid and Psyche, as embedded in *The Golden Ass,* is a witty and straightforward tale of the ways of gods and mortals with each other. Very likely it is also an allegory of the quest of the soul to achieve intellectual love.

But first of all, it is a good story, told with lighthearted wit and urbanity.

The parts of the story relevant to Lewis's version are briefly as follows: A king and queen have three daughters, the youngest of whom, Psyche (Greek for soul), is so fair that men blasphemously worship her and neglect Venus. No man dares seek her hand in marriage. In desperation, her father consults Apollo's oracle and is told that no human suitor is acceptable. Psyche must be chained to a tree on a mountain as an offering to a dragon. Her father sets out to follow these directions. But meanwhile, jealous Venus has other plans. She commands her son, Cupid, to set the girl aflame with passion for the basest of men. Cupid goes forth to accomplish this mission, but when he sees Psyche, he falls in love with her himself. After she is left on the mountain, he has her carried to his palace. By night he visits her as her lover and husband, but will not permit her to see his face. Psyche, lonesome for her sisters, wins Cupid's reluctant consent for a visit from them. They are magnificently entertained by Psyche. The divine splendor of her life fills them with envy and they resolve to destroy her happiness.

When they visit her again, they convince her that her mysterious husband must be a giant serpent. They leave her a lamp and a sharp knife, and instruct her to look upon the face of her husband and stab the monster to death. Cupid wakes from his sleep when a drop of hot oil falls on his shoulder. He rebukes Psyche for violating her promise, and vanishes from her sight.

Psyche wanders the face of the earth, an exile, and endures countless miseries until she falls into the hands of her deadliest enemy, Venus herself, who imposes on her a series of seemingly impossible tasks, such as sorting countless seeds into separate piles (she achieves this task with the aid of friendly ants). Finally, she is rejoined by Cupid, who has forgiven her. He intercedes with Jupiter, who consents to their marriage and makes Psyche a goddess. Even Venus is reconciled, and all live happily ever after.

Lewis, in his note at the end of *Till We Have Faces,* explains some of the ways in which he has modified the story:

> The central alteration in my own version consists in making Psyche's palace invisible to normal, mortal eyes. . . . This change of course brings with it a more ambivalent motive and a different character for my heroine and finally modifies the whole quality of the tale. I felt quite free to go behind Apuleius, whom I suppose to have been its transmitter, not its inventor. Nothing was further from my aim than to recapture the peculiar quality of the *Metamorphoses*—that strange compound of picaresque novel, horror comic, mystagogue's tract, pornography, and stylistic experiment. Apuleius was of course a man of genius: but in relation to my work he is a "source," not an "influence" nor a "model."[1]

Apuleius, therefore, provided the bare bones of the story but little more. Certainly, the tone is completely different. Apuleius's characters are all surface, hardly more than simple embodiments of one personality trait, such as envy. Lewis, by contrast, creates his most memorable character, Orual, in *Till We Have Faces.* Also, the mood of Lewis's tale is more troubled than that in *The Golden Ass.* Apuleius can treat the Olympian gods as quaint, almost comic figures. In the world that Lewis creates, the gods are not laughable. They are inscrutable, always intervening in human affairs when we wish they would leave us alone, but absent when we want them present. The central theme of the story is the attempt of Queen Orual to make the gods speak up and vindicate themselves.

The tone of the story is significantly affected by the ambiguity of time and setting. Perhaps the tale takes place somewhere on the fringes of Asia Minor, far away from the great civilizations of classical antiquity; possibly in what is now Turkey, or near the Black Sea. But no clear clues are given, except that we are in a semibarbaric world.

---

[1] *Till We Have Faces* (Grand Rapids, Michigan: W. B. Eerdmans, 1956, 1966), p. 313.

The time is apparently between the death of Socrates and the birth of Christ, that period when Greek philosophy and literature were slowly penetrating into the fringes of the classical world. Lewis is careful to keep explicit theologizing out of the book, but one senses that the world he presents is waiting for a more adequate revelation than either the cult of Ungit (a primitive Venus) or Greek rationalism. It unconsciously yearns for a religion that will be both "thick" (the sacrifice of Christ fulfilling the old pagan sacrifices) and "thin" (the ethic of biblical religion fulfilling the aims of Greek rationalism).

The king, more a barbaric chieftain than a regal monarch, reigns in a crude palace of wood and brick. He does make some faint efforts at refinement, as when he commands that a chorus of women be taught to sing a Greek wedding hymn upon his marriage to a new wife. But he is quick to kill a slave and he taunts Orual for her hideous face. His lack of sensitivity does not cloak strength as a ruler. He is in fact a brutal but incompetent monarch.

The middle sister, Redival, is a mixture of whining and coaxing. Psyche, born of the king's second marriage, would be too good to be believed if Lewis had not somehow made it seem plausible that she was potentially a goddess from the beginning. Her first epiphany comes when a plague strikes the land and she discovers that by touching victims she can often cure them.

Bardia, captain of the guard, is the archetypal gruff soldier with a heart of gold. One of the secondary themes of the story is the attraction Orual feels for Bardia, who is her companion in battle after he has trained her to be a female warrior. Orual and Bardia's wife, Ansit, are, half consciously, rivals for his person and most of all for his time.

One of the most interesting characters is the "Fox," a Greek who has been captured in some war and sold into slavery; he is purchased by the king as a tutor to his children, and gradually becomes one of the most trusted counselors, appreciated for his clear mind and common sense. He repre-

sents that generation of Greek philosophers who could never
return to the crudities of the Olympian gods. He is something of a Platonist, most of all a Stoic; to him man's felicity
consists of being a good (i.e., rational) part of nature. He
can accept the traditional gods only as convenient symbols of
rational truth. To one degree or another, the family falls
under his influence, for he speaks the most advanced thought
and the most sensible reasons are always on his tongue. Yet,
when real crises come, such as famine and drought, or the
question of what to do about Psyche and her mysterious
husband, the Fox seems to provide less useful guidance than
the high priest of the House of Ungit. A man hideously cos-
tumed, and reeking of the stale blood of sacrifices, the latter
seems in touch with realities and powers that Greek rationalism prefers to ignore.

Orual has a double misfortune. First of all, she is a girl,
one of three begotten by a father who regards daughters as a
curse, and is vocal in his resentment. In addition, she is hideously ugly, so that a glance into a mirror is a form of mental
torture. Eventually, she decides to wear a thick veil all the
time, and her hidden face becomes a legend.

Her life is mistake upon mistake. She permits her ugliness of face to become an ugliness of the soul, because she
deceives herself into believing that her fierce possessiveness,
which touches the lives of Psyche, the Fox, and Bardia, is
equivalent to the highest reaches of earthly charity. At the
same time, as life frustrates her plans and plots, and in particular as Psyche slips away from her control, she rages
against the gods, from whom she might have learned wisdom
and true love if she had listened to them. The central psychological theme, though not clear until almost the end of the
book, is the quest for self-knowledge. Orual's face is hidden
from the public, and her soul is hidden from herself until her
challenge to the gods leads to a confrontation in which they
make her see herself as she is, with a spiritual ugliness greater
than anything merely physical could be. The quest in this tale
is a more probing one than in *Out of the Silent Planet*.

Ransom's journey across the surface of Malacandra gives him deeper trust in God and banishes his fears, but this evolution of soul is in a direction he had already achieved on earth. Nothing can save Orual from the corruption of her soul except a complete turnaround, a literal conversion, so that she becomes a new being. This comes, but barely before death.

This psychodrama is set in the midst of political and military events, as the king struggles against foreign enemies and domestic unrest, and the country is afflicted by plague and famine. The Great Offering must be made to Ungit, whose house smells always of the blood of lesser sacrifices. The hazy legends of this religion talk also of a shadowbrute, perhaps the son of Ungit, who consumes the offerings. The general impression is that some kind of monster, somehow connected with Ungit, will devour the victim who is bound to a particular tree. The high priest explains in language that unconsciously foreshadows the coming of the Christian revelation:

> In the Great Offering, the victim must be perfect. For, in holy language, a man so offered is said to be Ungit's husband, and a woman is said to be the bride of Ungit's son. And both are called the Brute's Supper. And when the Brute is Ungit it lies with the man, and when it is her son it lies with the woman. And either way there is a devouring . . . For in sacred language we say that a woman who lies with a man devours the man. . . . The best in the land is not too good for this office.[2]

The "best in the world" is obviously Psyche. Her father, with much hypocritical lamentation, consents to the offering.

Psyche, bedizened like a temple prostitute, sets out on the procession to the sacred tree. She is curiously calm, almost eager to receive whatever bridegroom the gods have allotted to her. Orual falls ill and is unable to go along. During her convalescence she has countless dreams or visions in which Psyche is physically or psychologically tormenting her.

---

[2] P. 49.

Orual finally recovers, nagged by the persistent feeling that Psyche had done her some great, nameless injury. This long interlude in bed is the first clear warning to Orual that she is deceiving herself about her feeling for Psyche, but in her self-righteousness she is unable to receive the message.

The Great Offering works. Rain comes, the plague ends, military and political affairs take a turn for the better. Meanwhile, Orual does not forget her duties. She decides she must be an Antigone and find the bones of Psyche to give them proper burial. She chooses Bardia as her companion. They discover no trace of Psyche at the tree. After many hardships, they arrive at what Bardia says must be "the Secret Valley of the God":

> . . . At our feet, cradled amid a vast confusion of mountains, lay a small valley bright as a gem, but opening southward on our right. Through that opening there was a glimpse of warm, blue lands, hills and forests, far below us. . . . I never saw greener turf. There was gorse in bloom, and wild vines, and many groves of flourishing trees, and great plenty of bright water—pools, streams, and little cataracts. And when, after casting about a little to find where the slope would be easiest for the horse, we began descending, the air came up to us warmer and sweeter every minute.[3]

One recognizes here a recurring Lewis image. It is the earthly paradise or the land of "Joy." It figures in *The Pilgrim's Regress,* has kinship with the landscape of *Perelandra,* and is an echo of the fringes of heaven in *The Great Divorce.* It is god-country, and a place where spiritual power can be expected to reveal itself. All at once, a few feet away, stands Psyche. Her face shines with a more than mortal life, but she is dressed in rags. Now comes the main distinction between Lewis's tale and its source in *The Golden Ass.* Orual and Psyche do not see the same world. Psyche plucks some wild berries and gives them to Orual, extolling them as food for

---

[3] P. 100–01.

the gods. She offers water from a spring and praises it as the finest wine. Most of all, she expects Orual to marvel at her splendid palace, when her sister can see only the natural landscape.

Psyche now tells her story. She remembers being drugged and taken to the sacred tree where she was chained and left to await the arrival of the monster. Finally, the divine West-wind came and released her, and carried her to a palace whose splendor was beyond all description. There she heard a voice commanding, "Enter your House . . . Psyche, the bride of the god."[4] Cautiously she went into the palace where invisible voices sang a welcome to her, and unseen hands served a banquet of welcome. She was then led to the dark bridal chamber, and the invisible god himself entered to consummate their marriage. Psyche lives under one restriction: she must never try to see her husband. Apart from that, her life is one of complete content and bliss.

Orual has another chance to see truly. She recognizes that the gods have claimed Psyche as their own. Perhaps the palace is real. She even has a brief moment in which she beholds it as Psyche has described it. What a Christian might call salvation and a Greek call wisdom is rustling all about her, waiting only for her to recognize it. But she turns away from the opportunity. Her sense of duty, always conveniently ready to spring, comes to her rescue, and she resolves that she must rescue Psyche from the embraces of her monster lover.

On a second visit to Psyche, Orual extorts a tortured consent to her plans: Psyche must hide a lighted lamp in her chamber, and throw the beam on her husband's face, so she can at last know whether she is wed to man, god, or monster. When Psyche turns the lamp on the face of her husband, Orual is outside, waiting for a glimpse of the mysterious mate. For a brief flash she sees the face of Cupid, the god of love. She hears his voice, sweet still in its sternness, pro-

─────
[4] P. 113.

nouncing judgment on Psyche: "Now Psyche goes out in exile. Now she must hunger and thirst and tread hard roads. Those against whom I cannot fight must do their will upon her. You, woman, shall know yourself and your work. You also shall be Psyche."[5]

Thus Psyche presumably goes forth upon a life of wandering and exile. Orual meanwhile returns to the palace of her ailing father. It is about this time that she makes the veil a permanent habit. It is rich in symbolic implications, suggesting alienation both from others and from self, and a refusal to show or accept her true identity.

The memory of Psyche is always with her in the midst of her practical preparations for the crown:

> My aim was to build up more and more that strength,
> hard and joyless, which had come to me when I heard the
> god's sentence; by learning, fighting, and labouring, to
> drive all the woman out of me. Sometimes at night, if the
> wind howled or the rain fell, there would leap upon me,
> like water from a bursting dam, a great and anguished
> wonder—whether Psyche was alive, and where she was on
> such a night, and whether hard wives of peasants were
> turning her, cold and famished, from their door. But then,
> after an hour or so of weeping and writhing and calling
> out upon the gods, I would set to and rebuild the dam.[6]

The high priest of Ungit and the king are both approaching death. The new high priest, Arnom, and Orual work out a practical alliance between cult and state, and in time Arnom becomes one of the new queen's principal advisers, as do also the Fox and Bardia. Meanwhile, the Ungit religion is feeling the gradual impact of Hellenic modernism. A statue of Aphrodite, done in the realistic Greek style, soon shares the house of Ungit with the blood-stained shapeless image of the old Aphrodite. A two-level system of religion develops; the common folk regard the new Aphrodite as a god for

---

[5] Pp. 173–74.
[6] P. 184.

the upper class and the sophisticated, and continue to put their trust in the old Ungit, who in their experience gets results.

By the time the old king, Orual's father, dies, she has already effectively grasped the reins of power. She quickly proves to be an effective monarch, whether on the battlefield or in diplomatic exchanges. All in all, Queen Orual proves an admirable ruler, and manages the affairs of her nation far better than her emotional and often irrational father ever had.

With everything in good order at home, Orual decides to visit some of the neighboring kingdoms. This is uneventful until she comes to a small temple dedicated to Istra, the native name for Psyche. An old priest tells her the sacred legend, a mixture of historic fact, pious imagination, and echoes of ancient vegetation cults. According to it, both of Psyche's sisters visited her at her palace, and the palace was fully visible; their motive in urging her to put her husband to the test of sight was simple jealousy.

It is at this point that Orual resolves to write a book to state her case against the gods. *Till We Have Faces* is therefore her bill of indictment, designed to put the gods on the defensive, and to compel them to recognize the injustices they have perpetrated on humankind. Orual's hope is that the manuscript of her book will eventually be carried by some traveler to Greece, where the people are said to understand the ways of both the gods and humanity. The gods have dealt with her cruelly. They have taken Psyche away from her. They talk in riddles or they talk not at all. They demand utter obedience without explaining the purpose of half the things they command or forbid. They seem to be chuckling in some divine privacy as mere mortals seek to understand them. The injustice of it nearly drives Orual mad. She cries forth for an explanation.

The gods prepare her for the confrontation by a series of experiences. One of her fixed beliefs is that she was always loving and self-sacrificing with her two sisters. This illusion is destroyed when she meets a man who had once served at the palace, and indeed had been punished with castration for making advances to Redival. He recalls what she had said: "She was lonely. . . . Oh yes, yes, very lonely. . . . She used to say, 'First of all Orual loved me much; then the Fox came and she loved me little; then the baby came and she loved me not at all.' "[7]

In the course of writing her book, Orual must sort out motives; soon, in her dreams, she finds herself sorting out various kinds of seeds into separate piles. In some of these dreams, she becomes a little ant, straining her six legs to push seeds larger than herself. She is so preoccupied with the day-time and nocturnal sorting that she has hardly a thought for Bardia except irritation that he is wasting time by lying sick abed. Finally she listens to what Arnom is trying to tell her— that Bardia is gravely ill. A few days later he dies, worn out by years of service to his queen. Orual then pays a formal visit of condolence to the widow, Ansit. They begin with traditional courtesies, but the scene soon evolves into perhaps the most probing dialogue that Lewis has written in any book. The two women are rivals. Both have been in love with the same man—one consciously and one unconsciously. This realization, when they embrace, gives them a passing moment of understanding. At the same time, Orual is driven to see herself as she appears in Ansit's eyes—the woman who used up Bardia's strength and will to live, and who psychologically encroached on the marriage that she so much resented.

Orual experiences a more profound vision when she wakes from sleep and sees her father, long since buried, standing beside her. He commands her to arise, orders her to remove her veil, and leads her to the Pillar Room. The two of them take pickaxes and a crowbar and begin breaking up the paved floor in the center of the room. They find a dark hole that looks like a wide well. At the king's command, they jump into the hole, leaving the elegant room where so

---

[7] P. 255.

many formal events have been held. They are now in the
primitive world of darkness. This is another Pillar Room,
but smaller and made of earth. Again, her father commands
her to dig and they reach yet another Pillar Room, still
smaller. It is like the others, except that it is made of live
rock, and there is water trickling down the walls. In symbolic
terms, they are now deep in the unconscious, waiting to learn
what it can teach.

A mirror is hanging on the far wall, and her father insists that she look in it. What she sees is the face of Ungit.
Orual is one with the goddess who has tormented her whole
life. "That ruinous face was mine. . . . I the swollen spider
. . . gorged with men's stolen lives."[8]

She wakes from the dream or vision with suicidal
thoughts, and wanders to the edge of a river where she in-
tends to drown herself. But a voice, unmistakably of a god,
calls out in command, "Do not do it." The voice adds, "You
cannot escape Ungit by going to the deadlands, for she is
there also. Die before you die. There is no chance after."[9]

Finally Orual has a climactic vision. She finds herself in
a desert filled with serpents and scorpions. Then a gigantic
eagle of the gods appears and it asks what she is carrying. It
is the book containing her complaint against the gods. The
eagle proclaims, "She's come at last. Here is the woman who
has a complaint against the gods."[10] She is passed from hand
to hand until she reaches an enormous cave. Tens of thou-
sands watch her, including the ghosts of her father and the
Fox. At the command of the judge, she is stripped naked. She
is then ordered to read aloud her diatribe against the gods,
and as she reads it, her own nature becomes clearer to her.
She reveals to herself how from the beginning her heart has
been possessive, selfish, hiding its clutching desires under a
self-deceiving pretext of sacrificial love.

The judge finally stops her obsessive reading and reread-

---

8 P. 276.
9 P. 279.
10 P. 287.

ing of the book, her harangue of self-pity. There is a long silence. At last, he speaks. "Are you answered?" and she replies, "Yes." She has nakedly poured forth the viciousness of her spirit, and at last the gods can communicate with her.[11]

The Fox speaks up, taking the main blame upon himself. He now knows how shallow his Greek rationalism has been; that the worshippers of Ungit, though she is not final truth, are closer to that truth than the smooth debunkers of ancient legends. By the way he educated Orual he took her further away from the ultimate facts of human existence. The judge interrupts. It is the gods who are on trial, and they have made their answer through Orual's understanding of herself.

The Fox leads her to a cool chamber and points out to her the paintings on the walls. One by one she gazes at them, and each brings a new insight into her own life and nature. The first picture shows Psyche at a river's edge, apparently preparing to commit suicide. Orual cries out in the words she had earlier heard from the gods, "Do not do it." Psyche in the picture seems to hear her and goes away. Next Orual sees Psyche, in rags and fetters, sorting out seeds into separate piles. She looks like a serious child performing some assigned task. The floor is black with ants helping her. Next there is a scene of Psyche gaily plucking golden fleece from a hedge.

In the following picture, Orual sees both Psyche and herself, walking slowly over desert sands. Psyche carries an empty bowl; Orual, her book of bitterness. Psyche, though pale and thirsty, moves along singing. With the help of the Fox, Orual begins to understand the ways in which human beings flow in and out of each other, and even merge with the gods. "We're all limbs and part of one Whole," the Fox explains.[12] Orual, all unknowing, has helped bear the burden and anguish of Psyche's trials.

This section of the book shows the obvious influence of Charles Williams, with his doctrine of substitution or co-

---

[11] P. 293.
[12] Pp. 300–01.

inherence. In his book *Descent Into Hell* we observe the experience of a woman who takes into herself the terror of a distant ancestor who was put to death during the time of religious persecutions. Separated by centuries, she is able to work backward in time and make it possible for him to die with amazing courage. It appears that human beings are members of one another in a more literal way than commonly believed; in "real life" Lewis discovered he could receive the pain of his wife's cancer and make her condition more endurable.

Orual asks whether there is a real Ungit. The Fox explains:

> All, even Psyche, are born into the house of Ungit. And all must get free from her. Or say that Ungit in each must bear Ungit's son and die in childbed—or change. And now Psyche must go down into the deadlands to get beauty in a casket from the Queen of the Deadlands, from death herself; and bring it back to give it to Ungit so that Ungit will become beautiful. . . .[13]

The reader scarcely notices it at first, but a glimmer of Christianity is beginning to infiltrate into the rational world of the Greeks and the intuitive wisdom of the old pagans. This foreshadowing of the supreme revelation that lies perhaps several centuries in the future is done quietly and adroitly. There is simply the growing sense that neither the Fox's rationalism nor the bloody cult of Ungit is adequate to make sense of the insights Orual has so painfully arrived at. The meaning of her life lies in a future she will never see. Fox's remark that friends and family will conspire to separate the soul from the Divine Nature is a foreshadowing of Christ's implacable words (Luke 14:26–27): "If any man come to me, and hate not his father, and mother, and wife, and children, yea, and his own life also, he cannot be my disciple. And whoever doth not bear his cross, and come after me, cannot be my disciple."

---

[13] P. 301.

Orual begins to understand how much Psyche has suffered on her behalf. The Fox assures her that she, perhaps in a smaller way, has suffered for Psyche. Voices are now heard proclaiming the return of Psyche from the deadlands. She is safely back, with the casket of beauty that Ungit has commanded her to bring. Orual falls at the feet of Psyche and kisses them:

> "Oh Psyche, oh goddess," I said. "Never again will I
> call you mine; but all there is of me shall be yours. Alas,
> you know now what it's worth. I never wished you well, never
> had one selfless thought of you. I was a craver."[14]

A sudden rustle of sound is everywhere. A god is approaching, to pass judgment on Orual. The queen has a vision of two Psyches reflected in a pool. Both are beautiful.

A great voice cries out, "You also are Psyche." The vision ends; Orual is back in her palace gardens where she had lain speechless for many hours. Her silly book of accusation is still in her hand. Four days later she writes in the book:

> I ended my first book with the words *no answer*. I know
> now, Lord, why you utter no answer. You are yourself the
> answer. Before your face questions die away. What
> other answer would suffice? Only words, words; to be led
> out to battle against other words. Long did I hate you,
> long did I fear you. I might—

At this point Orual apparently falls across the manuscript and dies. A postscript is added by the high priest, praising her achievements as queen and instructing his successors to turn the manuscript over to anyone who will swear to take it to Greece.

A reader who feels at ease with the space trilogy and such fantasies as *The Great Divorce, The Screwtape Letters,* and *The Pilgrim's Regress* finds himself compelled to seek a new vocabulary and angle of vision when discussing the total effect of *Till We Have Faces*. Where once clarity prevailed,

---

14 Pp. 305ff.

with sharp outlines, clear colors, logically coherent ideas, he now finds a shimmering and fluctuating world, in which even the identity of characters is not a fixed thing. Dreams and visions abound, as in others of Lewis's books, but they do not carry a precise intellectual meaning. In most of the book, there is no solid floor to support the reader, for trapdoors are constantly letting him down into the dark depths of the unconscious where the archetypes have their home.

Certainly here the treatment of religious themes is far more problematical than in Lewis's other books. In *Out of the Silent Planet,* the reader quickly understands that the *eldila* are more or less equivalent to earthly angels, and that they function on an unfallen planet as a combination police force and cadre of counselors, smoothly implementing the will of Maleldil, whose divine reality is no new discovery to the person who has read his Bible. But though Ungit reveals something of the divine, it is difficult to equate her completely with Maleldil.

There is also a profound difference in the way mythology is used. All is clarity in the trilogy. We are permitted to behold an actual Mars and Venus. Not so the mythology in *Till We Have Faces.* Categories break down. We are in a world the anthropologists would find interesting, a prelogical world in which consciousness has not yet split into separate compartments.

It is a world in transition. Malacandra will maintain its supervised perfection until natural forces make it uninhabitable. Perelandra will see the fructification of its joyous, sweet splendor as more green people are born to the Green Lady and her husband. Sad Tellus, in *That Hideous Strength,* has had a dress rehearsal of Armageddon, but the real battle remains in the future. The world of *Till We Have Faces* differs from all of these, for an old spiritual order is dying and a new one is waiting to take its place. The worship of Ungit is begetting by a dialectic process the spread of Greek rationalism. But ultimately, neither world view is adequate. What the restless souls of Glome really want, though they hardly have words to express it, is a religion that fulfills the highest intuitions of both faiths.

Lewis has often been accused of making good and evil too neat; his characters, say the critics, are either basically good and becoming more so, or are already so far down the road to damnation that repentance and conversion seem rather distant and highly theoretical possibilities. This criticism overlooks some of the intermediate types, such as Mark and Jane Studdock, whose sins are more those of intellectual and psychological shallowness than a steadfast devotion to pure, metaphysical evil. It is true, however, that other Lewis characters seem damned before we meet them, and they never get within hailing distance of salvation. Weston is far advanced in the service of demonic powers when he first steps on the stage, and his further progress in *Perelandra* is merely to embrace the evil he has already learned to serve. Frost and Wither are further examples. As a Christian, Lewis is obliged to believe that his characters can, up to the last moment of life and perhaps even beyond that, be saved, but the plots of his tales suggest that this moral miracle is of rare occurrence. Mostly, good people get better, bad people get worse.

Till We Have Faces presents a strikingly different view. Most of the characters are mixtures of good and evil, and the proportions can shift in the course of one scene or another. It is as though the categories "good" and "evil" are no longer the dominant principle of classification. We are confronted by intricate and separate beings, and their measurement by some ethical yardstick is far from the only way they can be revealed. The one exception, perhaps, is Psyche, who seems love made incarnate, and has about her from the beginning an aura revealing her potential divinity.

Who has not met Orual? Any priest or psychiatrist will recognize in her the fierce desire to dominate others, and the deep-seated illusion that the correct name for dominance is self-sacrificing love. The mother who has devoted her life to ungrateful children, the artist whose dedication to his craft is really a lifelong indulgence of ego, the president who converts statutory crimes into acts of compassion and sees himself as an ethical martyr—the Oruals are all about us, never more so than when we stand off from ourselves and entertain the thought that the Oruals are not always "they." Nor is the Orual of the novel by any means wholly bad. Whatever mixed motives may drive her, she does prove to be an admirable queen, and the nation profits from her leadership. It is even revealed near the end, when she is stripped naked both physically and spiritually, that though her love for Psyche is tainted by egoistic grasping, it is not completely corrupt. Mixed in with the cries of the ego is enough genuine love so that during Psyche's long wanderings and trials, Orual's concern for her has, by a kind of pre-Christian communion of the saints, helped to sustain her, though not, of course, nearly as much as Psyche has sustained Orual.

The lesser characters stand out in their individuality. Batta, the nurse whom Orual finally has to hang to put a stop to her tattling and troublemaking, is a weak rather than a vicious person. Orual's father, a good deal of a barbarian and a brute, has his moments of insight and tenderness, and is more a candidate for psychiatric care than an incarnation of the fallen Oyarsa. Bluff, faithful Bardia has no sense of the more esoteric religious and ethical virtues, but is absolutely faithful to his queen and works himself to death in her service. The old high priest is a ghastly figure in his robes with the image of a birdlike head and the smell of blood, but he has retained an intuition of the nature of real existence, and why Ungit commands the Great Offering. As for the Fox, his heart is sounder than his intellect. He renounces homeland and family to throw in his lot with the queen who so sorely needs his wisdom, but in his work as teacher and adviser he too readily accepts a sunny and shallow rationalism. When the universe turns mysterious and threatening, he has little practical wisdom to offer.

As one reviews the main characters it becomes very difficult to place them in neat ethical or religious categories. They are as diverse as the membership of any army, college, or church. They exist in their own right, not as embodiments of particular character types. In short, in this book Lewis did what he had not done before: he created some characters as multidimensional as actual human beings, and he focused the tale on the characters themselves and not on the qualities they stand for.

Lewis may have attempted to banish the unconscious from his own understanding of himself, as Owen Barfield suggests in *Light on C. S. Lewis,* but in *Till We Have Faces* he invites those dark depths to emerge into the consciousness of Orual. The series of pictures presented to her near the end of the story are a kind of dramatized psychoanalysis, revealing to her the truths she has not previously dared to face.

The symbolism of the tale is far more mysterious than in Lewis's other fantasies. In *Perelandra,* the floating islands betoken faith in God; the green pair do not need the security of fixed land. The fruit that comes in a variant form, more delicious than the average, symbolizes the grace of God, and challenges one to accept grace with thanks but not go running around demanding it. In *Till We Have Faces* the great archetypes, with all their ambiguities, abound. One could, for instance, see symbols of the whole of human life in the images of water so abundantly found in the book. It stands for life and in particular for new life; it is a symbol of purification; it bespeaks sex; though a symbol of life, it also points to drowning and death. Lewis's book, if analyzed, does not yield a neatly charted symbology. But the symbols echo and vibrate, and as the tale progresses, the reader is caught up into the experience of death and rebirth.

There is a density to the story. The events that a camera would record are sharply etched, but it is as though one slide after another is fed into the projector and sometimes one shows through another. The difference is that much more is going on inside the characters. Orual lives a double life. She is the efficient and triumphant queen, waging successful wars and guiding her country with a firm and wise hand. At the same time, unsuspected by her admiring people, she is wrestling with her inner demons, trying to make sense of a personal life that is far more mysterious—and tormented—than the practical responsibilities of a dedicated monarch.

One way of understanding the difference between *Till We Have Faces* and, say, the space tales, is the recognition that in the hands of a less skillful writer the trilogy might slip over into the merely cute, as *Out of the Silent Planet* comes close to doing when Weston and Devine are confronted by Oyarsa. But *Till We Have Faces* never comes close to this peril. It is a psychodrama, and the reader is held engrossed not by marvels of angelcraft or biology, but rather by the meanings beneath meanings.

Intensely individualized, Orual is at the same time an Everyman, hurling the challenge of her will against the inscrutable voices of the mysterious gods, and enduring the torments allotted to anyone who must understand the gods—and himself—or perish. It is the least typical of Lewis's narratives and represents the surging breakthrough of an inwardness that Lewis had striven for years to suppress. Readers trained on Lewis's more typical works are still wrestling with this book which only slowly but with overwhelming power reveals the secrets at the heart of the gods.

8

THE HOPEFUL CRITIC

Lewis's published output of literary history and criticism, some of it posthumous, comes to about a dozen volumes. Most of these are focused on a single subject; the remaining ones are miscellaneous collections and partly overlap in content. The bulk of this assorted work is brought together in *Selected Literary Essays* (1969) and *Studies in Medieval and Renaissance Literature* (1966).

In 1936 Lewis published his first and most important work of literary criticism and history, *The Allegory of Love*. Three years earlier he had brought out *The Pilgrim's Regress*. The close juxtaposition of these two books, one a scholarly study of the allegory and the other a freshly composed allegory, may serve as symbols of Lewis in his thirties. He was deliberately choosing not to specialize. He was, and remained, both a scholar and a creative writer.

It is *The Allegory of Love* that sundry Oxford faculty singled out for praise when I first went to England in 1948. "If only the shoemaker had stuck to his last," they would sigh. They seemed to praise the *Allegory* all the more heartily when I mentioned, say, the radio talks or *The Screwtape Letters*. But what seemed to Lewis's detractors a kind of literary schizophrenia was so only when viewed from the outside. Studying the evolution of the allegory helped him compose one.

By the time he wrote *The Allegory,* Lewis's prose style had reached its full maturity. He could make words do anything he chose. Thus the first distinction of the book, a relatively rare one in scholarly work, is good writing. The book has a dual theme. One purpose of the study is social and psychic history. Lewis observes the sudden and ultimately mysterious rise of "courtly love" in eleventh-century southern France, and watches its gradual spread and development. It is a curious system of refined adultery. Indeed, it develops into a type of feudalism; the man is the vassal of the lady and she is his lord (the masculine word *midons,* "my lord," is actually used in Provençal poetry). The system clashes head-on with both classical and Christian ideals, although in many ways it is more tender and romantic than medieval marriage. Lewis skillfully traces the evolution of this alternative system of sexual relations—the "religion of love"—until in the time of Spenser it made its peace with marriage by merging into "romantic marriage."

The other theme is the literary one—the evolution of the allegory and its use to express courtly love. Lewis finds the roots in late Latin literature and in certain psychological events taking place toward the close of the classical period and early in the Christian. As he sees it, the old pagan gods, even before they faced the frontal assault of Christianity, were dying. They were evolving into abstractions that could be used as allegorical counters. Men's minds were turning inward. The allegory was a convenient form for depicting inner conflicts.

Lewis details the gradual process by which this form and the doctrine of courtly love came together. His key documents are Ovid's *Art of Love* (taken less seriously by Ovid than by the Middle Ages), the tales of Chrétien de Troyes, and above all *The Romance of the Rose.* Lewis continues straight forward through Chaucer and beyond, until he finds the culmination and transformation in Spenser's *Faerie Queene.*

From the moment of its publication, *The Allegory of Love* was hailed as a major and permanent contribution to literary history. But the book goes beyond mere scholarship. Lewis has a genius for finding redeeming passages in the most minor works, and holding these up for the reader's delighted attention. To read the book is to be introduced to the long history of Western sensibility, and to understand better the present era. As Lewis puts it:

> With Spenser my story comes to an end. . . . It is only after centuries that Spenser's position becomes apparent; and then he appears as the great mediator between the Middle Ages and the modern poets, the man who saved us from the catastrophe of too thorough a renaissance. . . . In the history of sentiment he is the greatest among the founders of that romantic conception of marriage which is the basis for all our love literature from Shakespeare to Meredith. . . . The whole conception is now being attacked. Feminism in politics, reviving asceticism in religion, animalism in imaginative literature, and, above all, the discoveries of the psychoanalysts, have undermined that monogamic idealism about sex which served us for three centuries. . . . What once was platitude should now have for some the brave appeal of a cause nearly lost.[1]

Lewis's next book of criticism, *Rehabilitations and Other Essays,* is a potpourri ranging from a vindication of Shelley and William Morris to thoughts on the English curriculum at Oxford, and a lively set of instructions on the use of the Old English alliterative meter. The final essay, "Christianity and Literature," is of considerable importance in understanding Lewis's approach to literature. He begins by listing the words most commonly used in discussing books: creative/derivative, spontaneity/convention, freedom/rules. He then points out how this corresponds to nothing in the New

---

[1] *The Allegory of Love* (London: Oxford University Press, 1936, 1938), pp. 359–60.

Testament. The latter is concerned with hierarchical relations that involve imitation, not originality. The woman reflects her husband; the husband reflects Christ; Christ reflects His Father. Applied to literature, this would mean that originality is unimportant. A writer may properly be occupied in retelling, to the best of his ability, some traditional tale, rather than dreaming up a completely new one. Or as Lewis states it:

> . . . an author should never conceive himself as bringing into existence beauty or wisdom which did not exist before, but simply and solely as trying to embody in terms of his own art some reflection of eternal Beauty and Wisdom. Our criticism . . . would be opposed to the idea that literature is self-expression.[2]

The Christian, Lewis argues, will be less solemn in his approach to literature than the unbeliever, less inclined to make a religion of art, more ready to enjoy the arts simply for the pleasure they can give. Finally, though, Lewis insists that the greatest literature involves something more than art for art's sake. Its content is crucial:

> When Christian work is done on a serious subject there is no gravity and no sublimity it cannot attain. But they will belong to the theme. That is why they will be real and lasting—mighty nouns with which literature, an adjectival thing, is here united, far over-topping the fussy and ridiculous claims of literature. And *a posteriori* it is not hard to argue that all the greatest poems have been made by men who valued something else much more than poetry—even if that something else were only cutting down enemies in a cattle-raid or tumbling a girl in a bed.[3]

In an earlier chapter I quoted Owen Barfield's comment that during the 1930's Lewis seemed to have turned outward, deliberately deciding that his own psychological

---

[2] *Rehabilitations and Other Essays* (London: Oxford University Press, 1939), p. 192.
[3] P. 196.

operations were less interesting than the world about him. This emphasis on impersonality and objectivity weaves in and out of his critical writings. *The Personal Heresy* is here a key document. It consists of a series of urbane essays carrying on a controversy with Professor E. M. W. Tillyard, apparently touched off by the latter's work, *Milton*. In this book, Tillyard contended that the only critics approaching Milton properly were those who studied Satan as the embodiment of Milton's most intense feelings and values. Such an attempt to double-guess an author was anathema to Lewis, who assumed that Milton knew what he was doing. He also disagreed with Tillyard's conviction that one purpose of poetry is to reveal the personality of the poet and even offer him as a model for life. To Lewis, the poet was mainly a person with unusual linguistic skills.

Lewis's gentlemanly manners mask the fierceness of his feelings. He abominated any confusion of poet with sage or saint or public figure. It is an interesting speculation. If he had lived longer and seen the rise and triumph of the American "confessional" poets (Sexton, Plath, Berryman, Lowell, etc.), what effect would it have had on his thinking? Surely he would have responded to their power at the same time probably maintaining that the reader need not trouble himself with inquiring how far their confessions were biographically exact.

The controversy with Tillyard, carried on in successive essays, leads to a narrowing of the critical gap between the two, but they never reach complete agreement. A difference in mindset becomes evident. Lewis wants to list pairs of opposites and say "either this or that." Tillyard is the synthesizer, the critic inclined to say "both/and." The controversy is complicated by varying interpretations of the word "personality." Lewis takes it on a simple level, such as speculation about the effect of a writer's stammer on his work. Tillyard sees personality as a "mental pattern," which can pervade a poem and be one of its greatest delights.

Lewis states: "The poet is not a man who asks me to

look at *him;* he is a man who says 'look at that' and points; the more I follow the pointing of his finger the less I can possibly see of him."[4] Tillyard argues that the poet's personality reveals itself in style and therefore constitutes an integral part of the poem. When Lewis, challenged by Tillyard, undertakes a definition of poetry he leans very hard on the special use of language, and agrees with the ancient tradition that the purposes of poetry are simply pleasure and profit. It says something worth saying, and in a pleasing way.

At times, Lewis comes very close to the theories of the New Critics. With Eliot, he agrees that the poet ought to put aside his own personality and create a work of art that exists in its own right, not as a psychological projection of the poet. Lewis differs from the New Critics mainly in his methodology. He seems to stand off at a middle distance, rather than applying the critical microscope to a poem and examining it, line by line or word by word, to see the mechanisms that make it function: imagery, rhetorical devices, levels of ambiguity, even puns, plus all the special effects created by particular poetic forms. He undertakes a more general overview, sufficiently detailed to help a reader respond to the poem, but not a complete dissection.

Lewis is willing to grant that sometimes poets come up with startling ideas, and that when these are incorporated into poems, with all the rich possibilities of language at top power, the effect on the reader can be revelatory. But he argues that more often the poet's ideas and themes are pretty much those of the world around him, and the novelty of his poem is not a new philosophy or religion, but a more effective way of expressing perfectly familiar things.

Who comes out ahead in the Tillyard–Lewis debate? On points, the victory goes to Lewis, whose dialectic skills were already highly developed at this time. We see him defining,

---

4 E. M. W. Tillyard and C. S. Lewis, *The Personal Heresy: A Controversy* (London: Oxford University Press, 1939, 1965), p. 11.

contrasting, presenting yes or no alternatives; he is an Ulster-man and intellectually tidy. Tillyard is less concerned with saying what something *isn't* than with trying to make sense of a total poetic experience which may include everything from the poet's aura to philosophic proclamations to a particular meter and rhyme scheme. One's analytic mind is swayed by Lewis but his total intuition is wooed by Tillyard. Meanwhile, the book is of great value to anyone wishing to observe how Lewis's critical mind functioned.

A book more sharply focused is *A Preface to "Paradise Lost."* As a background for this study of Milton, Lewis spends several chapters discussing the primary epic (Homer, *Beowulf*) and the secondary or literary epic (Virgil in particular) and moves on to a consideration of *Paradise Lost.* In Chapter IX, "The Doctrine of the Unchanging Human Heart," Lewis attacks the type of criticism which invites us, say, to forget about Milton's Christian obsessions and his benighted views of male dominance, and to enjoy the poem for its universal aspects. To Lewis, the unchanging human heart has so little content that it is not worth examining. The heart exists only in historical context.

Lewis sees Milton very coolly going about the process of writing a long poem. First, he chose a form, the epic, and only then did he choose a subject. Milton happened to select a major subject, the exile from Paradise, and whether or not the old tale is literally true, it is unquestionably a significant theme, conducive to great poetry. But form is important, too. Lewis says:

> Every poem can be considered in two ways—as what the poet has to say, and as a *thing* which he *makes*. From one point of view it is an expression of opinions and emotions; from the other, it is an organization of words which exists to produce a particular kind of patterned experience in the readers. . . . It is easy to forget that the man who writes a good love sonnet needs not only

to be enamoured of a woman, but also to be enamoured
of the sonnet.[5]

Lewis's main crusade in the book is to demolish the
Satan–Hero theory which has dominated so much Milton
criticism since the time of Blake. Lewis amasses the evidence
that Milton consciously depicted Satan as the villain of the
story. True, Lewis grants, the Satan–Hero theory cannot be
definitively refuted, for it is always possible for an author to
do the opposite of what he thinks he is doing. But it seems
highly improbable that as systematic and well organized a
person as Milton would so gravely deceive himself. Lewis
demonstrates that while Milton gave a splendid picture of the
Devil, he did not thereby make the Devil splendid. In fact,
Satan is at times close to a comic character as he deludes himself into believing that he is at war with Almighty God. Satan,
after all, is not a competitive deity but a lowly rebellious
angel.

Lewis brings his book to a conclusion with a listing of
the flaws he finds in *Paradise Lost:* too much theology packed
into the last two books; too anthropomorphic a God at times;
an unconvincing picture of unfallen sexuality. Finally, he
concedes that in most ways Dante is the greater writer, as
well as being a religious poet in a way that Milton is not.
Dante takes the reader inside the Christian experience; Milton leads him on a conducted tour outside its perimeters.

Lewis's most sustained work of literary history and
criticism is *The Oxford History of English Literature: English Literature in the Sixteenth Century Excluding Drama.*
He had been invited to write this study shortly after *Allegory*
was published and he labored over it off and on for several
decades until it was ready for print. The task became at times
a nagging chore, particularly when he had ideas for other
books teeming in his brain. In his letters he often ruefully

---

[5] *A Preface to "Paradise Lost"* (London: Oxford University Press,
1942), pp. 2–3.

refers to "Oh Hell." Still, when the book was at last published, it was everywhere recognized as a major achievement,
though the praise was not as unanimous and all-embracing
as that which welcomed the *Allegory*. The reason is that a
radically revisionist concept of history (not just literary history) underlies the whole book. It can be briefly summarized
by quoting an anecdote told by Neville Coghill:

> I remember, on one occasion, as I went round Addison's
> Walk, I saw him coming slowly towards me, his round
> rubicund face beaming with pleasure to itself. When we
> came within speaking distance, I said "Hullo, Jack! You look
> very pleased with yourself; what is it?"
> "I believe," he answered, with a modest smile of
> triumph, "I *believe* I have proved that the Renaissance
> never happened in England. *Alternatively"*—he held up
> his hand to prevent my astonished exclamation—*"that if
> it did, it had no importance!"*[6]

The same contention underlies the inaugural address,
"De Descriptione Temporum," which Lewis delivered when
installed as professor of Medieval and Renaissance English
Literature at Cambridge. Lewis argues that the continuities
from the ancient pagan world straight up to the Industrial
Revolution are more striking than the changes. The real
watershed of history, he is certain, occurred less than a hundred years ago. It is not a return to ancient paganism but the
transition into a post-Christian world view. Assuming there
were no language problem, Homer would understand *Beowulf,* and the author of *Beowulf* would understand *Paradise
Lost,* but Milton would not know what to do with Joyce's
Ulysses. Lewis proclaims himself "Old Western Man":

> I read as a native texts that you must read as foreigners. . . .
> It is my settled conviction that in order to read Old
> Western literature aright you must suspend most of the
> responses and unlearn most of the habits you have acquired
> in reading modern literature. And because this is the

---

[6] *Light on C. S. Lewis,* Jocelyn Gibb, ed. (New York: Harcourt,
Brace & World, 1965), pp. 60–61.

judgement of a native, I claim that, even if the defence of
my conviction is weak, the fact of my conviction is a
historical *datum* to which you should give full weight.
That way, where I fail as a critic, I may yet be useful as
a specimen.[7]

The first chapter of the book—more than sixty pages—
is devoted to expounding his theory. Lewis assembles weighty
evidence. He demonstrates, for instance, that serious magic
(commonly considered a medieval specialty) does not fade
away with Renaissance enlightenment but flourishes more
than ever. He also shows that the Humanists succeeded only
in killing Latin when they resolved to freeze the language at
its pure "classical" moment, renouncing the kind of linguistic
evolution that made medieval Latin so fluid an Esperanto. A
cataloguing of literary works by Humanists as contrasted
with those produced in the Middle Ages reveals one major
distinction: the latter are still widely read and the former are
not. Most of all, Lewis contends that the sudden and ultimately mysterious literary flowering around the time of
Shakespeare owes more to native roots than to any learned
attempt to imitate the classicism of the Greeks and Romans.

Lewis was never happier than when pushing a thesis to
its extremes, and some literary historians are convinced he
did so in this case. Obviously, he was operating with an *idée
fixe* and went looking for evidence. The truth seems to be
that Lewis was partially right; his extreme is a corrective to
another extreme. The great watersheds of history do not destroy all continuities. Much of the classical life-style survived
into the so-called Dark Ages, which were not all that dark;
medieval institutions like the jury system survive to the present; and Shakespeare points backward to medieval sensibility
as much as forward.

Most of the book is not as controversial as the first
chapter. One finds, as expected, a fresh and hopeful look at
the writers of the period, their achievements, their failures,

---

[7] *Selected Literary Essays,* edited by Walter Hooper (Cambridge:
Cambridge University Press, 1969), pp. 13–14.

their individual significance, and their place in literary trends. Lewis is singularly free from packaged judgments and is able to respond to a book as though he were reading it for the first time. He is happier to find a few lines to praise than to cast a whole work into outer darkness.

Lewis is at his appreciative best when he deals with Scottish literature. He resurrects a body of highly sophisticated work scarcely read by anyone except specialists, and reveals its elegance and vitality. The Scottish language of that time, he makes clear, was not merely the peasant dialect of small farmers; it was also the speech of the court. He illustrates its potentialities and achievements by considering Douglas's translation of *The Aeneid,* which he finds more "classical" than most readers, confused by linguistic problems, recognize.

The book is by no means restricted to the evolution of sixteenth-century literature. It traces religious and intellectual movements, and indeed builds up a convincing "feel of life" in the century. But most of all, it is an exploration of the period's literature—good, bad, and mostly mixed—conducted by a man with an endless zest for the written or printed word. His main instrument of perception and evaluation is the very love he brings to bear upon the texts under study. This book will for many decades to come be the starting point for anyone wishing a map of the broad sweep of English literature during the century that culminated in Shakespeare. Its specific judgments, of course, will keep the scholars busy confirming, modifying, and refuting, and the most blatant judgment of all—that the real mutation of Western man occurred a century or less ago—will continue to infuriate and challenge the historians.

To judge by casual conversations and newspaper editorials, everyone is something of an expert in semantics. Constant debates flare, followed by visits to the dictionary, which as often as not perpetuates the original confusion by ruling that both sides are right. Lewis has provided rich fare for those fascinated by the history of individual words. *Studies in Words,* in the form of its second and enlarged edition, traces the evolution of eleven families of words: nature, sad, wit, free, etc.[8] Lewis shows how these words ramify, developing multiple meanings and gradually undergoing semantic changes. The reader learns, for example, that the ancient Greek *eleutheros,* the Latin *liber,* and the English *free* all originally meant "not a slave." In English the word takes on the connotation of courteous manners—befitting a person who is free. *"Freedom"* then soon comes to mean, among other things, a gentlemanly generosity with one's possessions. At other times it has the sense of license as in a phrase like "taking liberties with a woman."

The final chapter, "At the Fringe of Language," reveals some of Lewis's presuppositions when he wrote literary criticism. He finds it more difficult to damn than to praise. He then explores why this is so. First, it is difficult to pinpoint what makes a bad book bad. Every negative feature the critic singles out can be found also in books that everyone agrees in calling good. Lewis points out that when I. A. Richards tried to reach a bedrock of badness by identifying it as an appeal to stock responses, the unquestioned power of Gray's *Elegy* defeated him.

Lewis's second misgiving about adverse criticism is more psychological than esthetic:

> The other difficulty lies within. As I said before, what we
> think thoroughly bad, we hate. If, besides being bad, it
> enjoys great popularity and thereby helps to exclude works
> that we approve from their "place in the sun," hatred
> of a somewhat less disinterested sort will creep in.
> Lower and still lower levels of hatred may open; we may
> dislike the author personally, he and we may belong
> to opposed literary "parties" or factions.[9]

---

[8] *Studies in Words,* 2nd ed. (Cambridge: Cambridge University Press, 1967). The earlier and shorter edition was published in 1960.
[9] P. 239.

One suspects this passage was written from agonizing experience, for Lewis had known what it was to see other poets exalted above himself, and in his heart he did not accept that judgment.

In *An Experiment in Criticism* Lewis comes as close as he ever does to giving a systematic account of how he approaches a work of literature. Here, in the role of critic, he analyzes the various ways a reader may respond to what he is reading. Bad reading involves *using* a book (for daydreams, pornographic fancies, confirmation of pet ideas, etc.), whereas good reading means *receiving* the book, laying yourself open to whatever it can do to and for you, finding yourself enlarged by the experience. When good reading is possible, this is prima facie evidence that the book has some value. Some books are so bad they can only permit bad reading. What this approach adds up to is a belief that over a period of time the successive readers of a book constitute a kind of jury. If even a few readers through the centuries can give a book a good reading, then that book cannot be without merit.

As he develops his general thesis Lewis takes up many of the traditional questions raised by literary criticism. Among these is the purpose of literature: "He [the best type of reader] never mistakes art either for life or for philosophy. He can enter, while he reads, into each author's point of view without either accepting or rejecting it, suspending when necessary his disbelief and (what is harder) his belief."[10]

Chapter X ("Poetry") is valuable as one of Lewis's clearest statements on contemporary poetry. He argues that modern poetry has drawn farther away from prose than was the case in any earlier period. To respond to it, "You must achieve a trance-like condition in which images, associations, and sounds operate without these [logical and narrative con-

---

[10] *An Experiment in Criticism* (Cambridge: Cambridge University Press, 1961), p. 68.

nections]."[11] One assumes Lewis is referring to such poets as Eliot and Pound. Small wonder, Lewis says, that so few people read modern poetry and that those who do differ violently in their interpretations of a given poem. Often a reader decides to settle for "what the poem means to me" and not worry about what the poet tried to make it mean. Lewis is willing to accept that as one legitimate pleasure, but pleads that you might as well have the best of both worlds by going on and seeking the poet's meaning also.

Chapter XI, which sums up the book, begins by listing some of the advantages of concentrating on how people read. Here the focus is on the work itself, not on theories about it. It is a remedy against changing literary fashions. It makes critical condemnation a more difficult task, and that in itself is a good thing; the judgmental stance is not the best way to approach a work of literature. Lewis asks from what sources he has derived most help in his own reading of literature. First of all, he says, comes Dryasdust. Textual critics, editors, commentators, and lexicographers have enabled him to find out what the author actually wrote and what the difficult words mean. Next come the literary historians, who helped him read books in the context of their own times. Then come the frankly emotive critics whose enthusiasm sent him eagerly to the authors they discussed.

And what of the great theoretical critics through the centuries? They are helpful in a minor way, Lewis grants, but mostly after one has already read and responded to a given book. It is then interesting to compare the verdicts of the critics with one's own.

Next Lewis pays his tart respects to "the Vigilant school of critics," who grimly evaluate a book not for its esthetic qualities but for its philosophy and ethics. On a low level this results in a witchhunt to eliminate "debasing books" from library shelves; on the higher level it encourages a kind of criticism which treats works of imaginative literature as though everything were a treatise in ethics and social policies.

---

11 P. 97.

The Epilogue is one of Lewis's most sustained treatments of the old literary question, Is form or content more important? We have seen that he wavers somewhat on this matter. Here, he tilts toward form, at times almost in an "art for art's sake" way, but then proceeds to show how the content can become one of the pleasures of literature. For instance, Dante's universe, though few readers accept it literally, is part of the esthetic structure of the work and is a means by which the poet opens new vistas (with their delights) to the reader who is receptive to *The Divine Comedy*.

Summarizing the thrust of his book, Lewis concludes:

> Literary experience heals the wound, without undermining
> the privilege, of individuality. There are mass emotions
> which heal the wound; but they destroy the privilege. In
> them our separate selves are pooled and we sink back into
> sub-individuality. But in reading great literature I become a
> thousand men and yet remain myself. Like the night
> sky in the Greek poem, I see with a myriad eyes, but it
> is still I who see. Here, as in worship, in love, in moral
> action, and in knowing, I transcend myself; and am never
> more myself than when I do.[12]

As previously indicated, various critical works by Lewis were published posthumously. *The Discarded Image* (1964) is based on a series of lectures. Written with great affection, its purpose is to outline the way the universe was conceptualized by medieval man. For the reader seeking to understand Lewis's books, *Image* has a number of insights to offer. For example, one recalls that in the space trilogy the moon's orbit is a celestial roadblock; this idea is derived from medieval cosmology.

As is so often true of his work, Lewis's book has a polemic purpose. He is out to destroy the idea that the medieval world view can best be understood by finding primitive parallels. These exist, he grants, but the direct sources are far more literary—scraps of classical learning pieced together

---

[12] Pp. 140–41.

into a cosmology. Lewis sees medieval man as bookish, tidy, systematic, at times pedantic—not romantic or deliberately launched on imaginative flights. Above all, not primitive.

Lewis argues that the medieval model was satisfying to the imagination in a way that earlier—and later—ones have not been. It was as beautifully constructed as a cathedral, and it made man feel at home in the universe. He does not claim literal truth for the model, but he contends that such a claim cannot be made for the modern model either. It too will yield to a yet newer model:[13]

> The new Model will not be set up without evidence, but the evidence will turn up when the inner need for it becomes sufficiently great. It will be true evidence. But nature gives most of her evidence in answer to the questions we ask her. Here, as in the courts, the character of the evidence depends on the shape of the examination, and a good cross-examiner can do wonders. He will not indeed elicit falsehoods from an honest witness. But, in relation to the total truth in the witness's mind, the structure of the examination is like a stencil. It determines how much of that total truth will appear and what pattern it will suggest.

Another of Lewis's posthumous books, *Spenser's Images of Life,* represents the collaboration of the dead and the living. The raw materials for the book were notes, in highly abbreviated form, that Lewis used when giving lectures at Cambridge. Another eminent Spenser scholar, Alastair Fowler, was persuaded to take these and expand them into a book, remaining faithful to Lewis's chain of thought so far as that could be ascertained.

In this book, Lewis functions more as critic than as historical scholar. He tackles the main difficulties a modern encounters in reading a book whose assumptions are far

---

[13] *The Discarded Image: An Introduction to Medieval and Renaissance Literature* (Cambridge: Cambridge University Press, 1964), pp. 222–23.

removed from those of today, and does this in such a way that the reader finds himself lured and wooed into exploration. Spenser is revealed as a joyous proclaimer of the *via affirmativa;* his great poem in fact is one sustained hymn of joy about the goodness and beauty of life. (One thinks of the epiphany at the end of *That Hideous Strength* when the energies of love and goodness and sheer joy turn earth temporarily into the dwelling place of Aphrodite.)

Don't expect, Lewis warns, that you will find in *The Faerie Queene* the kind of psychological realism you may expect in a nineteenth-century novel. It is closer to a pageant than a novel. (Indeed, one suddenly wonders, could the same thing be said of Lewis's space trilogy?) The particular pleasure the reader derives from a romance is not the contemplation of complex characters but the feel, the atmosphere, call it what you will. In *The Wind in the Willows,* Lewis says, the dominant appeal is the contrast between the growing unfriendliness of the Wild Wood and the homeliness of Badger's house—not the personality of Badger or the other animals. The characters in such a tale are like musical themes, weaving in and out in infinite variations of relationship, and producing an effect closer to the symphony than the novel. Possibly one ought also to recognize, Lewis adds, a strong Jungian presence in *The Faerie Queene,* with archetypes such as St. George and Prince Arthur (the Hero as Deliverer) and the hermit in Book VI (the Wise Old Man).

The Faerie Queene was perhaps Lewis's favorite book, and his love for it gleams though his posthumous guidebook and is summarized in the final paragraph:[14] "It is, as we say, a comment on life. But it is still more a celebration of life: of order, fertility, spontaneity, and jocundity. It is, if you like, Spenser's Hymn to Life. Perhaps this is why *The Faerie Queene* never loses a reader it has once gained. . . . Once

---

[14] *Spenser's Images of Life* (Cambridge: Cambridge University Press, 1967), p. 140.

you have become an inhabitant of its world, being tired of it is like being tired of London, or of life."

Of Other Worlds (1966) brings together a series of essays on the story as a literary form. The first of the essays, "On Stories," is interesting for spelling out in more detail the theory assumed in *Spenser's Images of Life*—that the main value of pure story is not the characters, not even the excitement of events, but the feel or atmosphere created by the events. Lewis recounts an experience with a pupil who greatly enjoyed James Fenimore Cooper. The pupil had been in a delightful state of agonized suspense, wondering whether the sleeping hero would wake up in time to escape the Red Indian approaching with tomahawk in hand. Lewis believed it was not the action that held his pupil, but the atmosphere created by a specifically Redskin peril:

> In such a scene as my friend had described, take away the feathers, the high cheek-bones, the whiskered trousers, substitute a pistol for a tomahawk, and what would be left? For I wanted not the momentary suspense but that whole world to which it belonged—the snow and the snow-shoes, beavers and canoes, war-paths and wigwams, and Hiawatha names.[15]

In his essay "On Three Ways of Writing for Children," Lewis lists three approaches: (1) Give them what they want —the assumption being that their literary appetite is different from that of adults; (2) Tell your story to a specific child, with attention to his responses, and let the written story evolve from this; (3) Write a children's story because it just happens to be the best form for the story you want to tell.

Lewis states that his children's stories all fall within this last category. A good children's story, he maintains, is equally attractive to adults unless they have been shamed and brainwashed out of their "childish tastes." He argues that fairy

---

[15] *Of Other Worlds: Essays and Stories.* Edited by Walter Hooper (New York: Harcourt, Brace & World, 1966), pp. 4–5.

tales and fantasies do not give children a false impression of the real world, and that indeed the argument against terrifying tales is a kind of escapism; the "real world" is itself not very safe. But how does a story get started? In Lewis's case, by seeing mental pictures. In "It All Began with a Picture . . . ," Lewis describes how he first "saw" a faun walking in a snowy wood, and more than twenty years later decided to make a story out of it. Then Aslan came bounding into the picture, and the story was fully launched. Another essay, "Unreal Estates," describes the beginning of Perelandra, as a vision of floating islands. Lewis admits he is happy enough to have a moral develop in the course of writing a story, but it should batter its way in, not be slyly planted by the author.

A miscellaneous collection of literary essays, *Studies in Medieval and Renaissance Literature* (1966), is interesting for showing the breadth of Lewis's scholarly interests, but is too specialized for discussion here. *Selected Literary Essays* (1969) has more essays of general interest, one of which, "Psycho-Analysis and Literary Criticism," especially merits discussion.

It is popularly believed that Lewis was hostile to psychoanalysis, but this is at most a half-truth. In *Mere Christianity* he grants it a role in straightening out the human psyche so that the real religious and moral life can begin, and in the present essay he adopts a moderate attitude. True, he is unwilling to accept any claim that symbols (such as a garden for the female body) are *merely* symbols, but he has no objection to seeing them as a partial revelation of a literal reality:

> Once it is allowed that our enjoyment of *Paradise Lost,*
> Book IV, is a compound of latent erotic interest and
> real though conscious interest in gardens, then it becomes
> impossible to say *a priori* in what proportion the two are
> mixed. And even if it could be shown that the latent
> erotic interest was as 90 and the interest in gardens as 10,
> that 10 would still be the subject of literary criticism.

> For clearly the 10 is what distinguishes one poem from
> another. . . . For we must remember that a story about a
> golden dragon plucking the apple of immortality in a
> garden at the world's end, and a dream about one's pen
> going through the paper while one scribbles a note, are, in
> Freudian terms, the same story. But they are not the
> same as literature.[16]

Lewis next turns to Jungian thought, with its doctrine of archetypal patterns. He acknowledges that the very mention of primordial images evokes a whole chain of imaginary pictures in his mind and deeply stirs him. But he remains an agnostic about the *source* of these images, neither affirming nor denying that they are part of mankind's common psychic heritage. In view of Lewis's differing reaction to the two masters of psychoanalysis, it comes as no surprise that archetypes are considerably more evident in his work than Freudian symbols.

If a systematic methodology of criticism cannot be deduced from Lewis's works of criticism and literary history, at least a series of practical axioms emerges. It is as notable for what it omits as for what it includes. The most striking omission is the detailed *explication de texte* approach favored by the New Critics. Lewis rarely goes in for line-by-line, word-by-word analysis of a work of literature. He seems to stand off a bit, exploring a book or poem with sufficient depth to increase his enjoyment of it, but not investigating every last ambiguity, level of meaning, and rhetorical device. He is also remarkably indifferent to the game of ranking authors and literary works in a hierarchy of merit. His approach is appreciative much more than evaluative.

Lewis's general critical stance has implications for his own writing. It is not too farfetched to imagine him at his writing table, about to begin a new fantasy, and saying to the imaginary reader: "This is going to be a work of litera-

---

[16] *Selected Literary Essays.* Edited by Walter Hooper (Cambridge: Cambridge University Press, 1969), p. 296.

ture, not a sermon or lecture sugarcoated with fine language. Its 'content' may be as much a feeling or mood as a narrative. If it ends up with some religious or philosophic theme, that will not be something inserted by force; it will evolve from my mental pictures, the story itself, the characters and their interactions. This book may have a pageant-like quality; I have a very dominant visual imagination. Don't be too solemn about my book. It isn't Holy Scripture. Writing books is not the most important thing a man can do. If you find ideas here you don't agree with, just temporarily suspend your disbelief, and go along for the pleasure of the tale. It won't hurt you. Maybe this will be a book in which the great nouns of major themes are more important than adjectival literary qualities; I see that I haven't quite made up my mind about the extent to which art is autonomous and the extent to which its highest purpose is to serve something beyond mere art. I probably shan't try for originality. The good old stories are as good as ever and the writer's main job is to use them freshly and effectively. (Still, I may do something original in spite of myself.) I'll try to keep out of the story. Forget about me. Well, dear Future Reader, above all don't be a slave of the Spirit of the Times. All such spirits change. My Spirit may seem out of date, but then again some day it may be the very latest thing. Well, enough of that. Let's start writing. I have an interesting picture in my mind."

9

APOSTLE AT LARGE

At the opposite extreme from his soaring feats of imagination are those books in which Lewis aims directly at instruction and even conversion. These are the apologetic works par excellence. In this category would fall such books as *The Problem of Pain* and *Miracles,* dealing with particular theological questions.

The most important of these directly apologetic books is *Mere Christianity,* which began as a series of short radio talks given in four series over the BBC, from 1941 to 1944. The talks, phenomenally popular, were promptly brought out in the form of three slender books which later were combined into *Mere Christianity.* In this book there is none of the flamboyant fantasy of the trilogy or Narnia. Here the Lewis at his desk, though now a Christian, is still the disciple of his logical and rational Ulster tutor.

That *Mere Christianity* has amply served its purpose, to instruct and if possible convert, is suggested by its continuously impressive sales and the testimony of many individuals who have found in it a book that makes sense of Christianity. Charles Colson is only one of many individuals who see this book as the religious turning point of their lives. The original talks were given a third of a century ago, but nothing has yet appeared in print that seems to reach so many literate doubters and questers.

This being the case, the temptation is to concentrate heavily on the theological content of *Mere Christianity* and to slide quickly over its literary qualities. This, indeed, has been the case with most of the scholars who have discussed it. The aim of this present book, however, is to see how Lewis functions as a writer, not to evaluate the truth or falsehood of the particular religious doctrines he advocates. We are concerned here with the literary methods Lewis uses to present and advocate Christianity, and what factors contribute to his obvious success. How does he argue? How does he win the reader over?

He does it first of all by meeting the reader where he is. He begins with elements of plain, everyday experience and then uses these to develop philosophic or religious concepts. Lewis, believing in a universal human nature which underlies our individual traits and quirks, assumes that the reader will be easily led to draw the same conclusions from a given experience that Lewis himself would draw. At the very beginning of *Mere Christianity,* he describes a perfectly ordinary quarrel:

> Everyone has heard people quarrelling. Sometimes it sounds funny and sometimes it sounds merely unpleasant; but however it sounds, I believe we can learn something very important from listening to the kinds of things they say. They say things like this: "How'd you like it if anyone did the same to you?"—"That's my seat, I was there first"—"Leave him alone, he isn't doing you any harm"— "Why should you shove in first?"—"Give me a bit of your orange, I gave you a bit of mine"—"Come on, you promised." People say things like that every day, educated people as well as uneducated, and children as well as grown-ups.
>
> Now what interests me about all these remarks is that the man who makes them is not merely saying that the other man's behaviour does not happen to please him. He is appealing to some kind of standard of behaviour which he expects the other man to know about. And the other man very seldom replies: "To hell with your standard."

> Nearly always he tries to make out that what he has been
> doing does not really go against the standard, or that if
> it does there is some special excuse.[1]

Thus Lewis takes a common experience and shows a possible basis for it—a shared if implicit belief in universal principles of human interaction. Later, of course, he deals with various kinds of relativistic arguments that would stress the wide variations of social morality from one culture to another, or the possibility that morality is a set of pragmatic habits rather than something absolute and binding on all cultures. How well he fends off the relativists is another question; the answer may depend more on the reader's unspoken metaphysical assumptions than anything else. The point is that by the end of the first page of the book, and without using any technical language of philosophy or religion, he has planted the idea that just possibly we all operate on the assumption of moral absolutes, however little we live up to them day by day. Once absolutes are accepted as a hypothesis, an absolute Lawgiver may not be far behind.

Closely related to the rhetorical use of little parables drawn from everyday experience is the employment of analogies both to make ideas clearer and to suggest their plausibility. Sometimes Lewis hits on a multiple purpose analogy and it recurs through several pages. For instance, he points out that when you have to decide between two instincts, whatever it is in you that decides cannot be one of the instincts.[2] "You might as well say that the sheet of music which tells you, at a given moment, to play one note on the piano and not another, is itself one of the notes on the keyboard. The Moral Law tells us the tune we have to play: our instincts are merely the keys." A little later, he keeps the same analogy but reinforces it simply by rephrasing it more tersely. "The thing that tells you which note on the piano needs to be played louder cannot itself be that note." Still farther on, maintaining that no one

---

[1] *Mere Christianity* (New York: Macmillan, 1943, 1960), p. 17.
[2] Pp. 22–23.

instinct is good by itself, Lewis argues that there must be some faculty that trains the instincts to work together in harmony. Reverting to the music analogy, he makes a more complex point: "Strictly speaking, there are no such things as good and bad impulses. Think once again of a piano. It has not got two kinds of notes on it, the 'right' notes and 'wrong' ones. Every single note is right at one time and wrong at another. The Moral Law is not any one instinct or any set of instincts: it is something which makes a kind of tune (the tune we call goodness or right conduct) by directing the instincts."

The effect of his unfolding analogy is twofold. First of all, it transforms an abstract philosophic proposition into a mental picture. In the second place, it suggests to the reader that if the musical analogy makes sense in the universe of music, it is quite possible that something similar makes sense in the world of social behavior. This use of analogy is no form of proof, though eager readers may seize upon it as such. A way of looking at things has simply been proposed, and the reader finds himself, if not persuaded, at least loosened up, ready to consider a possibility that, presented in the abstract, might stir the theorizing mind but not take on a kind of everyday plausibility.

Defending the transcendence of God, Lewis argues, "If there was a controlling power outside the universe, it could not show itself to us as one of the facts inside the universe—no more than the architect of a house could actually be a wall or staircase or fireplace in that house."[3] In this case a plausible analogy has been used to jump across acres of long-standing metaphysical controversy. The Hindus, with their concept of the universal Brahman represented inside the individual by the Atman, might not be impressed. Here, as in various other places, Lewis not only uses an analogy to present a concept, but uses it in such a way that debate is, for the moment at least, foreclosed; readers are swept along without realizing that they are being hustled forward by an analogy, not by a proof.

---

[3] P. 33.

Often his analogies appeal to more than the visual sense. In the next one, the reader feels in his muscles the attempts of an egg to fly, and smells the corruption of its decay—all to drive home the point that we must either become new creatures or deteriorate into something hideous:

> When He [Christ] said, "Be perfect," he meant it. He
> meant that we must go in for the full treatment. It is hard;
> but the sort of compromise we are all hankering after is
> harder—in fact, it is impossible. It may be hard for an egg
> to turn into a bird: it would be a jolly sight harder for
> it to learn to fly while remaining an egg. We are like
> eggs at present. And you cannot go on indefinitely being
> just an ordinary, decent egg. We must be hatched
> or go bad.[4]

Another way of looking at the analogies and the key role they play in the seductive power of *Mere Christianity* is to say that they are little poems interspersed in the prose text, bringing to full life the ideas that otherwise would smack of the scholar's study. Their poetic quality does not make them literally "true" but it makes them clear and appealing, and helps the reader imagine things that might just possibly be true, no matter how contrary they are to his daily common sense.

Another favorite rhetorical device of Lewis's is the either/or argument. Sometimes this leads him to oversimplify the terms of debate and rule out solutions that are at least conceivable. His essentially Western orientation and lack of familiarity with Oriental thought is particularly evident in one striking example, which is worth discussing at some length.[5]

> Among these Jews there suddenly turns up a man who goes
> about talking as if He was God. He claims to forgive sins.
> He says He has always existed. He says He is coming
> to judge the world at the end of time. Now let us get this
> clear. Among Pantheists, like the Indians, anyone might

---

4 P. 169.
5 Pp. 54–56.

say he was a part of God, or one with God: there would be nothing very odd about it. But this man, since He was a Jew, could not mean that kind of God. God, in their language, meant the being outside the world Who had made it and was infinitely different from anything else. And when you have grasped that, you will see that what this man said was, quite simply, the most shocking thing that has ever been uttered by human lips.

After spelling out this argument in more detail, Lewis moves on to his clincher:

A man who was merely a man and said the sort of things Jesus said would not be a great moral teacher. He would either be a lunatic—on a level with the man who says he is a poached egg—or else he would be the Devil of Hell. You must make your choice. Either this man was, and is, the Son of God: or else a madman or something worse. You can shut Him up for a fool, you can spit at Him and kill Him as a demon; or you can fall at His feet and call Him Lord and God. But let us not come with any patronizing nonsense about His being a great human teacher. He has not left that open to us. He did not intend to.

This is extremely powerful rhetoric, based on the ancient argument, "either God or not a good man." But, it is at least conceivable that Jesus was a spiritual mutant. Perhaps in his times of solitude and prayer He came to a new understanding of God and man. His extravagant claims, such as authority to forgive sins, may have been intended as *kōans,* designed to shake the mind loose from its accustomed patterns of thought, and liberate it for fresh insights. For example, the person hearing Jesus proclaim that He and the Father were one, would be led to his own moment of enlightenment, recognizing his personal divinity.

I confess that in my role as Devil's advocate I have striven to make the case stronger than I actually consider it to be. But the "third option" possibility is still sufficiently strong so that even in a brief radio talk, it needs a bit more refutation than Lewis offers. It is always possible, though not necessarily true in every controversy, that God can count beyond two.

Lewis writes at times as though the Christian life were a hurdle race and only one in fifty could jump successfully. But he does not leave it at that. He pictures the racer as having supernatural help. And most of all, he holds forth the hope that the hurdles are not the main or permanent point. Grim as man's state is, the glory of his final destiny (if he chooses the right path) is so blinding that it justifies all the pains of overcoming his own alienation from God. He will have become, or be in process of becoming, "a little Christ." The natural life within him (Bios) will have mutated into the eternal, spiritual life (Zoe). He will be a toy soldier who is now alive, a "little Christ" living "in Christ."

Here we see one of the main reasons for the remarkable effectiveness of *Mere Christianity*. It is all extremes. Instead of painting a moderately gray picture of the human condition and then offering a moderate kind of redemption—greater kindness, better psychological adjustment, more serenity—it depicts the earthly condition in the darkest possible way. At the same time it holds forth the hope of the beatific vision and the glory of God's direct presence.

Lewis has often been accused of legalism. If by this term, one means that he takes the moral precepts of the Bible literally, the charge is justified. Like all Christians, he is selective in the degree to which he applies casuistic principles to specific teachings. It would be easy, for instance, to take the saying of Jesus in Matthew 26:52 ("Put up again thy sword into his place: for all they that take the sword shall perish with the sword"), read it in the light of His general emphasis on love and forgiveness, and thus arrive at pacifism. This Lewis does not do. But when it comes to marriage, he uses a much more literal standard, seeing in divorce followed by remarriage a plain disobedience to the command of the Lord.

Lewis, as we have seen, is often accused of an obsessive

and excessive emphasis on Christianity as a series of moral rules. The truth seems rather that he dutifully presents the rules, but is impatient with too much discussion of them. Heaven is his destination, and his real eloquence is reserved for depicting that state of soul which is beyond the preoccupation with the rule book. One thinks of the beatific Sarah Smith of Golders Green in *The Great Divorce,* or the young Christian of *The Screwtape Letters* who at the moment of being blasted into bits by a German bomb experiences the vision of the gods and recovers the "central music" which had haunted him all his life. Lewis may imply that this state of beatitude is hard to achieve short of death, and that meanwhile it is well to review the rule book every day. But his final goal is not moral obedience so much as a goodness and joy that subsume and transcend the rule book.

How does *Mere Christianity* stand up when viewed in retrospect? It is, first of all, an amazingly effective job of presenting Christian belief in brief radio addresses. The achievement is all the more remarkable, for Lewis scorns any talking down. He assumes that a miscellaneous radio audience is capable of wrestling with the high points and complications of Christian theology. He does not spare them such austere mysteries as the Trinity, or the metaphysics of time. Theologically and philosophically the book is sophisticated, though the everyday diction may obscure this fact at times.

When Lewis writes of formal theology, or when his soaring imagination creates visions of heaven or hell, one never feels that he is doing his *duty;* rather, he is doing his pleasure. But when he sets out to defend every jot and tittle of the Christian moral law, the reader may sense that he is anxious to get it over with so he can romp again in the pastures of "Joy" where the Great Dance is woven more of streamers of theology and agape than of acceptable "Christian Behavior." If Lewis is a Christian legalist, it is only in an interim way.

His achievement, stated as a minimum, is simply that he makes a good enough case for Christianity so that anyone turning to it can do so with a clear conscience. He demonstrates that there is an intellectual coherence to Christianity, and that much human experience points toward a second story in the house of reality.

Lewis, like G. K. Chesterton in an earlier generation, competed with clever unbelievers to see whether Christian or skeptical wit would prevail. He more than held his own. He did it at a personal price, worrying about some of his rhetorical devices that he found most useful. For example, in a letter (October 12, 1940) to Brother Every he talks of how Every uses "liberal" and Lewis "fashionable" as smear words to imply "that something is bad which, if we attempted to *prove* it bad *en regle,* we should be very much less—well, impressive! But it is a question of method, I admit. I think a method of which all modern critics (and specially myself) are guilty contains a very dangerous element."

The brilliantly successful apologist had indeed a gnawing conscience, and was uneasy in the midst of his rhetorical victories.[6] Let him have the last word:

The Apologist's Evening Prayer

From all my lame defeats and oh! much more
From all the victories that I seemed to score;
From cleverness shot forth on Thy behalf
At which, while angels weep, the audience laugh;
From all my proofs of Thy divinity,
Thou, who wouldst give no sign, deliver me.

Thoughts are but coins. Let me not trust, instead
Of Thee, their thin-worn image of Thy head.
From all my thoughts, even from my thoughts of Thee,
O thou fair Silence, fall, and set me free.
Lord of the narrow gate and the needle's eye,
Take from me all my trumpery lest I die.[7]

---

[6] For a more technical discussion of Lewis's rhetoric when used for purposes of apologetics, see Richard B. Cunningham, *C. S. Lewis: Defender of the Faith* (Philadelphia: Westminster Press, 1967).

[7] *Poems* (New York: Harcourt, Brace & World, 1965), p. 129.

Altogether Lewis produced about a dozen additional books which deal in a straightforward manner with questions of religion, philosophy, and value systems. The order in which they were written seems of no vital importance, and I shall not be bound by it in discussing the individual books.

The Abolition of Man is one of the shortest books Lewis ever wrote. It is an eloquent example of his ruthless reasoning powers at their most effective. It is also of importance as a concise statement of his attitude toward values, and as such provides a background for assumptions taken for granted in many of his other works or more briefly treated, as in *Mere Christianity*.

Lewis uses as his target a textbook that had drifted across his desk. The Green Book, he calls it to conceal its identity. Its two authors are obviously followers of the logical positivism that then prevailed in British philosophy. They are out to debunk all value judgments. The procedure of Gaius and Titius (to use the pseudonyms assigned to them by Lewis) is illustrated in a commentary on their treatment of the famous waterfall episode:

> In their second chapter Gaius and Titius quote the well-known story of Coleridge at the waterfall. You remember there were two tourists present: that one called it "sublime" and the other "pretty": and that Coleridge mentally endorsed the first judgement and rejected the second with disgust. Gaius and Titius comment as follows: "When the man said *That is sublime,* he appeared to be making a remark about the waterfall. . . . Actually . . . he was not making a remark about the waterfall, but a remark about his own feelings. What he was saying was really *I have feelings associated in my mind with the word 'Sublime,'* or shortly, *I have sublime feelings.*" Here are a good many deep questions settled in a pretty summary fashion. But the authors are not yet finished. They add: "This confusion is continually present in language as we use it. We appear to be saying something very important

about something: and actually we are only saying something
about our own feelings."[8]

As Lewis points out, the schoolboy reading the passage
comes away with two convictions—that all sentences containing a value statement are simply statements about the
emotional state of the speaker, and that in any case, such
statements are of no importance. He is well on the way to
being debunked; henceforth he will laugh alike at patriots
asserting it is sweet and proper to die for one's country and
at lovers extolling their sweethearts.

Much of the reasoning in this book resembles the section in *Mere Christianity* where Lewis sets out to defend an
objective moral order and demonstrates that it cannot be a
purely instinctive evolution. In *The Abolition of Man* he
argues very effectively that a statement of fact can never,
without outside aid, turn into a statement of value. My service in the armed forces might protect the civil population,
but this *fact* can never compel me morally to enlist. Only the
Tao, eternal and substantially uniform throughout all cultures, can make me jump from mere statement to value
judgment. The path taken by Gaius and Titius leads ultimately to the replacement of teachers by conditioners, and
the latter can be governed only by their whims and impulses
of the moment.

One important way in which *The Abolition of Man*
differs from *Mere Christianity* is that Lewis is careful not to
introduce theism into his argument. Here he is arguing for
an objective moral law, a *Tao,* rather than for a divine Lawgiver. The *Tao* simply exists. A God is not required for the
bridge between *is* and *ought,* but an absolute metaphysical
order is.

In his conclusion, Lewis warns:

> But you cannot go on "explaining away" for ever: you
> will find that you have explained explanation itself away.

---

[8] *The Abolition of Man* (New York: Macmillan, 1947, 1965), p.
14.

You cannot go on "seeing through" things for ever.
The whole point of seeing through something is to see
something through it. It is good that the window should be
transparent, because the streets or garden beyond it is
opaque. How if you saw through the garden too?
It is no use trying to "see through" first principles. If you
see through everything, then everything is transparent. But
a wholly transparent world is an invisible world. To
"see through" all things is the same as not to see.[9]

The elaborate analogy just quoted (with its revelatory
pun on "see through") is typical of the many effective com-
parisons used in the book. The tone of the work becomes in
itself a demonstration of the *Tao*. It is righteous indignation,
the appropriate emotion when someone calls a sublime
waterfall *pretty*. But at the same time, Lewis maintains a
kind of grave courtesy in his attacks on Gaius and Titius. He
is careful to make the distinction between the sinner and his
sin that he defends in *Mere Christianity*. He tears the Green
Book into tatters but excuses Gaius and Titius from any
malicious intention. Of course, in exonerating the two
authors he does not pass up a chance to suggest that they
may not be the most gifted philosophers available. An example:

If *This is sublime* is to be reduced at all to a statement
about the speaker's feelings, the proper translation would
be *I have humble feelings*. If the view held by Gaius
and Titius were consistently applied it would lead to
obvious absurdities. It would force them to maintain that
You are contemptible means *I have contemptible feelings*:
in fact that *Your feelings are contemptible* means *My
feelings are contemptible*. But we need not delay over this
which is the very *pons asinorum* of our subject. It would be
unjust to Gaius and Titius themselves to emphasize what
was doubtless a mere inadvertence.[10]

[9] P. 91.
[10] P. 15.

In the last sentence one hears the echo of the Socratic Club where Lewis, while obeying the gentlemanly commandments of the *Tao,* was not inhibited from plunging for the jugular. The statement is generous in form and a put-down in fact—effective rhetoric. As in many of his other books, Lewis manages to turn the tables and leave the reader with the idea that really bright people are likely to share his supernaturalism, and that the unbelievers are intellectual drifters who simply seize on whatever ideas are floating about.

I come now to three books in which Lewis wrestles with prime trouble spots in the Christian gospel: how to reconcile miracles with the scientific view of the universe; how to reconcile a good and compassionate God with unmerited pain, and how to justify the more bloodthirsty passages in the Psalms.

In *Miracles: A Preliminary Study* Lewis makes it clear from the start that he is not a historian, and he does not intend to examine the historical evidence for specific miracles. His sole concern is to demonstrate by philosophic reasoning that miracles are not impossible; it is then up to the historians to study the evidence for each particular miracle that has been alleged. He defines a miracle[11] as "an interference with Nature by supernatural power," and posits the existence of a Supernature as well as Nature. If there is nothing but Nature, he grants, then everything is part of "the whole show," and events that may appear to be miraculous are actually the result of causes within Nature itself, and therefore destined to happen without any intervention from the outside. For miracles to be even theoretically possible, it must be demonstrated that Nature is not "the whole show," that certain realities exist outside Nature and are able to penetrate it, making it behave in ways that are not the mere result of natural cause and effect.

There is a bit of curious history about Chapter 3 of this

[11] *Miracles: A Preliminary Study* (New York: Macmillan, 1947), p. 10.

book, in which Lewis sets out to demolish Naturalism as a philosophic theory. In the original edition of the book, he tries to accomplish this in nine pages of well-leaded print. He drives the bulldozer of logic rather impatiently through a number of Naturalistic barricades and proclaims an easy victory. This particular chapter was challenged at the Socratic Club when G. E. M. Anscombe, a woman philosopher, made a highly technical and professional attack on Lewis's reasoning.[12] Some felt that for the first time in its history, the Club had seen Lewis defeated. Be that as it may, he promptly revised and expanded the chapter. The new version appeared in print when Fontana Books (Collins) brought out a paperback edition of the book.

In both versions of the chapter, the line of reasoning is essentially the same. The question revolves around the nature of thought. Is it possible to think true thoughts and know they are true? Or are thoughts simply by-products of the blind processes of Nature? In short, if Naturalism is true, how is one to *know* that it is true? To the Supernaturalist this line of reasoning demonstrates that Naturalism is a logical absurdity, for it contradicts itself. If thoughts come from blind natural processes, one theory is as good—or bad—as another. The Naturalist, of course, arguing for the truth of his position, suspects his adversary is trying to lure him into a semantic trap.

Temporarily postponing further discussion of miracles, Lewis argues that Reason looks beyond itself to its source, God. Another invader from the realm of the supernatural is Conscience. Thus our visible universe is infiltrated by God, Reason, and Conscience. At this point Lewis uses an ad hominem argument, stating that in actual practice the Naturalists who most vehemently deny any concept of objective moral values are prone to forget their theories and turn crusader in all manner of good causes.

---

[12] Roger Lancelyn Green and Walter Hooper, *C. S. Lewis: A Biography* (New York: Harcourt Brace Jovanovich, 1974), pp. 227–28.

Finally ready to deal with miracles head-on, Lewis maintains that a miracle is simply what we call an act of God when
He introduces a new situation into Nature. For example, the
virgin pregnancy of Mary is the result of a miracle, but her
delivery represents Nature responding to the miracle and
assimilating it into normal cause-and-effect operations.
Miracles do not destroy the normal course of nature; they
merely interrupt. Reverting to his long theoretical build-up,
Lewis now attacks the pantheistic concept of God and contends for a God who is sharply distinct from his creation.
This is followed by a chapter in which he argues not only that
God might produce miracles but that it would be appropriate
for Him to do so. Chapter 12 is particularly effective, drawing on many literary allusions to demonstrate that if miracles
do actually occur, they represent not God's arbitrary caprice
but rather a law above the law of Nature. God is like a poet
who knows when to suspend the metrical rules that are
ordinarily proper.

If miracles are possible, the criterion for any particular
miracle is fitness. Does it seem the kind of deed that would
be performed by the God of Reason and Morality? Does it
highlight God's relation to the universe rather than scattering
irrelevant events along the way?

By now the reader has reached the end of Chapter 13,
and one can almost hear Lewis's sigh of relief as he finishes
the theoretical and argumentative section of the book. He is
at last free to consider the central miracles that Christianity
proclaims and to apply the test of "fitness."

Lewis begins with the "Grand Miracle," the Incarnation. Nothing is better calculated to inspire his pen and set
his words aglow than this topic; from now on to the end of the
book it has almost the same kind of melody and majesty as,
say, *The Great Divorce*. He turns to an esthetic analogy:

> Since the Incarnation, if it is a fact, holds this central
> position, and since we are assuming that we do not yet know
> it to have happened on historical grounds, we are in a
> position which may be illustrated by the following analogy.

Let us suppose we possess parts of a novel or a symphony.
Someone now brings us a newly discovered piece of
manuscript and says, "This is the missing part of the
work. This is the chapter on which the whole plot of the
novel really turned. This is the main theme of the
symphony." Our business would be to see whether the new
passage, if admitted to the central place which the
discoverer claimed for it, did actually illuminate all the
parts we had already seen and "pull them together."[13]

Lewis argues that the descent of God to earth and His
subsequent ascent correspond to the archetypal patterns of
Nature itself. Nature belittles itself into tiny, hard seeds and
these are buried; out of this death new life comes. The pattern one finds in nature was first in God. Christ is the fulfillment of all the wistful dreams of a corn-God like Adonis or
Osiris. But Christ is not a vague legend; He is a man who
lived at a particular place and under a particular Roman
governor. Lewis maintains that God's visit to earth and return to heaven initiates a process leading not just to the
glorious transformation of humanity but to the reshaping of
Nature itself.

When he comes to discuss the miracles of Christ, Lewis
divides them into two categories: miracles of the Old
Creation (such as multiplying the loaves of bread by by-
passing the sowing and reaping of grain) and miracles of the
New Creation (walking on water will serve as an example).
The criterion for the authenticity of both kinds of miracles
is an esthetic one. Does each particular miracle have about
it the style of the God that Christians postulate? In short,
fitness.

When discussing the miracles of the New Creation,
Lewis focuses mainly on the resurrection and the ascension.
In these two events he sees a healing of that split between
body and soul, Nature and spirit, which has divided the consciousness of mankind since the Fall. There is an eloquent
passage evoking memories of places in so many of his other

---

13 *Miracles*, p. 113.

books where Lewis anticipates the healing of all psychic schisms.

> The whole conception of the New Creation involves the belief that this estrangement will be healed. A curious consequence will follow. The archaic type of thought which could not clearly distinguish spiritual "Heaven" from the sky, is from our point of view a confused type of thought. But it also resembles and anticipates a type of thought which will one day be true. That archaic sort of thinking will become simply the correct sort when Nature and Spirit are fully harmonised—when Spirit rides Nature so perfectly that the two together make rather a *Centaur* than a mounted knight. . . . Those who attain the glorious resurrection will see the dry bones clothed again with flesh, the fact and the myth re-married, the literal and the metaphorical rushing together.[14]

This last sentence might well serve as a brief statement of Lewis's particular angle of vision, the central melody that sings in the background of almost everything he ever wrote. Without it, his religious writings would be brilliant essays in logic but somehow hard and brittle. With the melody alone, there would be the suspicion that he was merely a day-dreamer and fantasizer. With the two together, the reader imaginatively experiences the reunion of spirit and Nature that Lewis sees as the divine goal of the universe.

Looking back at *Miracles,* almost any reader will recognize it as a more resonant book than *Mere Christianity.* Here Lewis can concentrate on miracles as prefigurements of a transformed universe—and not have to batter his way through such bread-and-butter doctrines as Christian morality, where he often is not at his best. But does he make his case? Poetically, yes. Intellectually—it depends on one's school of logic.

A striking contrast to *Miracles* is a book written slightly earlier, *The Problem of Pain.* Perhaps the difference in topic

---

14 Pp. 166–67.

predestined the great difference in tone. In *Miracles,* Lewis has occasion to soar in gleaming language and symbols. In *The Problem of Pain,* the subject matter is less conducive to epiphanies, and the style is (for Lewis) relatively dull. There is much well-honed thought here but few pages that sing.

The problem of pain is one that has baffled and ultimately defeated all who have dealt with it, as Lewis knew. He defends himself by constantly proclaiming his amateur status as a theologian; with dutiful humility he submits his speculations to correction by his theological betters. He is trying to do what Job first attempted, and achieves a partial but by no means complete success in the effort to explain why a good and omnipotent God permits or even inflicts pain.

His most plausible section is near the beginning when he argues that if human beings are to develop self-consciousness, they need to live in a stable, neutral world. It must have predictable laws. To make up an example, if A throws a stone at B's head, both of them recognize the laws of physics that control the ascent and descent of the stone. God might deflect it by a miracle. But not often. If He showered miracles right and left, we would live in a thoroughly confusing world. Thus, if a child tumbles from a third-story window and no divine hand intervenes, are we to say that God wills the death of the child? No. But he wills that the laws of physics shall operate. From the child's viewpoint, it doesn't matter whether God causes or permits.

The neutral environment in which the human drama is acted out can thus lead to suffering in two ways. First, by its very laws it makes suffering possible. The cure comes not from a miracle, but (as in the case cited) from better supervision on the part of parents so their children will not tumble from windows. The same neutral environment also makes it possible for one man to take a gun and insert a metal object and explosive powder, and be almost certain that God will not intervene if he points it at someone and pulls a trigger. The laws of nature are the same for a bad man and a good one.

This is stern doctrine although morally acceptable. If we want an environment in which our acts have real consequences, our free will is respected, genuine relations between individuals are possible, and growth in self-awareness is permitted, it must be one in which clear laws of cause and effect operate. At any rate, Lewis develops this point well and effectively reconciles this kind of pain—caused by disregard of natural laws or abuse of them—with the omnipotence and goodness of God.

Each reader will have to decide for himself whether he is convinced when Lewis extends his theory further and introduces demonic beings into the picture. Devils, he suggests, may sometimes exploit the laws of nature to bring about suffering and pain. They presumably do it for fun, and perhaps to weaken the faith of mortals. One can neither prove nor confute this theory. Demonic spirits by definition have powers of invisibility. If they are admitted as a possibility, the case of the child falling from the window becomes more complex: perhaps a devil pushed him out. At any rate, God, respecting the free will of his fallen creatures (demons) and resolved to save them by the same methods he uses with human beings, must honor their autonomy even when it leads to human suffering.

Lewis is less convincing when he argues that God sometimes directly inflicts pain as a way of bringing a person to his senses. Pain can be God's megaphone when the person will not listen to the well-modulated voice of conscience. The problem here is to confront specific cases of suffering and decide whether they fall in this category.

Take, for instance, a woman who has lung cancer. Maybe she is a heavy smoker. Then she brought it on herself. But suppose she doesn't smoke. She still belongs to a society which constantly fills the air with assorted carcinogenic fumes. Her cancer then becomes something akin to wounds in wartime. But maybe a demon is having fun with her. Or maybe God is the author of the cancer and is trying to tell her something through it.

How is she to know? She may find herself repenting imaginary sins on the mistaken assumption that the cancer is God's megaphone, when actually it is just a side effect of filthy air. Lewis's problem is that he offers too many different reasons for suffering, and too few criteria for pinpointing the sources.

As though he had not created sufficient problems for himself, Lewis then goes on to discuss animal pain. Here he is intolerably cozy and domestic. The true animal, he insists, is the one who has been "redeemed" by its association with human beings. The dog and horse become the archetype of what all animals ought to be, half-humanized creatures hanging upon the will of their master. Of course, the great majority of all earthly creatures are excluded from this kind of redemption. Where will an earthworm find a master to humanize him?

What we have is the cloying picture of the right kind of animal who exists to serve his human masters:

> You must take the whole context *in* which the beast acquires its selfhood—namely "The-goodman-and-the-goodwife-ruling-their-children-and-their-beasts-in-the-good-homestead." That whole context may be regarded as a "body" in the Pauline (or a closely sub-Pauline) sense; and how much of that "body" may be raised along with the goodman and the goodwife, who can predict? So much, presumably, as is necessary not only for the glory of God and the beatitude of the human pair, but for that particular glory and that particular beatitude which is eternally coloured by that particular terrestrial experience. And in this way it seems to me possible that certain animals may have an immortality, not in themselves, but in the immortality of their masters.[15]

---

[15] *The Problem of Pain* (New York: Macmillan, 1943, 1962), pp. 139–40.

What of wild animals? Lewis rather inconclusively discusses them, arguing that some may be taken into the New Creation because they serve a symbolic function to human beings—the "heraldic royalty" of the lion. All in all, the discussion of animals is blatantly anthropocentric and fails to cope with the possibility that God wants animals to be what they so magnificently are in the wilderness, and that the horse broken to the halter and bit represents as much mankind's exploitative lusts as a rightful exercise of dominion. Still, the section is redeemed by a beautiful passage which says little about the theological problem but prefigures the Aslan who, we all know, was not a tame lion:

> I think the lion, when he has ceased to be dangerous, will
> still be awful: indeed, that we shall then first see that
> of which the present fangs and claws are a clumsy, and
> satanically perverted imitation. There will still be something
> like the shaking of a golden mane: and often the good
> Duke will say, "Let him roar again."[16]

In Chapter 5 ("The Fall of Man"), Lewis gives one of his most complete theories of what the Fall actually involved. This chapter is written in Lewis's closest approximation to the "good drab" he singles out in his history of sixteenth-century literature. The result is that the reader finds himself less inclined to believe the entire theory than he is when reading the more poetic and imaginative works, where the primal loss of harmony, or the possibility of this loss, is dramatized so poetically—*Perelandra,* for example, or *The Lion, the Witch and the Wardrobe.*

Lewis depicts God's transformation of an almost-human animal into a fully human being:

> Then, in the fullness of time, God caused to descend upon
> this organism, both on its psychology and physiology, a
> new kind of consciousness which could say "I" and
> "me," which could look upon itself as an object, which
> knew God, which could make judgements of truth, beauty,

---

[16] P. 143.

and goodness, and which was so far above time that it could perceive time flowing past. This new consciousness ruled and illuminated the whole organism, flooding every part of it with light, and was not, like ours, limited to a selection of the movements going on in one part of the organism, namely the brain. Man was then all consciousness. . . . His organic processes obeyed the law of his own will, not the law of nature. His organs sent up appetites to the judgement seat of will not because they had to, but because he chose.[17]

If the passage above were expressed with Narnian language and symbols, the reader would imaginatively enter into the picture, however difficult he might find it to defend the idyllic vision of early man literally. But here the language is plain and businesslike, and the practical and factual questions keep crowding in—has the history of mankind really been the discontinuity of beast, quasi-angel, and fallen creature? Or has there been a smoother continuity as the beast evolved into some kind of man, and the man discovered the challenge and delights of the knowledge of good and evil, simultaneously falling downward into sin and disobedience and upward into the possibility of a heightened relation with God? Perhaps it is the Spirit of the Age, against which Lewis repeatedly warns us, that makes it difficult to imagine a creature so abruptly emerging from animalhood and possessing by nature such transcendent human qualities as subsequent saints have never quite achieved.

In fairness to Lewis, it must be pointed out that he presents his picture of early man as a myth. He uses that slippery word in the Socratic sense—"a not unlikely tale" or "an account of what *may have been* the historical fact."[18] The reader is thus free to take Lewis's theory of early man literally or as a symbolical representation of something we can never reconstruct in terms of linear time. The trouble comes when Lewis throws himself into the theoretical chronology

---

[17] Pp. 77–78.
[18] P. 77 *fn.*

with such zeal that the reader is tempted to say, "Either this is literally and historically true, or isn't true at all." The treatment needs to be either more tentative or more poetic.

Despite its ambiguities, *The Problem of Pain* is a highly intelligent book in its fine-grained analysis of many possible explanations. It is of little use in solving the more mundane problems of pain. But to be fair to Lewis, he did not offer the book as a practical treatise.

Reflections on the Psalms is devoted to a single book of the Bible.[19] Lewis makes no pretense of specialized knowledge; indeed he works with the handicap of having no Hebrew. He has, however, resources that balance his ignorance. He brings to bear a literary, indeed poetic sensibility on the personal and social significance of the Psalms. He is concerned with the question, What spiritual use can one make of these ancient poems? I shall concentrate on how he treats certain psalms that present ethical problems.

Anyone who has read through the book of Psalms will remember those occasional moments when he suddenly asked himself, "Does the Bible actually say this?" He is encouraged to hate his enemies, to dash their infants' heads against hard surfaces; he is left daydreaming about feasting while his enemies hungrily look on. Lewis, who likes to deal with extreme situations, does not rush in to say that God commands hatred. But neither is he willing to banish the "cursing Psalms" from the Bible.

Such hideous Psalms, Lewis argues, serve at least one humble purpose—they help us to recognize the vicious emotions inside ourselves. This is therapeutic. We come to know ourselves better. But Lewis moves on to point out that the kind of hate the Psalms often depict is not an accidental or capricious thing. It is most often the by-product of oppressive relations between individuals, classes, or nations. Such

─────────

[19] *Reflections on the Psalms* (New York: Harcourt, Brace & World, 1958).

Psalms may teach us to see the consequences of our own manipulation and domination of others.

Lewis has a double concern: to keep the Psalms part of the Christian tradition, and to avoid letting their surface meaning sometimes seduce people into sub-Christian states of mind. This approach to the Psalms introduces subtleties probably unknown to whoever originally composed them, but it also rescues them for the honest reader, permitting him to find in them new understandings and insights. It is a remarkable book, sketching out and demonstrating a fruitful approach to one of the most beautiful—and perplexing—books of the Bible.

Letters to Malcolm was written during Lewis's last months of life, when he was already gravely ill from a combination of heart and kidney afflictions. Malcolm is fictional—a convenient target for certain thoughts Lewis had about the theory and practice of prayer, liturgical matters, theological controversies, and the like. In *Mere Christianity,* Lewis had been careful to restrict himself to hard-core Christian doctrine and avoid theological speculation. In *Letters to Malcolm* we penetrate his screen of impersonality a little. We learn, for instance, that he had a low church background and that he found an empty church a poor place for private prayer (somebody was always practicing that abominable instrument the organ, or a charwoman was swishing around). We learn that he believes in Purgatory, not as a place for punishment but as the bathhouse of the soul. He does not pray to the dead, but he prays for them. As for the liturgy, his greatest desire is stability—let the theologians work out a liturgy and stick to it. The picture that emerges is of a man "protestant" in his relative indifference to the precise way holy actions are performed, and "catholic" in some of his personal beliefs and practices. All in all, a middle-of-the-road Anglican.

The book was written after the death of his wife, Joy, and this loss seems to color much of what he says. He refers to the event frequently, and there is also a curiously gentle, unglittering style. One thinks of the later poems of W. H. Auden, when the brilliance of his early work subsided into almost a domestic tone. In *Letters to Malcolm* Lewis speaks quietly, as one might converse with a friend when neither is trying to score debating points with the other. This tone is capable of its own subdued eloquence.

Here, also, one can find examples of Lewis's careless generosity with theological throwaways—concepts developed very briefly and then abandoned as he goes on to something else. For example, this advice about exegesis:

> I suggest two rules for exegetics: 1) Never take the images literally. 2) When the *purport* of the images—what they say to our fear and hope and will and affections— seems to conflict with the theological abstractions, trust the purport of the images every time. For our abstract thinking is itself a tissue of analogies: a continual modelling of spiritual reality in legal or chemical or mechanical terms. Are these likely to be more adequate than the sensuous, organic, and personal images of Scripture— light and darkness, river and well, seed and harvest, master and servant, hen and chickens, father and child? The footprints of the Divine are more visible in that rich soil than across rocks or slag-heaps. Hence what they now call "demythologising" Christianity can easily be "re-mythologising" it—substituting a poorer mythology for a richer.[20]

This book concentrates mostly on everyday religious questions: Should I pray for material things? Should I kneel? Is it all right to use ready-made prayers? Can drugs induce mystical states of consciousness? and so on. It lacks the dynamic thrust of many other books that Lewis wrote, but its very modesty gives it an endearing quality.

Letters to an American Lady is Lewis's correspondence, from 1950 almost to the end of his life, with a Southern lady

---

[20] *Letters to Malcolm: Chiefly on Prayer* (New York: Harcourt, Brace & World, 1964, 1973), p. 52.

who had turned to him for comfort, advice, and ultimately money. There is a good deal of theological talk, directed mostly to specific problems of ill health, aging, and personal relations, but little that is not better and more completely expressed in other books. As was often the case with Lewis's letters, some of these read like abridged passages from his books. But along the way there are the more human touches —such as Lewis's kindly criticism of the poems the American woman sent him. The main value of the book is the little sidelights we get on his daily life—Lewis desperately attempting to answer the mail, Lewis preparing his breakfast and doing his household chores early in the morning, the steady deterioration of his health; most of all, the entrance of Joy Davidman into his life and the story of her illness, recovery, relapse, and death.

The one general collection of Lewis's letters so far published is *Letters of C. S. Lewis*,[21] the result of a rather hasty editorial job done by his brother, W. H. Lewis, assisted by the publisher. These letters range in time from Lewis's early teens to within a few weeks of his death. The reader should be warned that they do not tell all. (Indeed, the manuscript letters, available for scholars at the Bodleian Library in Oxford and Wheaton College in Wheaton, Illinois, do not contain any sensational revelations; either Lewis did not have many scandalous experiences, or if he did, he declined to put them down on paper.) The published collection of letters is even blander than it might be, omitting, naturally enough, letters such as those dealing with the wild chases and rescues Lewis undertook when his alcoholic brother, Warnie, was on one of his nonstop drinking bouts.

They often read like foreshadowings of books yet to be written, or critical footnotes on books already written. Increasingly, as his fame grew, Lewis found himself explicating

---

21 Lewis's letters, of course, are not all about religion, but they seem to fit in this chapter better than anywhere else.

his own work in reply to letters of inquiry, or giving pastoral counsel. Much as he loathed the chore of letter writing (as he also regretted the time-consuming work of being an Oxford tutor) he felt morally impelled to answer all letters except the most insane ones, and often wrote in great detail about religious and personal problems. On the whole, the letters do not add much to what a reader of Lewis's books already knows about his religious and literary beliefs, but sometimes little nuances emerge that were only implicit in the formal books.

Major Lewis's selection of letters is only an appetizer. Several large collections of letters to specific persons cry out for publication as separate volumes. I am thinking, for example, of letters to Owen Barfield, the many theological and personal letters to Sister Penelope, and the letters, often discussing poetic theory, to the well-known poet Ruth Pitter. One hopes all these will be published in due course. Meanwhile, the letters he wrote from his early teens to Arthur Greeves are being edited, and will prove a valuable supplement to the biography, giving some insight into what Lewis was like as an ambitious young man before he became famous.

In the collected *Letters* we see Lewis as a soldier, trying to carry on the preoccupations of peacetime as much as possible:

> I make every effort to cling to the old life of books,
> hoping that I may save my soul alive, and not become a
> great, empty-headed, conceited military prig. I am
> finding out that the military ideal in our army differs from
> the German one only in degree, not in kind. The Sergt.
> Major told us the other day that "soldiering is more than
> 'arf swank. You've got to learn to walk out as if the bloody
> street belongs to you. See?"[22]

From the beginning Lewis had an observant eye for mortal foibles, as when he describes his formal "admission"

---

[22] *Letters of C. S. Lewis,* Edited, with a Memoir, by W. H. Lewis, (New York: Harcourt, Brace & World, 1966), p. 38.

at Magdalen. One can almost see in the future the forlorn Mark Studdock of *That Hideous Strength* worrying about his first meeting with the mighty ones of the N.I.C.E.

> Warren (the President) was standing, and when the V.P. laid a red cushion at his feet I realized with some displeasure that this was going to be a kneeling affair. Warren then addressed me for some five minutes in Latin. . . . no one had told me what response I was to make, and it was with some hesitation that I hazarded *do fidem* as a reply. . . . This appeared to fill the bill. I was then told in English to kneel. When I had done so, Warren took me by the hand and raised me with the words, "I wish you joy.". . . I was sent all round the table and every single member in turn shook my hand and repeated the words: "I wish you joy.". . . English people have not the talent for graceful ceremonial. They go through it lumpishly and with a certain mixture of defiance and embarrassment, as if everyone felt he was being rather silly, and was at the same time ready to shoot down anyone who said so.[23]

Lewis's love of hiking the countryside with a few male friends evokes some lovely descriptions, as in a letter to his brother:

> No one can describe the delight of coming to a sudden drop and looking down into a rich wooded valley where you see the roofs of the place where you're going to have supper and bed; especially if the sunset lies on the ridge beyond the valley. There is so much mixed in it; the mere physical anticipation, as of a horse nearing his stable, the sense of accomplishment and the feeling of "one more town," one further away into the country you don't know, and the old, never hackneyed romance of travelling.[24]

The letters often show Lewis engaged in literary scholarship and wishing there were more time for it. His love of the Bodleian Library, where most of his work was done, comes out in a letter to his father.[25] "I spend all my morn-

---

[23] P. 103.
[24] P. 117.
[25] P. 125.

ings in the Bodleian . . . if only one could smoke and if only there were upholstered chairs, this would be one of the most delightful places in the world."

In a letter "to a lady," Lewis states in plain language the doctrine dramatized near the end of *The Last Battle,* when the noble pagan finds that all unknowing he has served Aslan throughout his life: "I think that every prayer which is sincerely made even to a false god or to a very imperfectly conceived true God, is accepted by the true God and that Christ saves many who do not think they know Him."[26]

Poignantly enough, a few weeks before his death, we find Lewis writing: "Yes, autumn is really the best of the seasons; and I'm not sure that old age isn't the best part of life. But of course, like autumn, it doesn't *last.*"[27]

Back in the mid-forties, when I first decided to write a short book about C. S. Lewis, I communicated this ambition to Lewis, who sternly warned me to desist: one should, he said, write only about dead authors. Perhaps because he was becoming a public figure, he feared all the more the dramatization inherent in any book about him. One suspects that the same reticence lies behind the peculiar quality of *Surprised by Joy.* It is as though Lewis had reluctantly come to feel that he owed it to his reading public to present the record of his gradual loss of Christian faith, and the even more gradual return to it. But implicitly he says, "I'll be damned if I tell them anything else—the rest of it is my own business." He lifts the window shade just so much, and if curious eyes try to peer through the gap and observe the interior, he pulls the shade down with a jerk. As an example, take this passage:

> I came to know by experience that it ["Joy"] is not a
> disguise of sexual desire. Those who think that if adolescents
> were all provided with suitable mistresses we should soon

26 P. 247.
27 P. 308.

hear no more of "immortal longings" are certainly
wrong. I learned this mistake to be a mistake by the simple,
if discreditable, process of repeatedly making it. From
the Northernness one could not easily have slid into erotic
fantasies without noticing the difference; but when the
world of Morris became the frequent medium of Joy, this
transition became possible. It was quite easy to think
that one desired those forests for the sake of their female
inhabitants. . . . I repeatedly followed that path—to the
end. And at the end one found pleasure; which immediately
resulted in the discovery that pleasure (whether that
pleasure or any other) was not what you you had been
looking for.[28]

The reader pricks up his ears and waits to learn more
about these experiences. He is disappointed. Lewis has told
all that is needed to make his point.

For the religious reader, this semiautobiography is valuable as a roadmap of the twin paths—logic and "Joy"—that
Lewis followed, and which finally brought him back, first to
theism, eventually to complete Christian orthodoxy. One also
finds *Surprised by Joy* interesting in another way. It is evidence that had Lewis so chosen, he could have been an
effective realistic novelist. The realistic approach was not
Lewis's favorite mode—after all, he denigrates Chaucer and
seems more attracted to the writers of chivalric romances.
But when he wants to be plain realistic, his pictorial memory
and observation of small details stand him in good stead.
Consider his portrait of his father; the widower trying to be
one of the boys to his two sons and simply embarrassing
them; ranting about politics over dinner with the serene conviction that they are as interested as he is, misunderstanding
and reversing the intent of anything said to him. He really
lived, but as Lewis pictures him he is also straight out of
Dickens.

Lewis, who hated his succession of boarding schools
with a passion that erupts in so much of his adult writing, is

---

[28] *Surprised by Joy: The Shape of My Early Life* (New York:
Harcourt, Brace & World, 1955), pp. 169–70.

able to catch the personality of each master, no matter how bizarre or insane, and many of the individual pupils. Beyond this, he achieves a collective portrait of each school, so that the reader feels in his central nervous system what it would have been like to be a pupil there.

I come now to several books that cannot be adequately discussed without taking into account Lewis's marriage to Joy Davidman Gresham. By odd chance, my wife and I had known Joy and her husband, Bill, for several years before she met Lewis, though she had had a vigorous fan-letter correspondence with him for some time. When we first came to know them, the Greshams with their two young sons seemed an idyllic family; later, a second woman entered the picture and divorce finally ensued.

Joy, of secularized Jewish background and a convert to Christianity, had been a Communist in the 1930's, though in later life she became very conservative. She early established a literary reputation by winning the Yale Series of Younger Poets competition with a book of proletarian verse. Bill, a gentile, was best known for his novel which was made into a film, *Nightmare Alley*.

As I remember her, Joy had a plain face except for very large and luminous eyes. She possessed a formidably penetrating mind, a love of intellectual debate, unbounded contempt for sloppy or sentimental reasoning. In sheer I.Q. I suspect she equaled Lewis.[29]

In 1955 my wife, having a chance to observe Lewis and Joy together, firmly declared, "I smell marriage in the air." It is less certain whether Lewis smelled it at that time or wanted to.

Afflictions began to befall Joy. Early in 1956 the Home Office refused to renew her residence permit. Also, her health began to deteriorate. Diagnosed as acute rheumatism, it

[29] For fuller details of the marriage, see the *Biography* and my essay, "An Afterword," in C. S. Lewis, *A Grief Observed* (New York: Bantam, 1976).

turned out to be cancer. As an act of compassion, Lewis married her in a civil ceremony, thereby giving her and the boys British citizenship. There followed a long stay in the hospital. When it had done all for her it could, Lewis arranged a religious marriage ceremony so that he could, with a clear conscience, take Joy to live at the Kilns. Within the space of less than a year the cancerous bone reknit and Joy was able to walk with only a slight limp. She wrote us in mid-1957:

"Jack and I are managing to be surprisingly happy considering the circumstances; you'd think we were a honeymoon couple in our early twenties, rather than our middle-aged selves."

The recovery lasted only a few years until cancer struck again and this time there was no reprieve. But it lasted long enough to teach Lewis many things about love, himself, men and women, the role of emotions and feelings. The Orual of *Till We Have Faces* is not a portrait of Joy but is a character he could hardly have created if it had not been for what he learned from her. And in his book *The Four Loves,* the knowledge imparted by Joy enables him to move in one leap from legalist to existentialist.

Lewis's change in attitude was not without its problems. The Episcopal Radio-TV Foundation of Atlanta asked him to record a series of talks on varieties of love, which would be aired over their usual radio network and could eventually be published as a book. After the recordings had been made it became evident that some influential American bishops were worried about their squeamish public, fearing the talk on Eros was too strong for American taste. Considering how often Lewis had been deplored as a prig and prude, there was delicious irony in the implied accusation that he was a purveyor of pornography. Mrs. Rakestraw, executive director of the foundation, found herself caught between her cautious bishops and a furious Lewis and Joy. Eventually the talks were fairly widely used by various stations on an ad hoc basis, but were not aired on the whole network for Episcopal

radio programs. Meanwhile, Lewis went ahead and revised the lectures into his book *The Four Loves*. This deals
with four distinct yet partially overlapping species of love:
Affection, Friendship, Eros, and Charity.

The uneasy bishops did indeed put their collective
fingers on one striking aspect of the book. Its discussion of
sex and marriage has a down-to-earth, experiential tone that
was sadly lacking in *Mere Christianity*. It is not that the
stern divine laws, such as fidelity and the permanence of
marriage, are abrogated, but the inside view of what marriage is like is far removed from the logical and legalistic
pronouncements of the earlier book. Take, for instance, this
passage:

> A young man to whom I had described as "pornographic"
> a novel that he much admired, replied with genuine
> bewilderment, "Pornographic? But how can it be? It treats
> the whole thing so seriously"—as if a long face were a
> sort of moral disinfectant. Our friends who harbour Dark
> Gods, the "pillar of blood" school, attempt seriously to
> restore something like the Phallic religion. Our
> advertisements, at their sexiest, paint the whole business in
> terms of the rapt, the intense, the swoony-devout;
> seldom a hint of gaiety. And the psychologists have so
> bedeviled us with the infinite importance of complete
> sexual adjustment and the all but impossibility of achieving
> it, that I could believe some young couples now go to it
> with the complete works of Freud, Krafft-Ebing,
> Havelock Ellis and Dr. Stopes spread out on bed-tables
> all round them.[30]

Or the bishops may have been offended by this passage:

> She [Venus] is a mocking, mischievous spirit, far more
> elf than deity, and makes game of us. When all external
> circumstances are fittest for her service she will leave one
> or both of the lovers totally indisposed for it. When
> every overt act is impossible and even glances cannot be

---

[30] *The Four Loves* (New York: Harcourt Brace Jovanovich, 1960,
1971), p. 113.

exchanged—in trains, in shops, and at interminable parties—she will assail them with all her force. An hour later, when time and place agree, she will have mysteriously withdrawn; perhaps from only one of them. What a pother this must raise—what resentments, self-pities, suspicions, wounded vanities and all the current chatter about "frustration"—in those who have deified her! But sensible lovers laugh. It is all part of the game; a game of catch-as-catch-can, and the escapes and tumbles and head-on collisions are to be treated as a romp.[31]

These two passages point toward the more relaxed way the book is written. In most of his theological books, Lewis assaults the reader with phalanxes of logic, supported on both flanks by illuminating analogies, often of the multipart kind. He is out to take the high ground and hold it. In his more imaginative works, like the space novels and Narnia, he infiltrates the imagination and shapes it to his ends. *The Four Loves,* so far as its style is concerned, is a humbler book. It smacks less of the Socratic Club and more of a casual conversation about serious but also merry matters.

The analogies, of course, are not lacking. They are as accurate as ever, but less dazzling; for example, he remarks: "As gin is not only a drink in itself but also a base for many mixed drinks, so Affection, besides being a love itself, can enter into the other loves and colour them all through and become the very medium in which from day to day they operate."[32] At times the humility of language reflects a real universality of experience. In discussing need-pleasures and how quickly the desire vanishes once the need has been met, he says: "If you will forgive me for citing the most extreme instances of all, have there not for most of us been moments (in a strange town) when the sight of the word GENTLEMEN over a door has roused a joy almost worthy of celebration in verse?"[33]

---

[31] Pp. 115–16.
[32] P. 45.
[33] P. 22.

The Four Loves states its subject by its title. Lewis points out that most languages are like English: they have a general word for love which can cover everything from fondness for a dog to the love of God. Nuances or subspecies of love require the use of additional words—in the case of English, affection, friendship, eros, and charity. But, Lewis argues, the fact that there is one word, love, that embraces all these shadings of meaning is an indication that the race finds a partial overlap among the four varieties of love.

The chapter on Affection has nothing very startling in it, but is winsome for the friendly picture it sketches of the humblest of the loves. Affection is nonjudgmental. The man patting a dog on the head, the dog curling up against him, the old-shoe relation of people who happen to live in the same rooming house and find a fondness growing despite all their differences in outlook—these are examples of Affection, the love that blossoms from propinquity.

Friendship, Lewis argues, arises when two people discover they have an interest in common. It may be Stone Age men discussing the niceties of the hunt, or Oxford dons debating a crux in philosophy. The thing that unites them is that their eyes are fixed on the same object. Sexual lovers stand face to face; friends stand side by side. In his discussion of friendship, Lewis speaks very clearly as an Oxford man, content to live in a male bastion. It seems very natural to him that friends are usually of the same sex. In an anthropological speculation about paleolithic man, he pictures the band of hunters as the matrix out of which male friendships grew:

> In early communities the co-operation of the males as
> hunters or fighters was no less necessary than the begetting
> and rearing of children. . . . Long before history began
> we men have got together apart from the women and
> done things. We had to. And to like doing what must be
> done is a characteristic that has survival value. We not
> only had to do the things, we had to talk about them.
> We had to plan the hunt and the battle. When they were
> over we had to hold a *post mortem* and draw conclusions

for future use. . . . In fact, we talked shop. We enjoyed
one another's society greatly: we Braves, we hunters,
all bound together by shared skill, shared dangers, and
hardships, esoteric jokes—away from the women and
children. As some wag has said, palaeolithic man may or
may not have had a club on his shoulder but he certainly
had a club of the other sort. . . .

What were the women doing meanwhile? How should
I know? I am a man and never spied on the mysteries
of the Bona Dea.[34]

The general tone of the chapter on Eros has already
been suggested by the quotations from it. The most striking
thing, compared to his earlier work, is the frank sensuality
and the emphasis on the rough-and-tumble aspects of sexual
love. If Lewis at one time was something of a prig, as one
suspects he was, he had traveled a long distance at this point,
and one must give much of the credit to Joy.

The final chapter, "Charity," is not only on spiritual
love (agape) but on the ways it brings all other loves into
relation, and indeed takes them into itself. This chapter is
full of seminal insights and nuances, as Lewis proclaims that
all merely human loves must be submitted to the ultimate
love and die before they can be reborn within Charity. He
refuses to base the primacy of Charity on prudential grounds.
He even contradicts St. Augustine, one of the strong influences on his theological thinking. Augustine (*Confessions*
IV, 10) warns against giving your heart to anyone except
God because, after all, human beings die. Lewis grants that
this is practical advice, but after admitting that the cautious
side of his nature is strongly moved by this wisdom, he goes
on to reject it:

When I respond to that appeal I seem to myself to be a
thousand miles away from Christ. If I am sure of anything
I am sure that His teaching was never meant to confirm
my congenital preference for safe investments and limited
liabilities. I doubt whether there is anything in me that

---

[34] Pp. 75–76.

pleases Him less. And who could conceivably begin to love
God on such a prudential ground—because the security
(so to speak) is better? . . . Eros, lawless Eros,
preferring the Beloved to happiness, is more like Love
Himself than this.[35]

The Four Loves, less glittering than many other Lewis
books, is also less intimidating. For the person interested in
Lewis the man as well as the thinker and writer, the book indirectly says much about the human evolution going on in
him during those few years between the wedding service in
the hospital and the last days of Joy.

Of all Lewis's books, the most nakedly personal is *A
Grief Observed,* so much so that he originally published it
under the pseudonym of N. W. Clerk. The origin of the book
was first, Joy's death from cancer, and second, Lewis's
attempt to cope with a continuing storm of grief and anguish
which had no parallel in his life, except possibly after the
death of his mother. But now the blow hit him in full adult-
hood and he found that the usual comforts had forsaken him.
When Charles Williams, his closest friend, died, Lewis sensed
Williams's continued life and vitality, and could celebrate as
well as mourn. No such comfort was available at Joy's death.
As an attempted sublimation, he took some old composition
books and tried to come to terms with his feelings by record-
ing his changing moods.

There is a kind of indecency in attempting a literary
analysis of such a book. It is feeling nakedly revealed in language stripped down and making no pretensions of elegance
or eloquence, though by its very directness it achieves, in
places, great power. The record he is setting down holds the
reader intently, waiting to see how one mood shifts to another.

In a way, *A Grief Observed* is Lewis's answer to his own
book, *The Problem of Pain.* He had made it clear enough in

---
[35] Pp. 137–38.

the latter that he was talking in theoretical terms, and that he would not stand up well against overwhelming affliction. His prophecy was accurate. He came very close to falling apart. For a time, his old certainties about the goodness of God forsook him, and he was torn between believing in no God and a sadist God.

A Grief Observed is its own commentary, and can best be discussed by quotations. Early in the book, Lewis writes about the absence of God:

> Meanwhile, where is God? This is one of the most disquieting symptoms. When you are happy, so happy that you have no sense of needing Him. . . . you will be— or so it feels—welcomed with open arms. But go to Him when your need is desperate, when all other help is vain, and what do you find? A door slammed in your face, and a sound of bolting and double bolting on the inside.[36]

Or perhaps God is not what he had thought:

> Not that I am (I think) in much danger of ceasing to believe in God. The real danger is of coming to believe such dreadful things about Him. The conclusion I dread is not "So there's no God after all," but "So this is what God's really like. Deceive yourself no longer."[37]

It is interesting at this point that he apparently did not seek comfort in the theoretical solutions that he had so carefully developed in *The Problem of Pain*. He might have laid all the blame on a sadistic devil, but did not. He might have blamed the disorders of the "neutral environment" but again he did not. At all times he suspects that God was the author of Joy's cancer and all the pain that ensued. He tries, not too successfully, to believe that the pain is the megaphone of God, and that God is the skilled and loving surgeon who heals by hurting. The memory of the pain is too real, and the good surgeon concept seems too farfetched.

---

[36] *A Grief Observed* (Greenwich, Conn.: Seabury Press, 1963), p. 9.
[37] Pp. 9–10.

There is a Job-like theme in the book, with accusations and questions directed to a God who insists on keeping silent. He seeks the consolations of religion: "Talk to me about the truth of religion and I'll listen gladly. Talk to me about the duty of religion and I'll listen submissively. But don't come talking to me about the consolations of religion or I shall suspect that you don't understand."[38]

Conceiving of God as possibly the divine surgeon (and apparently He does not believe in anesthesia) Lewis faces the terrible possibility that even death is not the end of the surgery:

> "Because she is in God's hands." But if so, she was in God's
> hands all the time, and I have seen what they did to her
> here. Do they suddenly become gentler to us the moment
> we are out of the body? And if so, why? If God's goodness
> is inconsistent with hurting us, then either God is not
> good or there is no God: for in the only life we know He
> hurts us beyond our worst fears and beyond all we can
> imagine. If it is consistent with hurting us, then He may
> hurt us after death as unendurably as before it.[39]

It has sometimes been said that in his books Lewis treats women as types. There is the whining domestic creature, the frustrated intellectual type, the earth mother. He does not give Joy this treatment. As I read the following quotation, I remember her and see how exactly he has caught her essence:

> What was H. not to me? She was my daughter and my
> mother, my pupil and my teacher, my subject and my
> sovereign; and always, holding all these in solution, my
> trusty comrade, friend, shipmate, fellow-soldier. My
> mistress; but at the same time all that any man friend (and
> I have good ones) has ever been to me. Perhaps more.
> If we had never fallen in love we should have none the less
> been always together, and created a scandal. That's

[38] P. 23.
[39] Pp. 24–25.

what I meant when I once praised her for her "masculine virtues."[40]

The literary Job reaches his fourth notebook and resolves that he will not buy a fifth one to continue what could be an endless diatribe against God. Then comes an experience which results in the renewal of his agonized mind. He writes:

> It was quite incredibly unemotional. Just the impression of her *mind* momentarily facing my own. Mind, not "soul" as we tend to think of soul. Certainly the reverse of what is called "soulful." Not at all like a rapturous re-union of lovers. Much more like getting a telephone call or a wire from her about some practical arrangement. Not that there was any "message"—just intelligence and attention. No sense of joy or sorrow. No love even, in our ordinary sense. No un-love. I had never in any mood imagined the dead as being so—well, so business-like. Yet there was an extreme and cheerful intimacy. An intimacy that had not passed through the senses or the emotions at all.[41]

The momentary sense of Joy's presence somehow breaks the evil spell that has held him captive, and he finds life returning, even though his questions have not really been answered. He is ready to accept the meaning of Joy's act on her deathbed when she turned to the chaplain and said, not to Lewis but to the chaplain, "I am at peace with God."[42]

Little more needs to be said. Lewis's experience is the common enough one of faith proving half illusion when the test comes, and then returning in a more modest way afterward. Lewis says of himself many of the things his enemies had said of him. But when we leave him on page sixty of *A Grief Observed,* he is on the road back to trust in God, and

---

40 P. 39.
41 Pp. 57–58.
42 P. 60.

willing to leave Joy in the hands of the God whose ultimate
goodness he has come once more to trust if not understand.[43]

---

[43] A number of Lewis's essays on religious matters are found in
miscellaneous collections of his work. The three most important are:
They Asked for a Paper (London: Geoffrey Bles, 1962); *Christian
Reflections* (Grand Rapids: Eerdmans, 1967); *God in the Dock*
(Grand Rapids: Eerdmans, 1970). Included in these collections are
such memorable essays as "Transposition," "The Weight of Glory,"
and "Is Theology Poetry?"

A BACKWARD
AND FORWARD LOOK

Lewis is not a temporary phenomenon. His fame leaped the Atlantic around the middle of World War II. Today, more than a third of a century after the American edition of *Screwtape,* the sales of his books are running higher than ever. Meanwhile, he has acquired whole new audiences, such as the children who read and reread the Chronicles of Narnia.

This is clearly no transient reputation. In particular, one cannot explain and discuss Lewis as a shallow religious popularizer. If he were merely that, equivalent apologists would have taken his place by now. His books are read by sophisticated atheists as well as the simply pious—and the sophisticated pious.

It is not hard to enumerate the assets that Lewis brought with him when he set out to be a writer. First of all, intelligence. His mind, sharpened by lifelong training, was formidable in its power and precision. One can disagree with him to the point of fury, but not condescend. Coupled with the superb mind was solid erudition. He was master of classical, medieval, and Renaissance literature, so much at home in it that he could make use of its symbols and themes with unconscious ease and grace. Greek and Roman mythology and the legends of the Celts and Germanic peoples were as much a part of his literary frame of reference as the Bible. His

243

books grew out of the collective memory of Western mankind.

Lewis brought to traditional mythology as much as he took from it. His vivid imagination could transport his mind to the floating islands of a distant planet, and from there he would evolve the story of Paradise Retained. This absolute clarity of visual imagination is one of the main appeals of his more fantastic books. Anyone reading, say, *The Lion, the Witch and the Wardrobe* is given so distinct a picture of Aslan's death that he could reproduce the scene on canvas with photographic detail.

Lewis's intelligence and his imagination, taken together, are more than equal to the sum of the parts. In his fantasies one always senses barely beneath the surface a powerful mind controlling the movement of events. In the expository and argumentative books, when the tools of logic are at full strength, there are sudden epiphanies of "Joy," so that the rules of reason are sweetened by fragrances from a different land.

Lewis brought another asset to his writing. Conviction. There is something impressive and moving about a writer who genuinely believes in the world view he presents. Lewis's adult Christianity was not for him an optional frame of reference. It was the core of his being. If he had lived in a country where martyrs still perish, he would have suffered the flames and never recanted. This can be called fanaticism, but so can every ultimate commitment. The content of Lewis's conviction—traditional Christianity—may seem to many readers a misplaced loyalty, but when it is encountered as transmitted through his mind, it cannot be dismissed as superficial. And in ways his readers may not consciously recognize, it gives strength to all that he wrote.

No matter what great use he makes of pagan mythology, Lewis's central symbol system is biblical. The pagan gods must fit themselves into Jehovah's universe. It is easy to observe how, about the time he wrote *The Pilgrim's Regress,* he had come to view all experiences through the eyes of the

Christian faith and to express them through its symbols. The advantage of a traditional symbol is that it is always rooted in the eternal archetypes. Lewis's older contemporary, William Butler Yeats, regretfully found he could not believe in Christian doctrine, and as a substitute devised his own mythology and metaphysics, writing his book *A Vision* to explain it. His system worked well for his own creative imagination, giving him "metaphors for poetry," but most readers find something contrived about it. It does not resonate in the same way that Lewis's symbols do. From a purely literary point of view, the most fortunate thing that ever happened to Lewis was his embrace of Christianity in his early thirties.

Finally, to conclude this inventory of assets, there is Lewis's style. It can be seen evolving from two sources in his boyhood writing. There is first of all the "Boxen" style—brisk and businesslike, not poetic, but capable of irony and wit. The other source is represented by "Bleheris," with its euphuistic delight in fancy language and flowery turns of phrase. From the marriage of the two styles came the remarkably flexible and gracious style we have examined in a number of contexts. It is straight to the point, lean, free of inflated language and the technical jargon of the professions. At the same time, thanks particularly to the use of exact metaphors, it is capable of modulating into highly poetic effects—more poetic, in fact, than most of Lewis's verse. It is a modest style, summoning the reader to go beyond the exact words and to retain in his memory not the words but what they point to.

The question now is twofold. First, what is distinct and individual about Lewis's books, and secondly, how high a rank did he achieve as a writer? Will he be read for pleasure and profit a hundred years from now? Five hundred? All his books or only some?

Lewis's career as a published author began with two books of poetry, *Spirits in Bondage* and *Dymer*. He subsequently relegated verse to a corner of his life, making no serious attempt to bring out further books of poetry. Only after his death were two additional collections published.

His short poems frequently attempt to do in verse what he learned to accomplish equally well in prose. More problematical are the long narrative poems. *Dymer* is hopelessly confused and confusing, though with sections of brilliant writing. When it is compared with *The Queen of Drum,* the progress Lewis had made in a few years is startling. He was very close to becoming the modern Chaucer, though less tolerant of the foibles of daily existence. He backed away— perhaps as much because of public indifference as anything else.

One postscript on his poetry. It is strongly visual, turned outward, objective, far removed from the confessional tradition as represented, say, by Robert Lowell and Sylvia Plath. Such objectivity, though Homer would have understood it, is rare in modern poetry and not greatly in demand. All Lewis's qualities, handicaps today, could become assets if some vast psychic shift, a movement from subjectivity to objectivity, realigned the landscape of poetry. Lewis's verse, including the short poems, might suddenly speak with a much stronger voice. But no signs of such a psychic mutation are visible.

I come now to his achievements as a literary scholar. Such work is rather like scientific research. When a new theory is established, the monograph in which the theory was first stated becomes less essential. Good literary scholarship is absorbed into ongoing research. Sometimes, of course, the original, classical statement of new literary insights may continue to be read because it is well written and historically important. One can foresee such a future for Lewis's two major works in criticism and literary history: *The Allegory of Love* and the sixteenth-century volume (exclusive of dramatists) of *The Oxford History of English Literature.* In a more specialized way, Lewis's studies of Milton and Spenser will continue to be useful handbooks, and *An Experiment in Criticism* will long remain a valuable challenge to more conventional theories of literary criticism.

Lewis was as much out of step in his criticism as in his poetry. At times, it is true, he talks like a New Critic, empha-

sizing the need to concentrate on the text itself and not become bogged down in biographical and historical details. But
he seldom undertakes minute *explications de texte.* He also
shows little interest in other modern critical approaches,
such as the psychological or the archetypal. He is that type
of scholar least in fashion—the appreciative critic, whose
great gift is to whet a reader's appetite for a particular book
and to give him just enough practical guidance so he can
find his way through it.

Few major reputations are based solely on criticism and
literary history. Stubbornly and perhaps rightly, readers think
of writing about writing as a secondary thing. There is nothing secondary about the next category of Lewis's books—
those dealing directly with religion, metaphysics, and ethics.
The continuing popularity of these works, particularly *Mere
Christianity,* is emphatic evidence that they speak to listening
ears.

Perhaps part of the secret has been explored by Lewis
in his doctrine of "great nouns" as contrasted with the "adjectival" role of mere literature ("Christianity and Literature," in *Rehabilitations*). The overpowering effect of a book
like *Mere Christianity* reflects the way it transcends itself and
its author. The uncanny literary skill moves the reader's
thoughts beyond the gleaming metaphors and directs them
to concepts and hopes that leave language behind. It is as
though all the brilliant writing is designed to create clear
windows of perception, so that the reader will look *through*
the language and not *at* it. It is a kind of kenosis. Lewis with-
draws himself so that he will not distract the reader from
that which is visible through the clear panes of the writing.
Any literary critic determined to concentrate on purely literary considerations constantly finds himself analyzing and
debating Lewis's *ideas* and has to struggle against recalcitrant
forces if he wants to keep his analysis on purely literary
tracks.

Another source of power is Lewis's ability to use Aristotle's tools to maximum effect. Here a hypothetical shadow

hangs over these books. Only the future will tell whether this kind of logic will continue to seem as much a part of the structure of the universe as it has long appeared to Western man. Ways of thought from the Far East—where Aristotle is a recent arrival—call into question traditional assumptions. Within the framework of Western philosophy other doubting questions are being raised. Some vast shift in sensibility, with a new kind of logic, may arise, negating at one stroke Lewis's careful lines of reasoning. This would not necessarily mean that his argumentative books would lose all appeal. They might come to be enjoyed more as "poetry" than as "prose," as literature rather than as ideas, and the great nouns would yield to adjectival delights. As Lewis pointed out in *The Discarded Image,* the poetic mind can still respond to medieval cosmology, though few schools of astronomy require their students to master it.

The solid core of Lewis's achievement, however, consists of those more imaginative and mythological books in which his ability as a writer and his sensibility as a Christian are fruitfully wedded. These books are the space trilogy and Narnia, together with *The Pilgrim's Regress, The Screwtape Letters,* and *The Great Divorce.* (*Till We Have Faces* is a special case, to be discussed later.) In these books he puts to work every talent he possesses and raises to a high literary level the serious fantasy. The schism between logic and romance is healed, and myth, fact, and truth are revealed as mere interim categories.

Lewis is not the first writer to attempt serious fantasy, but he is one of the most powerful, haunting, and successful. Endowed with a tremendously effective visual imagination, he creates other worlds, including that supernatural realm where Maleldil reigns supreme, to set in juxtaposition with our familiar Tellus. He makes of this genre a means of dramatizing the human condition and posing the everlasting questions. He converts fantasy into a presentation of philosophic and theological insights. In so doing, he states a major question for literary critics, whose trade is analysis and evaluation: Can a book of one genre be usefully compared with one in another genre? Does it lead anywhere if you compare a sonnet and a haiku? An epic and a lyric? Grant for the sake of argument that *Perelandra* is as great an achievement of its kind as *King Lear* is of its kind, does it follow that the two works have equal standing in that select bookshelf displaying supreme literary achievements?

In theory, such could be the case. (Perhaps Dante achieved this triumph in his serious fantasy, *The Divine Comedy*.) But does Lewis accomplish this? Assume again that from a purely literary viewpoint *Lear* and *Perelandra* are literarily equal. But they are not humanly equal. The most lasting literature seems to tell us important and profound things about what it is to be a human being. Lewis's fantasies deal more with representative types—the Christian quester, the whining mother, the cosmic egoist. We are rarely permitted a glimpse into those churning depths where the individual and individualized soul finds and explores its confused destiny. In theory, Lewis could explore these depths and stand beside Shakespeare. But there would be loss as well as gain; the pageantlike quality of his tales would lose their clarity; fantasy would evolve into something closer to the realistic novel. With his love of mythology and his unerring visual imagination, Lewis was wise to stick to his last and exploit his special strength and gift.

What does he do for us in his fantasies? He creates new worlds, and in creating them he sets Tellus in sharper relief. We see it almost for the first time as we compare it with Narnia, Mars, or Venus. *Mere Christianity* may become less compelling if the canons of logic change, but this would not cancel out the imaginative reality of Lewis's worlds. Time cannot destroy them. We now know that Venus has a temperature of 900° Fahrenheit, and that Mars is a nightmare of desert and monstrous volcanoes. No matter. Any reader of Lewis, by the magic of his vision, explores not the spheres of the astronomers, but the planets of the restless spirit. Meanwhile, he comes to understand his own provincial planet more precisely because it is not the only theater of Maleldil's cosmic drama. Lewis's particular way of relating imaginary worlds to our empirical world—through theology and mythology as well as actual voyages back and forth—is distinctive and gives him a central claim to being master of this literary form.

In *The Pilgrim's Regress* we explore a parallel world of the spirit which illuminates the familiar world that cameras can photograph. In *The Great Divorce* the gray town, familiar here and now to us earthlings, is seen in contrast to the borderlands of heaven. In *The Screwtape Letters* we behold our world through demonic eyes and understand better each passing moment.

At any rate, these three books plus the trilogy and Narnia constitute the most distinctive achievements of Lewis's visionary mind. They shape the reader's consciousness to entertain thoughts of a dynamic cosmos in which supernatural dramas are acted out. These books take their places as a subdivision of the great mythologies that have supplied meaning to so many civilizations. Lewis is a myth adapter and a myth maker, expressing his mythology through the pageants enacted first in the theater of his own imagination and then on the stage of the reader's mind.

I have so far said nothing about *Till We Have Faces.* Its differences from the fantasies are much more striking than the similarities. True, mythology plays a key role, but not the same role. The Venus symbolized by blood-stained Ungit is more like a psychological or spiritual force surging inside the individual than the gloriously objective Venus of *Perelandra* and *That Hideous Strength.* In *Till We Have Faces,* Lewis turns to traditional mythology as a way of saying something about those depths of heart and soul that he had previously left alone. This book is not a fantasy. It is a realistic novel. It is closer in insight to Dostoevsky than to the ancient myth of Cupid and Psyche from which the narrative springs. If Lewis had lived longer, he might have explored these depths further. It is another "might have been."

As it is, the fantasies must be the centerpiece of his achievement. It is easy to point out their occasional defects and limitations. There is sometimes the playing for cheap effects as in the dunking of Weston, and some details of the N.I.C.E.'s downfall. Certain of the characters are close to straw men. The narrative is often interrupted by editorializing and sermonizing. But how petty this list seems. The clarity and majesty of Lewis's vision, and the literary skill with which he expressed it, engulf the minor defects.

Lewis fits so oddly in our accustomed literary categories that it will be a long time before we can see him in proper perspective. But as we meanwhile read him, our spontaneous responses tell us much. In a world where the sacred groves are being felled to make way for airports, he conjures into existence other worlds corresponding to the intuitions of mankind's mythological dreams. Choosing not to seek originality, he produces some of the most original books of the century. In him is combined the sophistication of an Oxford don and the primal intuitions of a shaman. The roots of his vision lie in the unconscious mind where we are still one with the caveman painting sacred pictures on the wall. Thus Lewis, far from being an escapist, is a writer who renews our contact with the ever-present but often ignored sources of our psychic life. His visionary books are destined to survive, as much in our collective memories as in the footnotes we dutifully add.

BIBLIOGRAPHY

A useful bibliography of writings by C. S. Lewis, listing his articles, book reviews, prefaces, etc., as well as books, is included in Jocelyn Gibb, ed., *Light on C. S. Lewis,* 1965. This bibliography is updated in *The Joyful Christian,* 1977 (books only). For books and articles *about* Lewis, see Joe R. Christopher and Joan K. Ostling, eds., *C. S. Lewis: An Annotated Checklist of Writings About Him and His Works,* 1974. The annual MLA *Bibliography* also supplies both types of information.

The first bibliography given below is restricted to Lewis's books and omits some of the minor collections of his work. The second consists of the principal books dealing entirely or in large part with Lewis.

When American paperback editions are available, these are indicated as well as the original hardcover editions. Most citations in this book are from American paperback editions.

1. BOOKS BY C. S. LEWIS

The Abolition of Man: Reflections on Education with Special Reference to the Teaching of English in the Upper Forms of Schools
    London: Oxford University Press, 1943.
    London: Geoffrey Bles, 1946.
    New York: Macmillan, 1947.
    New York: Macmillan, Macmillan Paperbacks, 1965.
The Allegory of Love: A Study in Medieval Tradition
    London: Oxford University Press, 1936, 1938.
    New York: Oxford University Press, Galaxy Books, 1958.
Beyond Personality: The Christian Idea of God
    London: Geoffrey Bles, 1944.
    New York: Macmillan, 1945.
Broadcast Talks. (In America, *The Case for Christianity*)
    London: Geoffrey Bles, 1942.
The Case for Christianity. (In England, *Broadcast Talks*)
    New York: Macmillan, 1943.

BIBLIOGRAPHY

Christian Behaviour: A Further Series of Broadcast Talks
    London: Geoffrey Bles, 1943.
    New York: Macmillan, 1943.
Christian Reflections. Edited by Walter Hooper
    Grand Rapids: W. B. Eerdmans, 1967.
The Dark Tower and Other Stories. Edited, and with a Preface,
    by Walter Hooper
    London: Collins, 1977.
    New York: Harcourt Brace Jovanovich, 1977.
    New York: Harcourt Brace Jovanovich, A Harvest/HBJ
    Book, 1977.
The Discarded Image: An Introduction to Medieval and Renais-
    sance Literature
    Cambridge: Cambridge University Press, 1964.
Dymer
    London: J. M. Dent, 1926; published under the pseud-
    onym of Clive Hamilton.
    New York: E. P. Dutton, 1926.
    New York: Macmillan, 1950 (with new Preface).
English Literature in the Sixteenth Century, Excluding Drama
    Oxford: Clarendon Press, 1954.
    London: Oxford University Press, Oxford Paperbacks,
    1973.
An Experiment in Criticism
    Cambridge: Cambridge University Press, 1961.
The Four Loves
    London: Geoffrey Bles, 1960.
    New York: Harcourt Brace Jovanovich, 1960.
    New York: Harcourt Brace Jovanovich, A Harvest/HBJ
    Book, 1971.
God in the Dock: Essays in Theology and Ethics. Edited, with a
    Preface, by Walter Hooper
    London: Geoffrey Bles, 1970; published as *Undeceptions.*
    Grand Rapids: W. B. Eerdmans, 1970.
The Great Divorce
    London: Geoffrey Bles, 1945.
    New York: Macmillan, 1946.
    New York: Macmillan, Macmillan Paperbacks, 1963.

BIBLIOGRAPHY

A Grief Observed
> London: Faber and Faber Limited, 1961. Published under the pseudonym of N. W. Clerk.
> New York: The Seabury Press, 1963. Published under the pseudonym of N. W. Clerk.
> New York: Bantam Books, 1976. Published under the name C. S. Lewis, with an Afterword by Chad Walsh.

The Horse and His Boy. Illustrated by Pauline Baynes
> London: Geoffrey Bles, 1954.
> New York: Macmillan, 1954.
> New York: Macmillan, Collier Books, 1970.

The Joyful Christian: 128 Readings from C. S. Lewis
> New York: Macmillan, 1977.

The Last Battle. Illustrated by Pauline Baynes
> London: The Bodley Head, 1956.
> New York: Macmillan, 1956.
> New York: Macmillan, Collier Books, 1970.

Letters of C. S. Lewis. Edited, with a Memoir, by W. H. Lewis
> London: Geoffrey Bles, 1975.
> New York: Harcourt Brace Jovanovich, 1975.
> New York: Harcourt Brace Jovanovich, A Harvest/HBJ Book, 1975.

Letters to an American Lady. Edited by Clyde Kilby
> Grand Rapids: W. B. Eerdmans, 1967.
> New York: Pyramid, 1971.

Letters to Malcolm: Chiefly on Prayer
> London: Geoffrey Bles, 1964.
> New York: Harcourt Brace Jovanovich, 1964.
> New York: Harcourt Brace Jovanovich, A Harvest/HBJ Book, 1973.

The Lion, the Witch and the Wardrobe. Illustrated by Pauline Baynes
> London: Geoffrey Bles, 1950.
> New York: Macmillan, Collier Books, 1970.
> New York: Macmillan. 1950.

The Magician's Nephew. Illustrated by Pauline Baynes
> London: The Bodley Head, 1955.
> New York: Macmillan, 1955.
> New York: Macmillan, Collier Books, 1970.

Mere Christianity. A revised and enlarged edition, with a new introduction, of the three books, *The Case for Christianity* —in England, *Broadcast Talks*—(London: Geoffrey Bles, 1942; New York: Macmillan, 1943), *Christian Behavior* (London: Geoffrey Bles, 1943; New York: Macmillan, 1943), and *Beyond Personality* (London: Geoffrey Bles, 1944; New York: Macmillan, 1945)

London: Geoffrey Bles, 1952.

New York: Macmillan, 1952.

New York: Macmillan, Macmillan Paperbacks, 1960.

A Mind Awake: Anthology of C. S. Lewis. Edited by Clyde S. Kilby

New York: Harcourt Brace Jovanovich, 1968.

Miracles: A Preliminary Study

London: Geoffrey Bles, 1947.

New York: Macmillan, 1947.

London: Collins, Collins Fontana Books, 1960 (revised edition).

New York: Macmillan, Macmillan Paperbacks, 1963.

Narrative Poems. Edited by Walter Hooper

London: Geoffrey Bles, 1969.

New York: Harcourt Brace Jovanovich, 1972.

New York: Harcourt Brace Jovanovich, A Harvest/HBJ Book, 1979.

Of Other Worlds: Essays and Stories. Edited, with a Preface, by Walter Hooper

New York: Harcourt Brace Jovanovich, 1966.

New York: Harcourt Brace Jovanovich, A Harvest/HBJ Book, 1975.

Out of the Silent Planet

London: John Lane, 1938.

New York: Macmillan, 1943.

New York: Macmillan, Macmillan Paperbacks, 1965.

Perelandra

London: John Lane, 1943.

New York: Macmillan, 1944.

New York: Macmillan, Macmillan Paperbacks, 1965.

The Personal Heresy: A Controversy (with E. M. W. Tillyard)

London, Oxford, Toronto: Oxford University Press, 1939.

London: Oxford University Press, Oxford Paperbacks,
    1965.

*The Pilgrim's Regress: An Allegorical Apology for Christianity,
Reason, and Romanticism*
    London: J. M. Dent, 1933.
    New York: Sheed and Ward, 1935.
    With the author's important new Preface on Romanticism,
    footnotes, and running headlines.
    London: Geoffrey Bles, 1943.
    New York: Sheed and Ward, 1944.
    Grand Rapids: W. B. Eerdmans, 1958.

Poems. Edited by Walter Hooper
    London: Geoffrey Bles, 1964.
    New York: Harcourt Brace Jovanovich, 1965.
    New York: Harcourt Brace Jovanovich, A Harvest/HBJ
      Book, 1977.

A Preface to "Paradise Lost"
    London, New York, Toronto: Oxford University Press,
    1942.

Prince Caspian. Illustrated by Pauline Baynes
    London: Geoffrey Bles, 1951.
    New York: Macmillan, 1951.
    New York: Macmillan, Collier Books, 1970.

The Problem of Pain
    London: Geoffrey Bles, 1940.
    New York: Macmillan, 1943, 1977.
    New York: Macmillan, Macmillan Paperbacks, 1962.

Reflections on the Psalms
    London: Geoffrey Bles, 1958.
    New York: Harcourt Brace Jovanovich, 1958.
    New York: Harcourt Brace Jovanovich, A Harvest/HBJ
      Book, 1964.

Rehabilitations and Other Essays
    Oxford, London: Oxford University Press, 1939.
    Norwood, Pa.: Norwood Editions, 1977.

The Screwtape Letters
    London: Geoffrey Bles, 1942.
    New York: Macmillan, 1943.
    New York: Macmillan, Macmillan Paperbacks, 1959.

The Screwtape Letters, with Screwtape Proposes a Toast. With a
new and additional Preface
London: Geoffrey Bles, 1961.
New York: Macmillan, 1961.
New York: Macmillan, Macmillan Paperbacks, 1962.

Selected Literary Essays
Cambridge, London: Cambridge University Press, 1969.

The Silver Chair. Illustrated by Pauline Baynes
London: Geoffrey Bles, 1953.
New York: Macmillan, 1953.
New York: Macmillan, Collier Books, 1970.

Spenser's Images of Life. Edited by Alastair Fowler
Cambridge, London: Cambridge University Press, 1967.

Spirits in Bondage: A Cycle of Lyrics
(Under the pseudonym of Clive Hamilton)
London: William Heinemann, 1919.
Ann Arbor: University Microfilms
International (Xerox copies available on demand)

Studies in Medieval and Renaissance Literature. Collected by
Walter Hooper
Cambridge: Cambridge University Press, 1966.

Studies in Words
Cambridge: Cambridge University Press, 1960; second
(enlarged) edition, 1966.

Surprised by Joy: The Shape of My Early Life
London: Geoffrey Bles, 1955.
New York: Harcourt Brace Jovanovich, 1956.
New York: Harcourt Brace Jovanovich, A Harvest/HBJ
Book, 1966.

That Hideous Strength
London: John Lane, 1945.
New York: Macmillan, 1946.
New York: Macmillan, Macmillan Paperbacks, 1965.

They Asked for a Paper
London: Geoffrey Bles, 1962.

Till We Have Faces: A Myth Retold
London: Geoffrey Bles, 1956.
New York: Harcourt Brace Jovanovich, 1957.
Grand Rapids: William B. Eerdmans Paperback, 1966.

Transposition. See *The Weight of Glory*

Undeceptions. See *God in the Dock*

The Voyage of the "Dawn Treader." Illustrated by Pauline Baynes
 London: Geoffrey Bles, 1952.
 New York: Macmillan, 1952.
 New York: Macmillan, Collier Books, 1970.

The Weight of Glory and Other Addresses
 London: Geoffrey Bles, 1949; published as *Transposition and Other Addresses.*
 New York: Macmillan, 1949.
 Grand Rapids: W. B. Eerdmans, 1965.

The World's Last Night and Other Essays
 New York: Harcourt Brace Jovanovich, 1960.
 New York: Harcourt Brace Jovanovich, A Harvest/HBJ Book, 1973.

2. BOOKS ABOUT C. S. LEWIS

Arnott, Anne. *The Secret Country of C. S. Lewis.* Illustrated by Patricia Frost. Grand Rapids: W. B. Eerdmans, 1975.

Carnell, Corbin Scott. *Bright Shadow of Reality: C. S. Lewis and the Feeling Intellect.* Grand Rapids: W. B. Eerdmans, 1974.

Carpenter, Humphrey. *The Inklings.* London: Allen & Unwin, 1978.

Christopher, Joe R., and Ostling, Joan K. *C. S. Lewis: An Annotated Checklist of Writings About Him and His Works.* Kent, Ohio: Kent State University Press, 1974.

Como, James, ed. *"C. S. Lewis at the Breakfast Table" and Other Recollections.* New York: Macmillan, 1979.

Cunningham, Richard B. *C. S. Lewis: Defender of the Faith.* Philadelphia: Westminster Press, 1967.

Gibb, Jocelyn, ed. *Light on C. S. Lewis.* Essays by Owen Barfield, Austin Farrer, J. A. W. Bennett, Nevill Coghill, John Lawlor, Stella Gibbons, Kathleen Raine, Chad Walsh, Walter Hooper. London: Geoffrey Bles, 1965. New York: Harcourt, Brace & World, 1965, and Harcourt Brace Jovanovich, A Harvest/HBJ Book, 1976.

Gilbert, Douglas and Kilby, Clyde S. *C. S. Lewis: Images of His World.* London: Hodder & Stoughton, 1973. Grand Rapids: W. B. Eerdmans, 1973, and Eerdmans Paperback, 1975.

Green, Roger Lancelyn, and Hooper, Walter. *C. S. Lewis: A Biography.* London: Collins, 1974. New York: Harcourt Brace Jovanovich, 1974. New York: Harcourt Brace Jovanovich, A Harvest/HBJ Book, 1976.

Hillegas, Mark R., ed. *Shadows of Imagination: The Fantasies of C. S. Lewis, J. R. R. Tolkien, and Charles Williams.* London and Amsterdam: Feffer & Simons, 1969. Carbondale and Edwardsville: Southern Illinois University Press, 1969.

Holmer, Paul L., *C. S. Lewis: The Shape of His Faith and Thought.* New York: Harper & Row, 1976.

Huttar, Charles, ed. *Imagination and the Spirit: Essays in Literature and the Christian Faith Presented to Clyde S. Kilby.* Grand Rapids: W. B. Eerdmans, 1971.

Keefe, Carolyn, ed. *C. S. Lewis: Speaker and Teacher.* Foreword by Thomas Howard. Grand Rapids: Zondervan, 1971. London: Hodder & Stoughton Paperback, 1974.

Kilby, Clyde S. *The Christian World of C. S. Lewis.* Grand Rapids: W. B. Eerdmans, 1964.

———. *Images of Salvation in the Fiction of C. S. Lewis.* Wheaton, Ill.: Harold Shaw, 1978.

Kreeft, Peter. *C. S. Lewis: A Critical Essay.* Grand Rapids: W. B. Eerdmans Paperback, 1969.

Lindskoog, Kathryn Ann. *C. S. Lewis: Mere Christian.* Foreword by Clyde S. Kilby. Glendale, Ca.: G/L Publications, 1973.

———. *The Lion of Judah in Never-Never Land: The Theology of C. S. Lewis Expressed in His Fantasies for Children.* With a Preface by Walter Hooper. Grand Rapids: W. B. Eerdmans, 1973.

Meilaender, Gilbert. *The Taste for the Other: The Social and Ethical Thought of C. S. Lewis.* Grand Rapids: W. B. Eerdmans, 1978.

Montgomery, John Warwick, ed. *Myth, Allegory, and Gospel: An Interpretation of J. R. R. Tolkien, C. S. Lewis, G. K. Chesterton, Charles Williams.* Essays by Edmund Fuller, Clyde S. Kilby, Russell Kirk, John W. Montgomery, and Chad Walsh. Minneapolis: Bethany Fellowship, Inc., 1974.

Purtill, Richard. *Lord of the Elves and Eldils: Fantasy and Philosophy in C. S. Lewis and J. R. R. Tolkien.* Grand Rapids: Zondervan Paperback, 1974.

Reilly, R. J. *Romantic Religion: A Study of Barfield, Lewis, Wil-*

liams, and Tolkien. Athens, Ga.: University of Georgia
Press, 1971.

Schakel, Peter, Jr., ed. *The Longing for a Form: Essays on the
Fiction of C. S. Lewis.* Kent, Ohio: Kent State University
Press, 1977.

Urang, Gunnar. *Shadows of Heaven: Religion and Fantasy in
the Writing of C. S. Lewis, Charles Williams, and J. R. R.
Tolkien.* London: Student Christian Movement Press, 1971.
Philadelphia: Pilgrim Press, 1971.

Vanauken, Sheldon. *A Severe Mercy.* London: Hodder & Stoughton, 1977. San Francisco and New York: Harper & Row,
1977.

Walsh, Chad. *C. S. Lewis: Apostle to the Skeptics.* New York:
Macmillan, 1949. Folcraft, Pa.: Folcraft Library Editions,
1974.

White, Luther. *The Image of Man in C. S. Lewis.* Nashville and
New York: Abingdon Press, 1969. London: Hodder &
Stoughton, 1970.

ACKNOWLEDGMENTS AND COPYRIGHTS

1972, 1975 by Alfred Cecil Harwood and Arthur Owen Barfield; C. S. Lewis, *The Last Battle,* © C. S. Lewis 1956; C. S. Lewis, *The Lion, the Witch and the Wardrobe,* copyright 1950 by Macmillan Publishing Co., Inc., renewed 1978 by Arthur Owen Barfield; C. S. Lewis, *The Magician's Nephew,* copyright 1955 by C. S. Lewis; C. S. Lewis, *Miracles,* copyright 1947 by Macmillan Publishing Co., Inc., renewed 1975 by Alfred Cecil Harwood and Arthur Owen Barfield; C. S. Lewis, *Out of the Silent Planet,* published in the United States by Macmillan Publishing Co., Inc., 1943; C. S. Lewis, *The Problem of Pain,* published in the United States by Macmillan Publishing Co., Inc., 1943; C. S. Lewis, *That Hideous Strength,* copyright 1945, 1946 by C. S. Lewis, renewed 1973, 1974 by Alfred Cecil Harwood and Arthur Owen Barfield.

Oxford University Press, for excerpts from C. S. Lewis, *The Allegory of Love,* 1936; *The Personal Heresy,* 1939; *A Preface to "Paradise Lost,"* 1942; and *Rehabilitations and Other Essays,* 1939.

Ruth Pitter, for excerpts from an unpublished memo on the poetry of C. S. Lewis.

Seabury Press, for excerpts from C. S. Lewis, *A Grief Observed.*

Trustees of the Estate of C. S. Lewis, for excerpts from C. S. Lewis, *Spirits in Bondage* (published under the pseudonym of Clive Hamilton) and from unpublished works of C. S. Lewis and Joy Davidman Lewis, all copyrighted by the Trustees of the Estate of C. S. Lewis.

INDEX

Italicized numbers indicate the principal discussion of a book.

Abolition of Man, The (Lewis), 12, 40, 114, *210–13*

All Hallows' Eve (Williams), 10

Allegory, 60, 132

Allegory of Love, The (Lewis), *179–81*, 246

Analogy, 203–06, 212, 215–16, 234; *see also* Metaphor

Apologetics, 202–09

Apuleius, *Golden Ass, The,* 12 159–61

Aquinas, 30

Archetype, 46, 108, 138, 195, 198, 216, 247, 251

Aristotle, 247–48

Art of Love (Ovid), 180

Arthurian legend, 12, 49–50, 112–22

Augustine, 236–37

Babbitt, Irving, 68

Babel, Tower of, 109, 116

Barfield, Owen, 13–14, 227; chapter in *Light on C. S. Lewis,* 8

Bible, 244–45

Blake, William, 12, 70

"Bleheris," 126–28, 245

"Boxen," 123–26, 245

Brave New World (Huxley), 45

Bunyan, Paul, 12; *The Pilgrim's Progress,* 62, 69

Chaucer, 14, 59–60, 180, 246; *Troilus and Criseyde,* 43

Chesterton, G. K., 13

Childhood's End (Clarke), 83

Chrétien de Troyes, 180

Christian World of C. S. Lewis, The (Kilby), 130

INDEX

"Christianity and Literature"
(Lewis), 247
Clarke, Arthur, *Childhood's End*,
83
*Confessions of a Well-Meaning
Woman* (McKenna), 21
Content, *see* Theme
Cosmology, 193–94
Criterion, The, 61
Criticism, literary, 246–47
*C. S. Lewis: Apostle to the
Skeptics* (Walsh), ix
C. S. Lewis: A Biography (Green
and Hooper), 3 fn.
Cupid and Psyche, 159–61, 250

Dante, 12, 186; *The Divine
Comedy,* 69, 80, 249
Dark Tower, The (Lewis),
96–98
Davidman, Helen Joy, 10, 224–
25, 231–34
Demonic powers, 100–10, 250
Descent into Hell (Williams),
172
Discarded Image, The (Lewis),
193–94, 248
Divine Comedy, The (Dante),
69–70, 80, 249
Dostoevsky, Feodor, 250
Dream vision, 60–69
Dymer (Lewis under pseudonym
of Clive Hamilton), 35,
43–49, 50–51, 245–46

Eddison, E. R., *The Worm
Ouroboros,* 12–13
Either/or argument, 205–06
Eliot, T. S., 55–56, 68
*English Literature in the Six-
teenth Century, Excluding
Drama* (Lewis), *186–89,* 246

Epic, 185
Epistolary form, 21–22, 31–32
Experiment in Criticism, An
(Lewis), 191–93, 246

Faerie Queene, The (Spenser),
180, 194–96
Fantasy, 11–12, 120, 244, 248–
51
Form, *see* Theme and form
Four Loves, The (Lewis),
232–37
Freud, Sigmund, 46, 61, 198

Genre, 248–49
Golden Ass, The (Apuleius),
159–61
Grahame, Kenneth, 12
Great Divorce, The (Lewis),
12, 23, 30–31, 60, *69–81,* 248,
250
Green, Roger Lancelyn, *C. S.
Lewis: A Biography* (with
Walter Hooper), 3 fn.; *The
Wood That Time Forgot,*
129–30
Greeves, Arthur, 227
Gresham, David Lindsay, 14–15
Gresham, Helen Joy Davidman,
see Davidman, Helen Joy
Grief Observed, A (Lewis),
237–41

Haggard, Rider, 11
History, literary, 246–47
Homer, 246
Hooper, Walter, xi, 49, 51, 53;
C. S. Lewis: A Biography
(with Roger Lancelyn Green),
3 fn.

Humanists, 61
Huxley, Aldous, *Brave New World,* 45

Imagination, 14, 59–60, 85, 94, 109, 129, 201, 248–50
Inklings, 10–11
Intelligence, 243–44

"Joy," 60, 128, 165–66, 230
Jung, Carl, 195, 198
Juvenilia, *123–28*

Keats, John, 50
Kilby, Clyde S., xi; *The Christian World of C. S. Lewis,* 130
Kirkpatrick, W. T., 4–5

Last and First Men (Stapledon), 83
Last Battle, The (Lewis), 147–57
Launcelot (Lewis), *49–51*
Lawrence, D. H., 61
Letters from Hell (Thisted), 21
Letters of C. S. Lewis, 226–29
Letters to an American Lady (Lewis), *225–26*
Letters to Malcolm (Lewis), *224–25*
Lewis, Helen Joy Davidman, *see* Davidman, Helen Joy
Lewis, Warren Hamilton, 8; Ed., *Letters of C. S. Lewis,* 226
Light on C. S. Lewis (various authors), 8
Lindsay, David, *Voyage to Arcturus,* 12, 21, 84
Lion, the Witch and the Wardrobe, The (Lewis), 123, *138–47*

Literary criticism, attitude toward, 190–93
Logic, *see* Reason
Longing for a Form (Schakel, ed.), ix fn.
Love, 29–30, 76, 232–37
Lowell, Robert, 246

MacDonald, George, *Phantastes,* 12
Maeterlinck, Maurice, 45
Magic, 133–34, 144
Magician's Nephew, The (Lewis), 132–38
Malory, Thomas, 50
Marriage, 117, 230–34
McKenna, Stephen, *Confessions of a Well-Meaning Woman,* 21
Mere Christianity (Lewis), 12 30–31, *201–09,* 233
Meredith, George, 12
Metaphor, 36, 48; *see also* Analogy
Milton, John, 185–86, 246
Miracles (Lewis), *213–17*
Moore, Janie King Askins, 9
Morris, William, 12, 181
Mythology, 12, 42–44, 92, 103, 106, 118, 136–37, 156, 174, 195, 217, 222, 243–44, 248, 251

Nameless Isle, The (Lewis), 51
Narnia, ix, x, 14, *123–57,* 197, 248, 250; and biblical parallels, 146; chronology of, 130
Narrative Poems (Lewis), *43–55*
Neo-Scholastics, 61
Nesbit, E., 12, 129
New Criticism, 184, 198, 246–47

Objective correlative, 136
Of Other Worlds (Lewis), 196–97
Originality, 14, 19, 181–82, 251
Out of the Silent Planet (Lewis), 83–96, 174
Ovid, *Art of Love,* 180

Pageant, 195, 249–50
Penelope, C.S.M.V., Sister, 227
Perelandra (Lewis), 10, 12, 14, 85, 98–109, 250
Personal Heresy, The (Lewis with Tillyard), 183–85
Personality, role of in literature, 183–85
Phantastes (MacDonald), 12
Pitter, Ruth, 9, 57, 227
Pilgrim's Progress, The (Bunyan), 62, 69
Pilgrim's Regress, The (Lewis), 3, 12, 31, 46, 60–69, 248, 250
Plath, Sylvia, 246
Poems (Lewis), 55–57
Poetry, 35–58, 245–46; confessional, 246; modern, 191
Political and social attitudes, 14–17
Pornography, 233
Potter, Beatrix, 12, 129
Preface to "Paradise Lost" (Lewis), 185–86
Problem of Pain, The (Lewis), 217–23, 237–38
Psychoanalysis, 197–98
Psychology, 247

Queen of Drum, The (Lewis), 51–54, 246
Quest theme, 24, 46, 61, 65–69, 122, 163–64

Raine, Kathleen, 8
Realism, 12, 52, 60, 94–95, 120, 125–26, 154–55, 230–31, 250
Reason, 59, 67, 201, 214–15, 230, 244, 247–49
Reductionism, 210–11
Reflections on the Psalms (Lewis), 223–24
Rehabilitations and Other Essays (Lewis), 181–82
Renaissance, 187–88
Robinson, E. A., 51
"Romance," *see* "Joy"
Romance of the Rose, The (de Lorris and de Meun), 180
Rubaiyat of Omar Khayyam, The (FitzGerald, trans.), 51

Santayana, George, 68
Schakel, Peter J., Ed., *Longing for a Form: Essays on the Fiction of C. S. Lewis,* ix fn.
Scholarship, literary, 246
Science fiction, 83
Scott, Walter, 12
Screwtape Letters, The (Lewis), 21–33, 248, 250
Selected Literary Essays (Lewis), 197
Shadows of Heaven (Urang), 62
Shakespeare, 14, 249; *Venus and Adonis,* 43
Shelley, Percy Bysshe, 180
Socratic Club, 11, 62–63
Song of Roland, 55
Space fiction, 83
Space trilogy, 83–122, 248, 250
Spenser, Edmund, 11–12, 246; *The Faerie Queene,* 180, 194–96
Spenser's Images of Life (Lewis), 194–96
Spirits in Bondage (Lewis under pseudonym of Clive Hamilton), 35–43, 245

INDEX

Stapledon, W. O., *Last and First Men*, 83
Studies in Medieval and Renaissance Literature (Lewis), 197
Studies in Words (Lewis), 189–91
Style, 245; *see also* Metaphor and Analogy
Surprised by Joy (Lewis), 3–4, 43, 61, 63, 229–31
Symbolism, 31–32, 38, 40–41, 61–69, 71–81, 85–94, 128, 130–31, 149–50, 154, 156, 176, 244

Tao, 40, 119, 142, 211–13
That Hideous Strength (Lewis), 5, 12–13, 17, 25, 85, *109–22*, 250
Tennyson, Alfred Lord, 51
Theme, 134–35, 157, 185
Theme and form, 182, 185–86, 193, 247
Thisted, Valdemar Adolph, *Letters from Hell*, 21
Till We Have Faces (Lewis), 12–14, 43, *159–78*, 232, 248, 250
Tillyard, E. M. W., *The Personal Heresy* (with Lewis), *183–85*
Tolkien, J. R. R., 13, 155, 156 fn.; *Lord of the Rings*, 10
Trilogy, *see* Space trilogy

Troilus and Criseyde (Chaucer), 43

Urang, Gunnar, *Shadows of Heaven*, 62
Utopia, 45

Venus and Adonis (Shakespeare), 43
Vision, A (Yeats), 245
Vision, angle of, 41–42
Voyage to Arcturus (Lindsay), 12, 21, 84

Wain, John, *Sprightly Running*, 10–12
Walsh, Chad, *C. S. Lewis: Apostle to the Skeptics*, ix
Wells, H. G., 84
Williams, Charles, 10, 13, 118, 171–72; *All Hallows' Eve*, 10; *Descent into Hell*, 172
Women, attitude toward, 17–18
Wood That Time Forgot, The (Green), 129–30
Worm Ouroboros, The (Eddison), 12–13

Yeats, William Butler, 45; *A Vision*, 245

Also published by Sheldon Press

Always Merry and Bright
The Life of Henry Miller

Jay Martin

Always Merry and Bright is Henry Miller's full life story including his boyhood in Brooklyn, his years in Paris with Anais Nin and Lawrence Durrell, and his memorable stay in Greece with Katsimbalis. Jay Martin gives us a clear view of Miller as he was seen by others, a close-up of the man who had a most profound effect on twentieth-century literature, and created literary history with a dazzling range of writing, from the lusty *Tropic of Cancer* to the romantic meditations in *Colossus of Maroussi* and the reflective *Book of Friends*.

Jay Martin is Professor of American Literature at the University of California, Irvine. He was born and brought up in the same Brooklyn area as Henry Miller, and knows well the areas that were prominent in Miller's boyhood.

Illustrated

ISBN 0 85969 166 7

Also published by Sheldon Press

The Dark Angel
Aspects of Victorian Sexuality

Fraser Harrison

A study of Victorian sexuality is virtually a study of Victorian marriage. Fraser Harrison begins his book by examining Victorian marriage during its hey-day and shows how deeply sexual and financial matters were entwined. Women were expected to be submissive and wives' primary function was to provide heirs at a time when personal wealth was being accumulated on an unprecedented scale. However, towards the end of Victoria's reign a declining economy and the female emancipation movement brought radical changes, and the author analyses the work of Frederick Leighton, Havelock Ellis, Kipling and other writers and scientists, to illustrate the fear men felt when faced with women's demands for social and sexual equality. The author describes the appalling conditions which dominated the personal lives of the working class, and which forced armies of women into prostitution.

Fraser Harrison is a freelance writer. He has given several radio talks on various aspects of Victorian sexuality and was editor of an anthology *The Yellow Book*.

Illustrated

ISBN 0 85969 094 6

Also published by Sheldon Press

Russian Fairy Tales

Aleksandr Afanas'ev

Nearly two hundred bewitching and colourful traditional tales selected from Afanas'ev's famous collection translated by Norbert Guterman. This is the first comprehensive edition available in the English language and is entrancingly illustrated by Alexander Alexeieff who has contributed illustrations to many Russian books, including *Doctor Zhivago*.

Aleksandr Afanas'ev (1826–71), a lawyer by education, was the Russian counterpart of the Grimm brothers. His collections of folklore, published from 1866 on, were instrumental in introducing Russian popular tales to world literature.

'A first-rate job and a most attractive book, of interest to children and to adults.' *Edmund Wilson*

'This book is indispensable.' *Time Magazine*

Illustrated

ISBN 0 85969 073 3

Also published by Sheldon Press

The Garden of the Beloved

Robert Way

A beautifully written and original fable of a rich young man who seeks to learn the art of loving from a humble gardener who tends the Garden of the Beloved. He becomes the gardener's Disciple and undergoes a long and difficult apprenticeship during which he comes to recognize that all creatures—even the most apparently loathsome—work for the glory of the Beloved. He learns humility and grows strong in his work until the gardener goes to join the Beloved. Then, when he is alone, he is tempted by the enemies of the Beloved and forced to choose between defending the Garden against sacrilege or joining them in using it for personal profit. In his decision to defend the Garden and suffer death at the hands of the enemies he finally gazes upon the Beloved and is filled with joy.

Robert Way's masterpiece reflects the same beauty of thought as *The Prophet* of Kahlil Gibran and will be a source of inspiration to all who read it. It is illustrated with seventeen delicate pen-and-ink drawings by Laszlo Kubinyi.

Illustrated

ISBN 0 85969 061 X

Also published by Sheldon Press

If You Meet the Buddha on the Road, Kill Him!

Sheldon Kopp

In this highly original book Sheldon Kopp, a practising psychologist and teacher, challenges the techniques employed by analysts and psychiatrists in guiding their patients. Dr Kopp argues that there are no hidden meanings in life and that our lives have only the significance which we give them. Thus 'Killing the Buddha on the Road' means destroying the hope that anything outside ourselves can be our master. No one is greater than anyone else. There are no mothers or fathers, only sisters and brothers.

Drawing on the writings of Hesse, Chaucer, Büber, Ginsberg, Shakespeare, Kafka, Dante, Jung, and Anais Nin the author illustrates his viewpoint by retelling some of the most memorable tales of men and women throughout history. Dr Kopp also writes movingly about some of his own patients and in so doing tells his own remarkable and often disturbingly honest tale. This is a wise and seminal book of major importance. It is written both for those who seek guidance as well as for those who seek to guide.

ISBN 0 85969 023 7